The Pluralistic Philosophy of

Stephen Crane

Patrick K. Dooley

Foreword by John J. McDermott

UNIVERSITY OF ILLINOIS PRESS
Urbana and Chicago

1-6529

The chronology in this book is from *The Correspondence of Stephen Crane,* volume 1. Edited by Stanley Wertheim and Paul Sorrentino (New York: Columbia University Press, 1988). Used by permission. Holographs reproduced in the book are through the courtesy of Columbia University, Syracuse University, and the Clifton Waller Barrett Library, Manuscripts Division, Special Collections Department, University of Virginia.

This book is printed on acid-free paper.

Library of Congress Cataloging-in-Publication Data

Dooley, Patrick Kiaran.
    The pluralistic philosophy of Stephen Crane / Patrick K. Dooley ;
    foreword by John McDermott
       p. cm.
    Includes bibliographical references and index.
    ISBN 0-252-01950-4 (cl)
    1. Crane, Stephen, 1871–1900—Philosophy. 2. Philosophy in
    literature. I. Title.
    PS1449.C85Z5795 1993
813'.4—dc20
                                             92-3183
                                              CIP

To Nora

Contents

Foreword

I detest dogma.
Stephen Crane, 1896

Rarely does the pervasive vice of our own procrastination so depress us as when we reflect on the life of Stephen Crane (1871–1900), dead at the premature age of twenty-eight. They say that he died of tuberculosis and, symptomatically, at least, that seems to be so. Yet, one can see his death as the direct result of spiritual and experiential exhaustion. No procrastinator, he! Despite his tragically short span of life, Crane bequeathed to us a marvelous body of literary works; novels, stories, travelogues, poems, and precious letters. More, far more, as Patrick Dooley elicits in this fine, intelligent, and inspiring book, Crane teaches us, over and over again, the deep, abiding, and irresolute character and quality of simply being humanly alive.

Stephen Crane's writing is not didactic, nor does it have the ring of the preacher. Yet, there is a message that resonates throughout both his life and his work. As Crane sees it, the human task is to eat the world, to sing its song in all the perturbations of sadness, joy, admiration, disdain, confusion, and loneliness. For Crane, the writer is the ideal messenger for the message. Better and more true to the life of Crane, we are called upon to report what is happening, every day, every way. Initially, professionally, Stephen Crane was a reporter, a brilliant, original reporter. Such reporting was a sacred calling for Crane, and to it he brought to bear a precocious sense of human subtlety. Further, his prose style has an extraordinary ability to match both the obviousness of the events witnessed and undergone as well as their symbolic significance, without damaging the story.

It can be said of Crane that he limns the human setting, its actions, its interpersonal transaction, and the environ in a way that is both utterly convincing and telling. No surprise here, for Crane began the right way, playing as a catcher in the American game—baseball. Anyone who has donned the mask, the chest protector, and the shin guards, allegedly the 'tools of ignorance,' knows full well the reverse is true. The baseball catcher is master of all surveyed, con-

troller of the game, and the one who sees everything, for everyone on
the team faces the catcher. Stephen Crane lived that way, seeing everyone face out and seeing everything in terms of ambience, symbol,
and drama, which eludes all but a few of us. For example, while a
reluctant student at Syracuse University, Crane writes in a letter,
"When I ought to have been at recitations, I was studying faces on
the streets, and when I ought to have been studying my next day's
lesson I was watching trains roll in and out of the Central Station."
Ordinary experience captivated Crane, and Patrick Dooley has it
right when he subtitles his second chapter "Exploring the Epiphanies
of Experience."

This study of Stephen Crane is not to be read as biographical and
literary history, although it contains much of that approach. Nor is
it to be read as literary theory, and certainly not as the imposition of
some procrustean critical bell-jar imposed from outside and understood only by the author and select academic epigones. And it is not
to be understood as a work in philosophy as such, or as an attempt to
show that Stephen Crane was a philosopher, *malgre lui.* He was not
a philosopher.

Rather, Patrick Dooley contends that the themes, outlook, and
diagnosis of the human condition as found in Crane's work are strikingly akin to those espoused and developed by his philosophical contemporaries, especially William James (1842–1910). Gratefully, there
is nothing forced, ideological, or manipulative about this interpretation of Crane by Dooley, who is a teacher and writer of philosophy.
Actually, his reading of Crane's text and his discussion of Crane's life
turns out to be a very fruitful and insightful way to read literature
with a philosophical vantage point in mind, especially as his interpretation enhances rather than blurs the literary quality.

Both the experiential precocity and the pragmatic sensibility of
Crane is revealed early in the book, when Dooley cites a remem-
brance of Post Wheeler, a boyhood friend. The day after a temperance
rally, featuring Mrs. Wheeler as a leader, young Crane, then about
ten, took his friend Post to a parade, where he introduced him to cigarettes and beer. Nervous about this profilgacy, Post Wheeler appa-
rantly protested. Crane responded: "'Pshaw! Beer ain't nothing at all.'
Then he added defensively but emphatically, 'How was I going to
know what it tasted like less'n I tasted it. How you going to know
about a thing at all less'n you *do* it?'"

Put differently, to be sure, but the gist of young Crane's response
is reminiscent of Meno's sharp rebuke of Socrates when he asks "And
how will you inquire, Socrates, into that which you do not know?"

or in a more colloquial version, "How will you look for something when you don't in the least know what it is?" (*Meno*, 30d). How indeed! Well, Crane tells us that knowing is a function of doing, and that happens to be the centerpiece of pragmatic epistemology. And, as William James warns and Crane came to realize deeply, the corollary to trying rather than simply watching is the ever-presence of risk, physical, professional, and personal.

In the Preface, Dooley sets out what he takes to be the dove-tailing of Crane's personal assumptions and approaches with the central strands and contentions of the major American philosophers at the end of the nineteenth century. Dooley believes that

> Crane, along with the classical American pragmatists, holds that reality's rich and teeming resources are so complex and overflowing—and humanity's awareness of and access to the world so limited and partial—that no more than a highly selective interpretation is possible.
>
> Crane shares with other American philosophers the view that there is no Reality, only realities; no Truth, only truths. "Reality" and "Truth" are, for them, mere abstractions. In theory, the former refers to the totality of experiences, and the latter stands for an objective account of the given order of things. In practice, however, humans must acknowledge the irreducible plurality of experiences and the inescapable lens of perspective. Accordingly, any search for Truth and Reality in Crane begins and ends with his highly charged depiction of fluid and interpenetrating experiences.

Surely the "inescapable lens of perspective" characterizes many writers other than Stephen Crane. What fascinates Dooley with regard to Crane is his stubborn refusal to become trapped in judgments before letting the experience run its course. And even then, when the hand seems to be played and the event undergone, Crane's creative restlessness wanders over the terrain, seemingly waiting for more, a surprise, a shift in what seemed to be obvious.

Following the thought of William James, we can say that so long as there is one of us left to witness, no experience ever runs its course. More, James stresses that unity of any kind is but a construct, a mock-up, a holding pattern, for there is 'separateness to the end.' It is this loose end that intrigues Crane, as if he were creatively filling out John Dewey's subsequent stress on the systemic relationship between the 'stable' and the 'precarious.' Although he confronts the world face-up, Crane, nonetheless, is never satisfied that what he hears or sees is 'all they wrote.' With abiding literary integrity and moral courage, Crane chases the hints, resonances, and left-over traces that leak from every face, every thing, every event, and every place.

Patrick Dooley sees an active pragmatic strain in the work of Crane. That seems to be so, and Dooley's gleaning of his text provides support for this contention. Dooley also stresses Crane's inveterate sensitivity to plurality and to the processive, floating character of reality and truth as filtered through the writing of Stephen Crane. In Dooley's book, that interpretation also is given sustenance.

Still another way to recognize Crane's subtle yet pervasive philosophical sensibility is to revisit a powerful metaphysical position of William James, which he named "radical empiricism." In brief terms, James holds that we experience, affectively, relations between things as directly as we experience the things themselves. In a famous passage from *Principles of Psychology*, James writes that "we ought to say a feeling of *and*, a feeling of *if*, a feeling of *by*, quite as readily as we say a feeling of *blue* or a feeling of *cold*" (1:238).

If James is correct about how we prehend things, persons, and events, as I think he is, then the texture of our experience as had by us is richly thickened. Objects do not float loose, for all of our experiences are of a webbing, an affectively undergone mosaic. As Dooley makes clear, Crane has a superb ability to penetrate this webbing in a highly selective, brilliantly evocative, and powerfully enlightening way.

For those who are long-time readers of the writings of Stephen Crane, this book will introduce a fresh, vital, and seminally new angle of interpretation. For others, Dooley's study should certainly engender a trip into the human landscape as bequeathed to us by Crane. Patrick Dooley's study of the philosophical pluralism of Stephen Crane has taught me anew that the tissue of human experience is both many-splendored and many-pockmarked, proceeding in a tandem, ineluctably related and necessarily feeding off each other. William James knew, talked, and wrote about that relationship. Stephen Crane, however, lived it, voraciously, incessantly, and sensitively. Few writers have rendered real the world as William James intuited. Patrick Dooley has shown us that Stephen Crane is premier among those writers.

John J. McDermott

Chronology

1871   Stephen Crane born November 1 in Newark, New Jersey, fourteenth and last child of Jonathan Townley Crane, presiding elder of Methodist churches in the Newark district, and Mary Helen (Peck) Crane, daughter of a clergyman and niece of Methodist Bishop Jesse T. Peck. Only eight of the thirteen Crane children who preceded Stephen were living at the time of his birth. His Revolutionary War namesake (1709–80) had been president of the Colonial Assemblies and delegate from New Jersey to the Continental Congress in Philadelphia. He returned home shortly before the Declaration of Independence was signed.

1874–80   Jonathan Townley Crane serves as minister of Methodist churches in Bloomington and then Paterson, New Jersey. Mrs. Crane active in the Women's Christian Temperance Union. Family moves in April 1878 to Port Jervis, New York, on the Delaware River, where father becomes pastor of the Drew Methodist Church, a post he holds until his death on February 16, 1880.

1883   Mother and younger children move to Asbury Park, a resort town on the New Jersey coast. Stephen's brother, Townley, operates a summer news-reporting agency for the New York *Tribune*. Another brother, William Howe Crane, remains in Port Jervis, where he practices law and becomes a founding member of the Hartwood Club, an exclusive hunting and fishing preserve in nearby Sullivan County.

1884   Agnes Elizabeth, a sister who encouraged Stephen's first writings and was his closest companion, dies in May at the age of twenty-eight.

1885–87 Stephen attends Pennington Seminary (New Jersey), a
         Methodist boarding school where his father had been prin-
         cipal, 1849–58.

1888   In January Crane enrolls in Claverack College and Hudson
         River Institute, a co-educational, semi-military high
         school and junior college in Columbia County, New York.
         In summer months from 1888 through 1892 he assists
         Townley in gathering shore news at Asbury Park.

1890   Publishes first sketch, "Henry M. Stanley," in the Febru-
         ary issue of the Claverack College *Vidette*. Is first lieuten-
         ant in the school's military regiment and adjutant to its
         commander, Colonel A. H. Flack. Writes the "Battalion
         Notes" column in the June issue of the *Vidette*, in which
         he is gazetted captain. Leaves Claverack, having complet-
         ed only two and a half years of the four-year curriculum
         and in the fall enters Lafayette College (Easton, Pennsyl-
         vania) as a mining-engineering student. Joins Delta Upsi-
         lon fraternity. Withdraws from the college in the first
         month of the second semester, "without censure," accord-
         ing to minutes of the faculty.

1891   Transfers to Syracuse University in January. Plays catcher
         and shortstop on the varsity baseball team. Becomes Syra-
         cuse stringer for the New York *Tribune*. First short story,
         "The King's Favor," appears in the *University Herald* in
         May. Also publishes a literary hoax, "Great Bugs in Onon-
         daga," in the June 1 *Tribune*. In August Crane meets Ham-
         lin Garland, who was presenting a lecture series on Amer-
         ican literature at Avon-by-the-Sea. Reports Garland's
         lecture on William Dean Howells in the August 18 issue
         of the *Tribune*. Becomes familiar with Garland's "verit-
         ism" and Howells's theories of literary realism. In mid-
         June Crane goes on a camping trip in Sullivan County,
         New York, near Port Jervis, with Syracuse Delta Upsilon
         fraternity brother, Frederic M. Lawrence, and two other
         friends, Louis E. Carr, Jr., and Louis C. Senger, Jr. This ex-
         perience contributes to the background of his Sullivan
         County writings. Fails to return to college in the fall. Be-
         gins to explore the slums of lower Manhattan while living
         with his brother, Edmund, in Lake View, New Jersey.
         Mother dies on December 7.

1892　　A number of the Sullivan County tales and sketches appear in the *Tribune*. Also a New York City sketch, "The Broken-Down Van" (July 10), which anticipates *Maggie*. The *Tribune*'s columns are closed to Crane shortly after his article, "Parades and Entertainments" (August 21), offends both the Junior Order of United American Mechanics and *Tribune* publisher Whitelaw Reid, Republican candidate for vice president. In October Crane moves into "The Pendennis Club," a rooming house at 1064 Avenue A in Manhattan inhabited by a group of medical students. Shares a room with Frederic M. Lawrence overlooking the East River and Blackwell's Island. Revises *Maggie*.

1893　　*Maggie: A Girl of the Streets* privately printed in March under the pseudonym of Johnston Smith. Crane is introduced to Howells by Garland. Begins composition of *The Red Badge of Courage*, probably in late March or April. Shares a loft in the old Needham Building on East 23d Street, recently abandoned by the Art Students' League, with artist and illustrator friends and lives in poverty in various New York City tenements.

1894　　Writes social studies such as "An Experiment in Misery" and "In the Depths of a Coal Mine." Begins *George's Mother* in May and completes the novel in November. Takes some of his poems and the manuscript of *The Red Badge of Courage* to Garland in the spring. In August Crane camps with Lawrence, Carr, and Senger in Milford, Pike County, Pennsylvania. The *Pike County Puzzle*, largely written by Crane, is a burlesque account of this experience. Negotiates with the Boston publisher Copeland and Day over *The Black Riders*. Retrieves the manuscript of *The Red Badge* from S. S. McClure, who had held it from May until October, and sells it to the Bacheller, Johnson and Bacheller newspaper syndicate. A truncated version of the war novel appears in the Philadelphia *Press*, the New York *Press*, and an undetermined number of other newspapers in December.

1895　　Crane journeys to the West and Mexico as a feature writer for the Bacheller syndicate. Meets Willa Cather in the office of the *Nebraska State Journal* in February. His first western sketch, "Nebraska's Bitter Fight for Life," describing drought and blizzard conditions in the state, is widely syndicated on Sunday, February 24. Sends final revision of *The Red Badge* to D. Appleton and Company in early March. *The Black Riders* is published in May. Crane becomes a member of the Lantern Club on William Street in Manhattan, founded by a group of young journalists. Spends summer at the home of his brother Edmund in Hartwood, New York, where he writes *The Third Violet*. Publication of *The Red Badge of Courage* in autumn projects Crane to fame in the United States and England.

1896   *George's Mother*, an expurgated version of *Maggie*, and *The Little Regiment* are published. *The Third Violet* is serialized by the McClure syndicate. Crane visits Washington in March to gather material for a political novel. Joins Author's Club. Becomes member of the Sons of the American Revolution in May. In September he becomes persona non grata with the New York City police by appearing in court to defend Dora Clark, a known prostitute who had falsely been arrested for soliciting while in his company on the night of September 16. Leaves for Jacksonville, Florida, at the end of November on his way to report the Cuban insurrection for the Bacheller syndicate. Meets Cora Taylor at her "nightclub," the Hotel de Dream.

1897   The *Commodore*, carrying men and munitions to the Cuban rebels, sinks off the coast of Florida on the morning of January 2. Crane and three others, the ship's captain, the steward, and an oiler, spend thirty hours on the sea in a ten-foot dinghy. Incident is the source for "Stephen Crane's Own Story" (New York *Press*, January 7) and "The Open Boat." Crane goes to Greece to cover the Greco-Turkish War for the New York *Journal* and the Westminster *Gazette*. Cora, who accompanies him, sends back dispatches under the pseudonym Imogene Carter. *The Third Violet* published in May. Stephen and Cora settle in England at Ravensbrook, Oxted, Surrey, as Mr. and Mrs. Stephen Crane. In September they visit Ireland with Harold Frederic and Kate Lyon. Sidney Pawling, editor and partner in the firm of William Heinemann, Crane's English publisher, introduces him to Joseph Conrad in October. They become close friends. Also meets Ford Hueffer (later Ford Madox Ford). "The Monster," "Death and the Child" and "The Bride Comes to Yellow Sky" are written this autumn.

1898   "The Blue Hotel" is completed in the first week of February. The sinking of the *Maine* impels Crane to return to New York. He attempts to enlist in the United States Navy but fails the physical examination. *The Open Boat and Other Tales of Adventure* appears in April. Crane goes to Cuba as a correspondent for the New York *World*. Reports the landings at Guantanamo, the advance on Las Guasimas, and the Battle of San Juan Hill. When he is discharged from the *World* in July, he contracts with Hearst's New York *Journal* to cover the Puerto Rican campaign. After the Protocol of Peace is signed in August, he enters Havana and leads a semi-underground existence for three months, communicating infrequently with Cora and his family. Returns to New York at the end of December and sails for England on the 31.

1899   In February the Cranes move to Brede Place, Sussex, rented by Cora from Moreton Frewen, whose wife, Clara, is a sister of Lady Randolph Churchill. They form friendships with Henry James, H. G. Wells, and Edward Garnett. Crane's second book of poems, *War Is Kind*, appears in May. Completes *Active Service*, which is published in October. Writes a series of stories about children set in the Whilomville (Port Jervis) setting of "The Monster." *The Monster and Other Stories* published by Harper in December. Finishes Cuban War stories and sketches of *Wounds in the Rain*. Increasingly forced into hackwork to repay enormous debts incurred through his and Cora's extravagance. Suffers tubercular hemorrhage at the conclusion of an elaborate three-day house party at Brede Place.

1900   Continues struggle to control debts and meet deadlines. *Whilomville Stories* and *Wounds in the Rain* published. Suffers new hemorrhages at the beginning of April. Travels to Germany's Black Forest in May, although little hope is held for his recovery. Dies on June 5 of tuberculosis in a sanitarium at Badenweiler. Body is returned to the United States for burial at Evergreen Cemetery in Elizabeth (now Hillside), New Jersey.

1901   *Great Battles of the World* appears. Researched and in part written by Kate Frederic.

1902   *Last Words,* an anthology compiled by Cora, published in England only. Contains a number of early pieces and eight new stories and sketches, two of which were completed by Cora.

1903   *The O'Ruddy* appears after delays caused by the reluctance of other writers to finish the novel, which was finally completed by Robert Barr, whom Crane had originally designated for the task.

Preface

No man of self-respect ever now states his result
without affixing to it its *probable error.*
C. S. Peirce

I am a philosopher. Perhaps readers will want to know this biographical fact; whether it affixes the amount of probable error in my study of Stephen Crane waits to be seen. In any case, training in philosophy is the source of this perspective on Crane.

My area of philosophical specialization is the classical American pragmatists, especially William James. In the early 1970s while I was at Harvard, reading James's unpublished papers and revising my dissertation, my wife insisted that we travel to Concord and Salem to visit the shrines of Thoreau, Emerson, Alcott and Hawthorne. She, not I, was a student of American literature. Our shrine-visiting had little immediate impact, for I continued to view James as a philosopher; his Americanness was peripheral and incidental. It was only later, after I completed a series of articles on conscience and civil disobedience in Thoreau and Emerson, that the American cultural setting moved closer to the center of my concerns.

In 1978 I participated in a National Endowment for the Humanities summer seminar for college teachers at Kansas University. The seminar, "Literature and Culture in Nineteenth-Century America," directed by Stuart Levine, made lasting impact; my scholarly interests have never been the same. That summer I was introduced to American studies and read for the first time *Moby Dick, The Prairie, McTeague, The Damnation of Theron Ware, The Rise of Silas Lapham,* and *Maggie.* Levine's seminar was an introduction to Stephen Crane.

It was Crane's style that attracted me. After *Maggie,* I read *George's Mother,* then a collection of his short stories, later his war dispatches, and eventually the University Press of Virginia's critical edition. Although my fascination with Crane's literary artistry did not wear off, my attention was drawn to the philosophy in his works. It was a familiar philosophy—pragmatic, contextual, melioristic, and pluralistic—akin to the views of William James, C. S. Peirce, Josiah Royce, John Dewey, and George Santayana.

In my pre–American studies days I believed that William James had, all by himself, worked out the main components of his philosophical vision: the strenuous and genial moods, a finite God, the steam of thought, a pragmatic theory of truth, and a pluralistic universe. The more I learned of late-nineteenth-century American culture, the more it became obvious that although James was an original and seminal thinker, his thought was a response to a cultural endowment of concepts and problems. So, for example, in an attempt to capture the exhilarating and transforming impact of actions beyond the routine and ordinary while James extolled the value of the strenuous mood, Theodore Roosevelt offered the benefits of the strenuous life—and Stephen Crane marveled at "The Mystery of Heroism."

Accordingly, Crane absorbed and reacted to an agenda of intellectual issues that other nineteenth-century Americans confronted, and in the process his prose and poetry engaged the issues that his philosopher counterparts addressed. In fact, Crane grasped philosophical developments (notably process thought and phenomenology) that did not gain wide currency until the middle of the twentieth century.

This study is an exposition and analysis of Stephen Crane's philosophy from a consideration of his entire body of work. The discussion will range throughout Crane's work—early, middle, and late, novels, sketches, short stories, news dispatches, and poems. For the purpose of this discussion, it is not especially relevant whether a Crane piece has been generally ignored—for example, "An Episode of War" or *George's Mother*—or frequently discussed—for example, "The Open Boat" or *The Red Badge of Courage.* Although my criterion for selection has been a work's underlying philosophical content, countless items in the Crane corpus are worthy of both literary and philosophical study. It is my hope that this volume will provide sustained, direct discussion Crane's philosophy, as well as fresh observations on philosophical issues. With reference to the latter, philosophers have applauded and used Crane's masterful exploration of an indifferent universe in "The Open Boat" but—to cite only two examples—few know about the keen moral analysis of "The Monster" or the epistemological sophistication of "The Clan of No-Name" and "Death and the Child."

Although my purpose has been neither to support nor displace items in the secondary Crane literature, a correct understanding of his philosophy inevitably contributes to an appreciation of his art. Instances that bear upon an interesting aspect or a controversial matter in the secondary literature are taken up in the notes. Although some notes are lengthy, this strategy has kept primary and secondary matters separate.

In sorting out Crane's philosophical positions on the nature of reality, the nature of human knowledge, the significance of moral actions, and the existence of God, it is evident that literary scholarship had so scrambled the medium and message that a coherent statement of his positions seems precluded. On the contrary, Crane consistently delineated a subtle epistemology and metaphysics. Perhaps, with attention that is appropriately focused upon Crane's basic philosophical positions, interminable and often wrong-headed debate can be put to rest about his secondary philosophical positions, his worldview, and his "outlook."

It is clear that Crane's beliefs and thought reflect the beliefs and thought of late-nineteenth-century American culture. The same matrix that nourished the era's intellectuals, artists, scientists, jurists, clergy, and philosophers also influenced Crane. In his works there is an acute and penetrating statement of the contextual epistemology and pluralistic metaphysics developed by his contemporary, the philosopher William James. Crane, along with the classical American pragmatists, holds that reality's rich and teeming resources are so complex and overflowing—and humanity's awareness of and access to the world so limited and partial—that no more than a highly selective interpretation is possible.

Crane shares with other American philosophers the view that there is no Reality, only realities; no Truth, only truths. "Reality" and "Truth" are, for them, mere abstractions. In theory, the former refers to the totality of experiences, and the latter stands for an objective account of the given order of things. In practice, however, humans must acknowledge the irreducible plurality of experiences and the inescapable lens of perspective. Accordingly, any search for Truth and Reality in Crane begins and ends with his highly charged depiction of fluid and interpenetrating experiences.

Much of Crane's writing focused on the impact of change. In his depiction of the processes and consequences of change, some of his protagonists experience merely the debunking of beliefs about themselves and reality. Often, though, the deflation of old views also includes the development of the reliable insight of "new eyes."[1] By end of *The Red Badge of Courage*, Henry Fleming has been weaned of his fantasy of self-importance. However, beyond demolishing young

Fleming's faulty reality principle, it is a matter of controversy whether the older Fleming is only older, settling into another faulty self-concept, or whether his initiation confers upon him maturity and sober realism. More generally, has Crane described, through Fleming's eyes, growth or mere change?[2]

Any consideration of the meaning and significance of change in Crane leads directly to fundamental questions about reality and human knowledge. Does change imply a positive theory of knowledge and a substance ontology? That is, does Crane assume a world wherein careful and rational persons can progress from appearances to reality, from false beliefs to the truth, from faulty, subjective perceptions to reliable, publicly verifiable knowledge? Or does change require a tentative epistemology and a process metaphysics? Does Crane assume a world in which, amid the ever-changing parade of events, processes, and experiences, human understanding must acknowledge inherent limitations due to partiality, perspective, and purpose?

The components of Crane's pluralistic metaphysics are especially obvious in several of his middle and late tales. Although other tales have been used for illustration and clarification, I have given special attention to "The Clan of No-Name," "An Episode of War," and "Death and the Child." In these middle tales, Crane was eager, on the one hand, to display the richness and fecundity of experience. On the other hand, he sought to destroy the pretense of ultimate answers, be they centered in God or humanity.

Crane lived in a society that had lost confidence in religion's ability to furnish unassailable answers to ultimate questions about the nature of reality, the significance of human actions, the meaning of truth, and the validity of morality. However, the difficulty was that as the replacement voice of authority, science offered—instead of answers—more questions and added qualifications. Beyond that, the ascent of Darwin forced a commitment to process and change; reality no longer contained fixity or stable natures to anchor certitude and permanent ethical values.[3] Crane sensed, as did the American philosophers of the 1890s, that the difficulty was not the lack of answers, but the multiplicity of them.

With all the scholarly attention paid to Crane since Knopf issued the twelve-volume *The Work of Stephen Crane* in the mid 1920s, little systematic investigation of his philosophy has occurred, despite the fact that nearly every critic has commented upon his philosophical "outlook." Although some attention has been given to his epistemology and humanism, Crane's metaphysics has been ignored.[4]

His fundamental philosophical stance is metaphysical—reality consists of changing and interpenetrating processes. Subordinate to and dependent upon his metaphysics, Crane adopts a contextual epistemology. In addition, his view of human action and ethic of social solidarity are likewise derived from his fundamental metaphysical commitments.[5] Above all, as the title of this book indicates, Crane's philosophy is pluralistic. His conclusion is that in the world we inhabit, human purposes and perspectives stand alongside a multitude of others that likewise are valid and worthy of regard.

Chapter 1 of this book is a detailed examination of the formative influences on Crane and shows him to be in close touch with contemporary American intellectual life, philosophical discussions included. The emphasis upon his early life is aimed at two considerations. First, several mentors encouraged him and shaped his creed; second, Crane's magazine reading immersed him in the intellectual mainstream of late-nineteenth-century American society. By the 1890s, American philosophy was not a specialized, academic, technical discipline; and there were very few philosophical journals. Not only did Peirce, James, and Crane read general interest and polite magazines, but all three also submited articles to *Nation, Atlantic Monthly, Scribner's,* and the like.

Chapter 2 is an investigation of Crane's fundamental metaphysical and epistemological stances. Because, for Crane, we confront realities instead of reality, and because experiencers, in part, constitute realities, the worlds of spectators and participants are not just different, they are often incompatible. Given his suspicions about the existence of Truth and Reality and his insistence upon the legitimate standing of multiple perspectives, Crane's metaphysics forces readers to question the existence of comprehensive schemes or even a widest possible context, and his epistemology cast doubts upon ultimate answers and final assessments.

What used to be known as the philosophy of man and what is now sometimes described as philosophical anthropology is the subject of chapter 3. Crane's humanism investigates the efficacy of human actions and the possibilities of community and solidarity in the face of an indifferent universe. More precisely, he explores the situation of human beings amid uncaring and unconcerned entities.

Chapter 4 follows Crane's ethical investigations of our special obligations to treat experiencers morally. His reflections range from the barely ethical (duties toward animals) to the properly ethical (conduct toward other humans in ordinary situations) to the supererogatory (heroic actions above and beyond ethical obligation).

What Crane termed his "ideas of life as a whole," his poetry, is the topic of chapter 5. Although God figures prominently in his "pills" or "lines," Crane's philosophy does not culminate in an easy, orthodox theism. He was wary of any single-answer solutions, even God. And so he sought a measure of religious security yet was unwilling to undermine the integrity of lived experience or to diminish the significance of human efforts—precisely the reasons Crane's nineteenth-century American philosopher counterparts offered for a finite God. A finite God substantially reduces the tensions between the agnostic repudiations and the theistic affirmations in Crane's "ideas of life as a whole."

Quotations used herein from Crane's work have been taken from *Stephen Crane: Prose and Poetry*, edited by J. C. Levenson. Because Levenson has made available, in a readily accessible volume, almost all of the University Press of Virginia's edition, I have cited page numbers from the Library of America edition. Note that Levenson has used the 1893 edition of *Maggie* and the 1895 Appleton edition of *The Red Badge of Courage*. When I quote from shorter sketches and newspaper dispatches not included in the Library of America edition, the Virginia edition is cited by volume and page number. I have also quoted reviews from *Stephen Crane: The Critical Heritage*, edited by Richard Weatherford (cited as *Critical Heritage*) and letters from *The Correspondence of Stephen Crane*, edited by Stanley Wertheim and Paul Sorrentino (cited as *Correspondence*). Both reviews and letters have been referred to by numbers (#) rather than pages. In the Notes, authors' names are followed by year and page numbers keyed to the Works Cited. Occasionally, primarily in chapter 1, authors and works listed in Works Cited are referred to directly.

Acknowledgments

Above everyone else, Louis J. Budd helped make this volume a reality. From beginning to end, he was unstinting with advice, encouragement, and support. When I took a semester sabbatical leave at Duke University during the spring of 1986, I planned to write an article on philosophical themes in Crane. Upon reading and commenting on the first draft of the projected article (now expanded into chapter 2), Budd urged me to think in book-length terms. His belief in me and my project gave me the will to believe in myself. Without him I would not have persevered.

Others, too, were supportive and helpful. My colleagues at St. Bonaventure University, Edward K. Eckert and William Wehmeyer, have read the manuscript and offered valuable suggestions. Michael Robertson also made comments on the sections dealing with Crane's newspaper days, and Donald Vanouse read my treatment of Crane's poetry. No scholar could have a better interlibrary loan librarian than Theresa Shaffer; Sandra Goodliff helped with word processing.

Bonaventure administrators John Watson, academic vice president, and Richard Reilly, dean of arts and science, have been generous with financial support for an initial sabbatical at Duke University, for summer research grants to spend two months each at Duke in 1987 and at Virginia University in 1989, as well as for trips to the libraries at Syracuse and Columbia universities to study Crane's manuscripts.

In August 1988, I was invited to give a paper on William James as part of a symposium sponsored by the Society for the Advancement of American Philosophy at the Eighteenth World Congress of Philosophy at Brighton U.K. John Watson found funds for me to attend and also to visit Rye and Brede Place in Sussex. Shortly before I left for England, I read a 1908 letter from Henry James to Mrs. Ford Madox Ford, describing the neighborhood around Lamb House. "Rye meanwhile is going to the dogs—with increase of population, villas, horrible cheap suburbs, defacements, and general ruination" (Lindberg-Seyersted 57). It was not like that at all. Rye was quaint and charming, Brede Place was stunning. On the other hand, the Master was on target about the golf club at Rye. The links were bracing and challenging, and the club secretary as interesting and congenial as the one in James's day.

Finally, I am grateful for the support I received from my wife, Nora, and our children Gregory, Hester, Rupert, and Edith. They not only put up with sublet apartments at Duke and Virginia, but they have also begun to ask where my next book will take us.

CHAPTER 1

Mentors, Backers, and a Literary Creed

Take the diamond out of that man's shirt immediately.... It is of
the utmost importance that you remove the diamond at once for our
fin de siecle editors have keen eyes for that sort of mistake.

Crane to Belle Walker, September 8, 1896

The war-correspondent [was]...a sort of cheap telescope for the
people at home...one spectator whose business it was to transfer,
according to his ability, his visual impressions to other minds.

Active Service

William Dean Howells, upon first reading *Maggie,* baffled by such
precocity, decided "this man has spring into life full-armed" (quoted
by Elbert Hubbard, *Critical Heritage* #23) Now much more is known
of Crane's authorial apprenticeship. Although the sources of his style
and literary creed are elusive, it is not remarkable that he should
have become a writer; after all, his father and grandfather, his uncles
and great-uncles, mother, brother, and sisters were writers. Crane's
independent and rebellious streak was no delicate veneer, but even a
stubborn young writer needs affirmation from family, friends, other
reporters, newspaper editors, and magazine publishers. Indeed, a
good number of mentors and backers, in B. O. Flower's phrase, gave
Crane "intellectual hospitality" (21) from his earliest newspaper
days until the runaway success of *The Red Badge of Courage* led him
to engage Paul Revere Reynolds as his literary agent.

A Family of Writers and Journalists

Crane was surrounded by a family of writers and by shelves of books,
including volumes written by his father, grandfather, and great-uncle.[1] And so, Crane wrote—very early, the story goes. At the age of
three, scribbling at his mother's feet, he asked, "Ma, how do you spell
'O'?" (Beer [1923] 38). Young Stephen Crane wrote because everyone
around him wrote. His grandfather, the Reverend George Peck, wrote
serious, killjoy theological volumes, *Christian Perfection* (1853),
Manly Character (1853), and *Rule of Faith* (1853). Alongside Grand-

father Peck's books on the family's shelves were such popular, none-theless stern, tomes as *What Must I Do to Be Saved?* (1858) written by Crane's great-uncle, the Methodist Bishop Jesse Trusedell Peck. This great-uncle was not only a successful writer, but he was also a co-founder of Syracuse University. A generation closer, Crane's fa-ther, the Reverend Jonathan Townley Crane, wrote articles for the *Methodist Quarterly Review,* several pamphlets, and *An Essay on Dancing* (1849), *Popular Amusements* (1869), *Arts of Intoxication* (1870), *Methodism and Its Results* (1876), and *Holiness: The Birth-right of All God's Children* (1874). After she was widowed, his moth-er, Mary Peck Crane, sought to turn her hobby of writing religious articles into a means of support for her family.[2] Another notable model in the generation preceding Stephen's was Robert Newton Crane, his uncle. In 1869 Robert Newton joined with a reporter from the Newark *Advertizer,* Richard Watson Gilder, to found the New-ark *Morning Reporter.* Later, young Crane submitted the first version of *Maggie* to Gilder; the improbable choice of Gilder and *The Cen-tury* becomes understandable given the family connection.

Three of Crane's siblings were also important influences, although he was so much their junior that brothers Wilbur and Townley and sister Agnes were practically half a generation older. Agnes was fif-teen when Stevie was born; she, more than his widowed mother, raised him. Later, as a school teacher, she nurtured Crane's literary talents by example; she wrote poetry and short stories and was a de-voted diarist.[3] Wilbur, twelve years older, was briefly a correspondent for the New York *Tribune.* Clearly, though, Townley was the most influential sibling.

Nearly twenty years Crane's senior, Townley, a practicing journal-ist, gave his little brother example and, as manager of the New Jer-sey Coast News Bureau in Asbury Park, gave him a job. Sixteen years old, and after one semester at a military boarding school, Claverack College, Crane spent the summer of 1888 working as Townley's aide. That summer and the next, he placed, through the New Jersey Coast News Bureau, more than two dozen unsigned pieces in the New York *Tribune.*

An early childhood friendship is also worthy of note. Post Wheel-er met Crane when both were about ten; his "A Rebel in Embryo" describes the event. Mrs. Wheeler, herself a temperance leader, had brought her son to hear speeches by the celebrated secretary of the WCTU, Frances E. Willard, and Mrs. Jonathan Crane. The next day, the temperance rally over, Crane took Wheeler to a parade, where he introduced Wheeler to cigarettes and bought a ten-cent beer.

"'Pshaw!' said Stevie. 'Beer ain't nothing at all.' Then he added defensively but emphatically, 'How was I going to know what it tasted like less'n I tasted it. How you going to know about a thing at all less'n you *do* it?'" (Wheeler 22). A few years later, Wheeler learned that both he and Crane were reporters: "It was a red letter day for me when the Stevie of my boyhood days and I renewed our ancient friendship. He was, I learned, living on the Jersey shore with his older brother Townley, who was correspondent of the New York *Tribune* for north Jersey, and I joined them to talk old times" (Wheeler 99). When Crane moved to New York City, Wheeler was there to greet him. Wheeler rose to become editor of the New York *Press* and figured in Crane's invitation to join the Lantern Club.

Two more Crane family involvements in newspapers are significant. Mrs. Crane used her influence to help Townley set up his news bureau.[4] Several years later, Stephen helped his mother place articles in the New York *Tribune* and the Philadelphia *Press*. The *Press* was among the largest and most influential papers in America to print the syndicated version of *The Red Badge of Courage* in January 1894.

Newspaper Stringer

Crane's early newspaper success confirmed his choice of vocation. Others have examined his early stories, especially their stylistic and thematic anticipations of Crane's mature works.[5] More important, however, is the warm encouragement he received from his New York *Tribune* editor, Willis Johnson, and his friendship with Hamlin Garland and William Dean Howells, both of whom he interviewed as a reporter.

Crane and newspaper reporting were not a natural fit. Joseph Pulitzer passed out cards to his New York *World* staff embossed "TERSENESS—ACCURACY—TERSENESS" (Churchill 39). Crane's natural bent was to be terse, but accuracy was a problem. His vibrant, chromatic, impressionistic prose usually got the better of the who, what, when, where, why, and how of a reporter's checklist. Further, he was not as keen on recording the literal facts of particular occurrences as in selecting details to capture typical events. Crane's forte lay in sketches like "The Fire" or "When Man Falls, a Crowd Gathers" published in the New York *Press* in late 1894. Both pieces were imaginative reconstructions and, significantly, both appeared in middle-page, supplement sections of Sunday papers.

Crane's newspaper mentor, Willis Johnson, was central to his writing career because he did not so much seek to alter Crane's approach as to find a way for newspapers to accommodate his genius. Johnson, a long-time family friend (he had been a student at Pennington Seminary when Crane's father was its president), was the day editor of the New York *Tribune* and in charge of all its news correspondents. During the summer of 1890 Townley informed his *Tribune* boss Johnson "that his 'kid brother' was assisting him" (Johnson 288).

In the fall, Stephen was off to Lafayette College. Several years later, he wrote about his initial college experience to John Northern Hilliard, a fellow New York City reporter who had lent Crane a suit so he could accept William Dean Howells's luncheon invitation. "I went to Lafayette College but did not graduate. I found mining-engineering not at all to my taste. I preferred base-ball" (*Correspondence* #169). He dropped out of Lafayette just after the winter term began. Crane's mother, however, was determined that college ought to be pursued, and she thought that Stephen's waywardness might be curbed by the religious atmosphere of Syracuse University. She no doubt imagined progress reports from the founder's widow, Mrs. Jesse Trusedell Peck. Learning that Crane was going to Syracuse, Johnson hired him as a *Tribune* stringer: "His work at Asbury Park had convinced me that he was competent for the job; besides, I felt a warm personal interest in both the Crane boys on account of my former friendship with their father" (Johnson 228).

Crane managed to evade the religious influence of Syracuse University, and the inside of most of its classrooms as well. Again writing to Hilliard, he confessed that "I did little work at school, but confined my abilities, such as they were, to the diamond. Not that I disliked books, but the cut-and-dried curriculum of the college did not appeal to me. Humanity was a much more interesting study. When I ought to have been at recitations I was studying faces on the streets, and when I ought to have been studying my next day's lessons I was watching the trains roll in and out of the Central Station" (*Correspondence* #78). Crane's baseball skills were to gain him easy introductions to an influential critic (Hamlin Garland) and a syndicate owner (Irving Bacheller). Both men were to play important roles in his career.

Even if Syracuse University (beyond its baseball team)[6] did little for Crane, the city offered him its slums and red-light district as a background for an early draft of *Maggie*. He also had journalistic success there. Crane expanded one of his *Tribune* dispatches, "Avon's School by the Sea" (August 4, 1890) into "The King's Favor" pub-

lished by the *Syracuse University Herald* in May 1891, and he sent
Johnson "Great Bugs in Onondaga." Crane's tall tale about "strange
insects of immense proportions" that crawled out of a limestone
quarry onto a railway, covering "a space of not less sixty feet along
the tracks" (7:579), appeared in the Syracuse *Daily Standard* and the
New York *Tribune* on June 1, 1891. Johnson endorsed his stringer's
tale by writing an editorial spoof that appeared in both papers the
next day.

The following summer, Johnson, vacationing at Asbury Park, saw
Townley and Stevie (back home from Syracuse University) almost
daily. Townley told him that Stevie had written several stories. "So I
sent for the boy, reminded him of my friendship with his father and
other members of his family, and told him that I should be glad to see
anything he had written, to talk with him about his work at any
time, and to give him the benefit of any advice which my experience
might suggest" (Johnson 288).

The stories Stevie brought him were the Sullivan County tales.
Eventually, between February and July of 1892, thirteen sketches
were published (all unsigned) in *Tribune* Sunday supplements. Accordingly, during the summer of 1892 Crane's Asbury Park news reports appeared in the same *Tribune* Sunday papers, as did the first of
his Sullivan County sketches. Although Johnson boasted, in the title of his reminiscences, that the Sullivan County sketches marked
"The Launching of Stephen Crane," Crane was still unknown outside of a small newspaper circle. Besides a classroom exercise and a
baseball story, both published in Claverack College's *Vidette*, his
first signed pieces did not appear until late 1892, and then not in
newspapers but in magazines. But even in the world of newspapers,
Crane was not quite launched. In fact, he had run aground just before
Labor Day of 1892.

In the Sunday, August 21, issue of the *Tribune*, the Asbury Park
item "Parades and Entertainments" described a parade of the Junior
Order of the United American Mechanics, which made "furious dis-
cords." Worse, Crane caustically compared the marchers, "bronzed,
slope-shouldered, uncouth and begrimed . . . the most awkward, un-
gainly, uncut and uncarved procession that ever raised clouds of dust
on sun-beaten streets," with Asbury Park tourists and sidewalk spectators, "composed of summer gowns, lace parasols, tennis trousers,
straw hats and indifferent smiles" (463). The piece got both of the
Crane boys fired. The owner and editor-in-chief of the *Tribune* was
Whitelaw Reid, the Republican vice-presidential candidate. His and

Benjamin Harrison's careful courting of the labor vote was undermined when rival Democratic papers cited Crane's article as proof of the antilabor bias of Reid, the *Tribune*, and the Republican party.[7]

New York City, Free-lancing, and *Maggie*

On August 25, 1892, before the unemployed Crane left Asbury Park for an annual camping trip in the woods and mountains of Pike County in northwestern Pennsylvania, he sent out an interesting job application. On letterhead that read "Memorandum/The/New Jersey Coast News Bureau/J. Townley Crane, Manager,/Stephen Crane, Secretary,/Edgar G. Snyder, Treasurer," he wrote to the American Press Association: "I am going south and, also, west this fall and would like to know I could open up a special article trade with you. I have written special articles for some years for the Tribune and other paper. Much of my work has been used by the various press associations; and I would like to deal directly with you if possible" (*Correspondence* #12).

There was no western trip, and in October Crane moved to New York City, where his living conditions with a group of medical students in an old house on Avenue A amounted to an urban campout. Crane's plan was to support himself with free-lance work while he studied the city and continued work on his first novel, *Maggie*. Rooming with an old Syracuse University friend, Frederic Lawrence, Crane prowled the Bowery, visited night courts, made the rounds of saloons, wrote stories, and collected rejection slips. Despite having published more than fifty articles before he had moved to New York City, Crane found the going very tough.[8] In December 1892, he finally sold an article to *Cosmopolitan* and placed another in the *Syracuse University Herald*. During all of 1893 only three more were accepted, all by *Truth*.

By the early spring of 1893, Crane finished *Maggie* and sought out his old *Tribune* editor, Willis Johnson, who warned that "it would be difficult to find a reputable publisher who would dare to bring it out" (Johnson 289). Crane tried at least one main-line publisher, Richard Watson Gilder. Gilder's *Century* magazine was prestigious; it was also ultra-prim and proper. When Gilder, shocked by *Maggie*'s harshness and profanity, found it cruel and revolting, Crane reportedly replied, "you mean the story's too honest?" (Beer 1923:83). Convinced that Gilder had a good sense of book publishers, Crane borrowed money and had *Maggie* printed at his own expense by a medical publishing firm. Although *Maggie* was a sales failure,[9] it would connect

Crane with Garland and Howells. Then, through the Garland-Howells alliance, an even larger circle of literary critics, magazine editors, and syndicate owners learned of Crane and his work. From this group Crane received both affirmation of his literary creed and advice about a writing career. Crane had first met Garland two years before, in August 1891, at Asbury Park when he attended Garland's lecture series on American literary history and theory.[10] Crane had been sent to file a dispatch for the *Tribune,* published on August 18 as "Howells Discussed at Avon-by-the-Sea." After Crane heard Garland speak, baseball proved to be the catalyst for a relaxed conversation as the two men played catch outside the lecture hall.[11]

Both had tried to place stories in *Century.* Predictably, Gilder had objected to profanity in Garland's homesteading stories. On the matter of swearing, Garland, unlike Crane, was willing to compromise. Writing to Gilder in the fall of 1889, he said, "I have also stricken out most if not all of the profanity. It does not seem to me to be profanity at all but it does to others and you are reasonable in asking its removal" (Holloway 40). While he patiently negotiated with Gilder, Garland found a very willing publisher, B. O. Flower of *Arena.* In accepting Garland's story "A Prairie Heroine," Flower wrote:

> If satisfactory to you I will send you a check for seventy-five dollars for this story. I notice you seem to suppress your thoughts in two or three instances, and have erased some lines from your story. In writing for the Arena, either stories or essays, I wish you always to feel yourself thoroughly free to express any opinions you desire or to send home any lessons which you feel should be impressed upon the people. I for one do not believe in mincing matters when we are dealing with great wrongs and evils of the day. . . . I do not wish you to feel in writing for the Arena at any time the slightest restraint. (Holloway 53)

Flower was a man of his word. From 1890 to 1892, a Garland story or article appeared in nearly every issue of *Arena.*

In the spring of 1893 Garland still considered Boston his home, but he was frequently in New York City, where Crane sent him a copy of *Maggie.* He was familiar enough with Crane's style and themes to guess that the author, identified as "Johnston Smith," was really Crane. More important, he talked Flower into letting him review *Maggie* for *Arena.*

Garland's review was *Maggie*'s first, the only one printed in 1893, and easily the book's longest and most encouraging notice. In either its circulation or its clout, *Arena* was not in the same league as more genteel magazines; nonetheless, Crane's first novel had been recommended by an established critic to a hundred thousand readers.[12] Garland's essay celebrated a new apostle of realism who dealt with the city out of "the desire to utter in truthful phrase a certain rebellious cry. It is the voice of the slums." Beyond its veritism, *Maggie* "is a work of astonishingly good style . . . crisp, direct, terse . . . [of] unequalled grace and strength" (*Critical Heritage* #1). Garland's conclusion must have been especially gratifying to a first-time novelist: "Mr. Crane need not fear comparisons so far as *technique* goes."

Crane was heartened by Garland's review. At the time, one of Crane's roommates was the artist R. G. Vosburg, who wrote that the public's response to *Maggie* was "the darkest hour in the life of Stephen Crane . . . [so] a critical article by Hamlin Garland . . . which appeared in the *Arena* during that winter was of immense value to him" (Vosburg 26–27).

Garland next worked up a list of potential literary benefactors for Crane: critics, editors, university professors, and reform ministers who should receive complimentary copies of *Maggie*.[13] Not everyone responded to these gift volumes, but the book and the young novelist were taken seriously. Crane's reflection upon these responses and his consideration of the four reviews (beyond Garland's) refined and solidified his literary creed.[14]

Meanwhile, there was still the matter of making ends meet with free-lance work. But with *Maggie* and the help of Garland (and Howells) Crane had entree with publishers, newspaper-syndicate owners, and magazine editors.[15] By 1894 he had arrived. He sold nearly two dozen stories and sketches. Most of his work—thirteen items—appeared in the New York *Press*, but equally significant were two pieces in *Arena*, an illustrated feature article in *McClure's*, and a Howells interview circulated by the McClure syndicate. He was also at work on *George's Mother* and seeking a publisher for *The Red Badge of Courage*.[16]

In his 1894 New York City sketches, Crane settled upon theme, style, and subject matter, clearly departing from his tall-tale Sullivan County sketches. As he wrote to Lily Brandon Monroe in early 1895, "when I left you, I renounced the clever school in literature. It seemed to me that there must be something more in life than to sit and cudgel one's brains for clever and witty expedients." He had, he explained, abandoned his "clever Rudyard-Kipling Style. . . . So I developed all alone a little creed of art which I thought was a good one. Later I discovered that my creed was identical with the one of Howells and Garland and in this way I became involved in the beautiful war between those who say that art is man's substitute for nature and we are the most successful in art when we approach the nearest to nature and truth, and those who say—well, I don't know what they say" (*Correspondence* #31).

Of course, there had been no overnight literary conversion; the Asbury Park dispatches and *Maggie* aimed at truthful reporting. Nevertheless, the vibrant realism of "An Experiment in Misery," "When Man Falls, a Crowd Gathers," "In a Park Row Restaurant," and "The Fire" exhibit much of the power and craft of Crane's mature works. Still, it was *Maggie* that opened doors for Crane, one of the most important being the one that led to the office of Edward Marshall, editor of the New York *Press*.

Maggie's influence on Crane's newspaper career is incontrovertible. In the April 15, 1894 Sunday edition of the Philadelphia *Press*, Marshall published Howells's praise of *Maggie*. On the same day, Marshall's own New York *Press* contained an announcement: "It is interesting to note that in next Sunday's 'Press' Mr. Crane will describe the experiences of a student of human nature among the tramps in a Bowery lodging-house, under the heading of 'An Experiment in Misery'" (Stallman and Gilkes, *Stephen Crane: Letters* 35n). The sketch was Crane's first signed New York City newspaper piece. Garland wrote his congratulations, "I saw your study in the *Press* today. It reads amazingly well" (*Correspondence* #34). Garland also offered to lend Crane money.[17] "Experiment in Misery" was only the first of the newspaper sketches Crane published in 1894; eleven more appeared, all but two signed.

Maggie, and Garland's sponsorship, gained Crane's admittance to the Boston reform magazine *Arena.* In April 1893, Crane bragged to Lily Brandon Monroe, "B. O. Flower of the '*Arena*' has practically offered me the benefits of his publishing company for all that I may in future write" (*Correspondence* #25).[18] Scarcely a year after this boast, "An Ominous Baby" appeared in the May 1894 issue, paving the way for one of his most significant sketches, "The Men in the Storm," in October.

Arena had appeared in December 1889, with Flower's declaration that it was to be a "progressive exponent of modern thought, giving special prominence to the leading moral, social, and economic problems that are today so profoundly agitating society" (quoted by Pizer [1960a]:67). In his retrospective, *Progressive Men, Women, and Movements of the Past Twenty-Five Years,* Flower explained that his magazine waged war against "the advancing despotism of privileged wealth" (156) with "enlightened veritism" (220). Flower worried that his magazine might suffer from over-seriousness and over-anxious propagandizing, and so used truthful fiction as a buffer. As he wrote in the April 1890 issue, "to quicken the public conscience, to awaken the multitude, to make the people think, act, and grow morally great—all this, it seems to me, should engross the heart, brain, and soul of the true novelist" (quoted by Pizer 1960b:68).

In January 1891 Flower announced *Arena*'s policy: "Each issue of the *Arena* during the ensuing year will contain a well-written story which will point a moral or illustrate vividly some great truth" (quoted by Cline 1940a:144). The regular contributor of *Arena*'s didactic fiction was Garland. Seeing effective slum sociology in Crane's New York City sketches, Garland brought Crane to Flower's attention. Flower agreed with Garland's assessment and wrote a testimonial about "The Men in the Storm": "Mr. Stephen Crane's little story is a powerful bit of literature. This young writer belonging to the new school is likely to achieve in his own field something like the success Hamlin Garland has attained in his" (*Arena*, October 20, 1894, xlvii). No doubt Garland and Crane did work in different fields.[19] Crane could educate without preaching, a skill that emerging muckrakers did not require but found an important bonus.

Newspaper Syndicates and Muckraker Magazines

In 1894, Crane's fortunes were bolstered by meeting Irving Bacheller, a newspaper-syndicate owner, and S. S. McClure, a syndicate owner who also published a leading muckraker magazine. McClures's Associated Literary Press Syndicate was formed in 1884 to provide material for the newly developed Sunday supplements.[20] After several expansions in the United States, McClure's syndicate was extended to England in 1887, paying unheard of royalties to R. L. Stevenson, Arthur Conan Doyle, and Rudyard Kipling.

By 1890, McClure's enterprises included book publishing. Three years later he offered the public *McClure's Magazine*, which had an initial run of twenty thousand copies. It was Crane's good fortune that the social consciousness of his sketches matched both the popular taste and the moral urgency of the muckrakers. In 1897, when *McClure's* reached a circulation of three hundred thousand, its editor explained his objectives: "Myself and the group of young men around me, endeavor to magazinize the noveler tendencies and movements of what is most important and optimistic in the world's progress. . . . What I have always felt is that a magazine, to be successful, must have a distinctly ethical background" (French 1897:140)

The 1893 Columbian Exposition and World's Fair in Chicago celebrated progress. McClure, who had visited the fair, was impressed with the Armour Institute and the New Chicago displays. Early in 1894 his magazine ran an approving feature story about Phillip Armour, the meatpacker and beef-trust king. But 1893 was also a year of great economic depression in the United States. McClure had no illusion that all progress brought improvement. Industrial growth had profoundly changed society, leaving a large segment of the American population at the margin. McClure's sober and considered response to progress and the World's Fair was to be a series of reports on American industrial workers.[21] First to appear, in June and July 1894, was a two-part article on the steelworkers of the Homestead Mill near Pittsburgh written by Hamlin Garland.

Six months earlier Crane had called upon McClure with a letter from Garland: "If you don't have any work for Mr. Crane talk things over with him and for Mercy Sake! Don't keep him *standing* for an hour, as he did before, out in your pen for culprits" (Lyon 129). Crane brought along the typescript of *The Red Badge of Courage.* While McClure postponed a decision about syndicating *Red Badge,* he commissioned Crane to visit the coal mines at Scranton, Pennsylvania. He also hired an illustrator. Thus, in early June 1894 Crane and his friend C. K. Linson boarded a train for the Lehigh Valley. Composition and editing went quickly, and on July 22 McClure syndicated Crane's account and three of Linson's drawings of the Scranton mines in five newspapers, the Detroit *Free Press,* St. Paul *Pioneer Press,* Buffalo *Express,* Philadelphia *Inquirer,* and St. Louis *Republic.* More important, "In the Depths of a Coal Mine," with fourteen of Linson's drawings, was the feature article in the August 1894 *McClure's.*

The mix of realism, art, and muckraking presented difficult challenges. To a muckraker, art was subordinate to reform; as Flower of *Arena* put it, "I have no sympathy with the flippant, effeminate and senile cry, 'Art for art's sake'" (Fairfield 279). Flower, McClure, and the others did not object to the sort of impassioned indictment with which Garland had concluded his July 1894 *Arena* article on the Homestead steel mills. (As opposed, for example, to Gilder of *Century,* who found Garland's fiction, let alone his documentary articles, saturated with "too-obvious didactic purpose" [Herbert Smith 92].) The steel mills, the steel industry, and Pittsburgh, too, Garland alleged were inhumane; "the town and its industries lay like a cancer on the breast of the human body" (Wilson 113). Muckrakers expected social protest, "a literature that was direct, enthusiastic, and partisan, projected not only to inform but also to reform" (Cassady 136).

However, unlike Garland's finger-wagging, Crane used craft and literary discipline to inform and powerfully move his readers by art and indirection.

It is fortunate that Crane's first draft as well as several published versions of "In the Depths of a Coal Mine" are still extant. A comparison of these versions provides fascinating glimpses of how Crane edited himself to achieve both realistic reporting and potent moral suasion. All five newspaper versions omitted, apparently for space considerations, the two initial paragraphs' wide-angle setting of the colliery breakers on the hillside. One printed none of Linson's drawings, another used one drawing, and the rest used all three.

Crane made a few purely stylistic alterations. For example, he removed the comparison of the breakers to an "extravagant Swiss chalet" (8:600), and "A mighty banging and clattering filled the ears" (8:601) was changed to "A mighty gnashing sound filled the ears" (606). More important was his scrupulous removal of all editorial comment—what remains are simply the details of the dust, din, and danger found "In the Depths of a Coal Mine." Crane's art leads readers to make their own damning conclusions about the coal industry. His first draft, including a description of the never-ending procession of coal cars from the cavern, closes with the observation: "They suggested to us then the misery of toil in the earth's heart" (8:601). Crane excised that comparison along with the sentence, "After *I* had come to know . . . *I* discovered . . . *I* had yet experienced" (8:602, emphasis added), about the slate boys.

Linson recalled that Crane composed the first draft in their Scranton hotel room. In the initial version, Crane's outrage and indignation simmered onto his pages; however, upon his return to New York City, his artistic sense reasserted itself.[22] For example, the phrase comparing the mine to "a penitentiary for bandits, murderers, and cannibals" (8:606) undercut the moral message that these workers did not see themselves trapped by the mine. Indeed, the ambitious ones "freely" aspired to be promoted deeper and deeper into the mine for the important, dangerous jobs. Crane did not need to point up the coal industry's inhumanity to miners; the treatment of the mine mules made his moral point for him (chapter 4).

Crane's most extensive and important deletions reflect a reporter's commitment to neutrality. He wondered why the miners did not organize a strong union. "When I had studied mines and the miner's life underground and above ground, I wondered at many things but I could not induce myself to wonder why the miners strike and otherwise object to their lot" (8:605). His sardonic comment that a coal

First page of the draft of "In the Depths of a Coal Mine" (1894). From the Stephen Crane Collection, Clifton Waller Barrett Library, University of Virginia.

miner's retirement bonus, "mine asthma . . . the joy of looking back upon a life spent principally for other men's benefit until the disease racks and wheezes him into the grave" (8:606), anticipates the final audit in "The Blue Hotel," when the Swede's dead eyes look atop a cash register, "This registers the amount of your purchase" (826). Perhaps tidy summaries can be used in short stories, but Crane decided they were unsuitable in documentary journalism.

Finally, Crane eliminated four paragraphs that denounced exploitation: they stressed the fact that miners' hardship provides comfort for coal-burning homeowners, the fact that miners' grime gives livelihood to "virtuous and immaculate coalbrokers," and the fact that miners' asthma brings financial health to "the impersonal and hence conscienceless thing, the company" (8:607). He refrained from the obvious: "One cannot go down in the mines often before he finds himself wondering why it is that coal-barons get so much and these miners, swallowed by the grim black mouths of the earth day after day get proportionately so little" (8:606).

Crane's improvements upon his first draft concretely illustrate the editorial principles he had outlined for the editor of *Demorest's Family Magazine:* "I have tried to observe closely, and to set down what I have seen in the simplest and most concise way. I have been very careful not to let any theories or pet ideas of my own be seen in my writing. Preaching is fatal to art in literature. I try to give to readers a slice out of life; and if there is any moral or lesson in it I do not point it out. I let the reader find it for himself. As Emerson said, 'There should be a long logic beneath the story, but it should be kept carefully out of sight'" (*Correspondence* #240).

McClure, confident of Crane's grasp of literary theory, next sent him to visit Howells for an interview syndicated for newspaper publication on Sunday, October 28, 1894. In "Howells Fears the Realists Must Wait," the "other man" reports Howells's observations decrying soapbox fiction because "it does no good to go at things hammer and tongs in this obvious way . . . a novel should never preach and berate and storm" (617). Howells agrees at interview's end with the "other man's" observation, "last winter, for instance, it seemed that realism was almost about to capture things, but then recently I have thought that I saw coming a sort of a counter-wave" (617). "Last winter" coincided with the initial issue of *Maggie.*

Following "Coal Mine" and "Howells Fears," *McClure's* published and syndicated a half-dozen of Crane's New York Tenderloin sketches, travel reports from Mexico, England, and Scotland, reports from the Spanish-American and Greco-Turkish wars, and several short stories including "The Veteran," "The Bride Comes to Yellow Sky," and "Three Miraculous Soldiers." His fourth novel, *The Third Violet*, was also serialized by *McClure's*.

All of this lead McClure to exaggerate, announcing in 1896 that "Mr. Crane has been added to the McClure staff, and his writings will be placed before the public exclusively through the newspapers of the Syndicate and McClure's Magazine" (Lyon 140). Actually, Crane's dealings with McClure and his magazine were mixed and often strained. McClure stalled, for example, on the decision to print *Red Badge*, and his indecision lasted through most of 1894. As Crane wrote to Garland on November 15, "I have just crawled out of the fifty-third ditch into which I have been cast and I now feel that I can write you a letter that wont make you ill. McClure was a Beast about the war-novel and that had been the thing that put me in one of the ditches. He kept it for six months until I was near mad. Oh, yes, he was going to use it but—Finally I took it to Bacheller's. They use it in January in a shortened form" (*Correspondence* #52).[23]

Irving Bacheller accepted Crane's war novel nearly overnight, and an abridged version was serialized by the Johnson-Bacheller syndicate in the Philadelphia *Press* in early December 1894. Bacheller was pivotal in the publication of *The Red Badge of Courage*, the climactic event in Crane's career. He had formed his pioneer news organization, the New York Press Syndicate, with James W. Johnson in 1884. When Crane brought him *Red Badge* in 1894, Bacheller was already an established and affluent literary power. He vigorously supported Crane's work, including, among other things, Linson's oil portrait of Crane for publicity.[24] In 1895 Bacheller syndicated three of Crane's "Little Regiment" stories, as well as several travel reports and stories that he had bankrolled by sending Crane to the Midwest, Southwest, and Mexico as a feature writer. A year later, Bacheller gave Crane an advance of $700 in cash so that he could cover the the Cuban insurrection. The money was lost at sea; however, for the literary world at least, "The Open Boat" was a fair return.[25]

The nearly unlimited line of credit Bacheller opened for Crane included an invitation to mix with New York City's literary establishment. In the winter of 1894, with Bacheller as president and with the help of Willis B. Hawkins and Howard Fielding, the Lantern Club was formed.[26] Members gathered over lunch or Saturday dinner to read their work aloud; "free criticism—brutally free—was expected and offered, and in this honest if rough school some very fine literary training was given and received" ("Irving Bacheller" 323). Crane joined the club in May 1895, welcomed by Bacheller, Hawkins, and

Fielding along with his other long-time friends Edward Marshall, Richard Watson Gilder, and Post Wheeler. He obviously felt at home there, for he told Copeland and Day that for letters concerning publication details of *The Black Riders:* "my address will be c/o Lantern Club, 126 Williams St, N.Y.C." (*Correspondence* #86).

Hard on the heels of the Lantern Club hospitality, Elbert Hubbard, the Roycroft maverick and publisher of *Philistine,* invited Crane to attend a dinner given in his honor on December 19, 1895 at Buffalo: "we will send out invitations to 200 of the best known writers publishers and newspaper men of the United States and England" (*Correspondence* #126). Crane hesitated, but fellow Lantern Club member Willis B. Hawkins insisted that Crane attend. In fact, Hawkins, coaxed Crane through the whole affair, including outfitting him with the proper formal dress, an overcoat, and shoes, and then meeting him at the Genesee Hotel in Buffalo on the afternoon of the dinner to buck up his courage.

"The Magazine Revolution and Popular Ideas in the Nineties"[27]

Free-lancer Crane knew the magazine market, and he knew how to deal with editors. When the *Youth's Companion* wrote to him on October 31, 1895, "In common with the rest of mankind we have been reading The Red Badge of Courage and other war stories by you. And our editors feel a strong desire to have some of your tales in the The Youth's Companion" (*Correspondence* #118), Crane's literary savy was evident in his November 5 response: "I am very grateful for your letter of October 31st., and I am sure that I would be very glad to write for the Companion. My time is just now possessed by a small novel [*The Third Violet*] but in the future, I might perchance do a story that you would like. Such possible stories I would send you, if I was informed of your literary platform and I would be happy to hear from you concerning it" (*Correspondence* #123).

Besides learning what might sell, Crane's magazine reading immersed him in the intellectual environment of the United States in the late-nineteenth century. For example, his first signed piece in a commercial magazine was "A Tent in Agony" in the December 1892 *Cosmopolitan. Cosmopolitan,* selling for a dime (as did *McClure's* and *Munsey's*), challenged the established polite magazines; the big three were *Harper's Monthly, Atlantic,* and *Century.* "The noble old thirty-five cent magazine had always to aim at the educated and moneyed audience, and naturally it was inclined to be aristocratic in taste and in political and social attitudes" (Mott 1954:196). Quality magazines did not appeal to the average reader. "Priced beyond his means and edited beyond his scope of interests" (Peterson 2), they did not have huge circulation, but they were influential. They also paid well, especially for the serialization of novels. "For the novelist of the period, to quote Howells again, the reward was 'in the serial, and not in the book.' Established writers were paid $1,500 to $10,000 for serials, which apparently helped rather than hindered the book sale" (Charvat 964).

Early on, Crane aimed for the polite magazines, hoping for a hit novel serialized in one of the big three. When Gilder and *Century* rebuffed *Maggie* in 1893, Crane retreated to study popular magazines, and the eighteen-year-old college dropout found much to learn.

Cosmopolitan had begun in 1886 in Rochester as a popular family magazine (U. S. Grant had been an early vice president on its staff); it was then moved to New York City, where Howells was a joint editor for several months in 1892. Shortly after Howells left *Cosmopolitan*, it published "A Tent in Agony." With a circulation of a hundred thousand, it was one of the nation's leading illustrated magazines. It presented a wide variety of light fare: "Beauties of the American Stage" (illustrated); articles on fly fishing in Canada, baseball, lawn tennis, yachting, and long-distance riding (with illustrations by Frederick Remington); "Bathing at the American Sea-shore Resorts" (profusely illustrated); and travel pieces on lumbering in the Northwest, the Grand Canyon, several American and European cities, China, and Japan, as well as "The Great Rail Road Systems in the United States." Not every article was meant for diversion, however. Some discussed contemporary authors and literary theories: "Literary Boston," "Mr. Howells and His Work," a piece on Ibsen's *A Doll's House*, as well as regular columns by Brander Matthews on, for example, "Jules Le Maitre," "Cervantes, Zola, Kipling & Co.," "Muses of Manhattan," and "Recent British Fiction." Of special interest to Crane would have been "French Journalists and Journalism" and—by John A. Cockerill, editor of the New York *Advertizer* and four-time president of the New York Press Club—"Some Phases of Contemporary Journalism." Cockerill warned that "the thousands of brilliant youths who, year after year, are lured to the pursuit of the ignis fatuus of fame and fortune through the portals of the newspaper" (696) to expect that "salaries for day work are from twenty per cent. to twenty five per cent. less than those paid to journalists for night work" (702). He did not, however, provide the base salary.

In 1889, Cardinal James Gibbon's treatise "On the Dignity of La-

Letter (5 November 1895) from Crane to *The Youth's Companion*. From the Stephen Crane Collection, Clifton Waller Barrett Library, University of Virginia.

informed of your literary platform and I would be happy to hear from you concerning it.

Very truly yours,

Stephen Crane.

bor" appeared; from May 1892 on, *Cosmopolitan*'s motto declared, "From everyone according to his ability: to everyone according to his need." The intellectual questions of the day were aired. In the same issue as Cockerill's journalism article were four essays on evolution and Christianity and, in later months, Jacob A. Riis on "The Riverside Hospital," "Workings of the Department of Labor," a discussion of the Chautauqua movement, and pictorial articles on several colleges, including "College Education in Relation to Business."

Also popular in the late 1890s was *Arena*, which had a narrower range of articles that focused on social and intellectual controversies. Typical were "Woes of the New York Working-Girl" and "The Economic and Social Influences of the Bicycle." *Arena*'s treatment of intellectual issues was extensive, with a roster of articles scheduled a year in advance. In December 1893 the editors announced, "we propose to make The Arena a library of the best new progressive and reformative thought in the world" (xxxix). Planned for the 1894 issues were symposia on the land question and the slums of America's largest cities, as well as articles on the rational dress movement, religions and higher criticism, educational reform, and psychical research.

Arena's treatment of current philosophical issues was noteworthy. The science versus religion, heredity versus environment, secular versus religious morality controversies were thoroughly discussed. Some articles were cursory, but many reflected sound scholarship. It is important to remember that William James, America's leading philosopher of the day, urged his colleagues to make sure that at least some of their deliberations used nontechnical language and were addressed to general readers. James practiced what he preached.[28]

James welcomed the sort of philosophical discussion that *Arena* featured. The distance between Boston and Cambridge was negligible; conversation between Harvard's James and *Arena*'s Flower was effortless. In 1899 *Arena* published a series by Horatio W. Dresser on American philosophers and contemporary philosophical topics. Volume 21 contained Dresser's "Has Life Meaning?" and "The Genesis of Action," quoting extensively from James's *The Will to Believe* and *Talks to Teachers*. The subtitles of these two books are significant; the former is *and Other Essays on Popular Philosophy*, and the latter is *and Students on Some of Life's Ideals*. Further, Dresser's "Has Life Meaning?" was a response to James's 1895 address before the Harvard YMCA, "Is Life Worth Living," which was later published in *The Will to Believe*. Dresser's "The Genesis of Action" was an analysis of James's "What the Will Effects," published first in *Scrib-*

ner's in 1888, and later incorporated into his treatment of voluntary action, the "Will" chapter of *The Principles of Psychology.*

James began his career by writing book reviews for *Nation.* Throughout his life, even after his philosophical reputation was well-established by several books and many technical articles in specialized journals, he continued to write for *Nation, Atlantic Monthly,* and *Scribner's.* His "Great Men, Great Thoughts and the Environment" appeared in *Atlantic Monthly* in October 1880, and "Talks to Teachers" was a five-part series in *Atlantic* in 1899, before it was expanded into a book for Henry Holt. The differences between philosophical discussions by James and competent essays in *Arena, Forum,* or *Cosmopolitan* were small and more a matter of degree than kind. Junius Henri Browne's "The Philosophy of Meliorism" in *Forum* in 1895, for example, compares favorably with James's "The Importance of Individuals."

Forum's assistant editor, John Barry, was a steady, long-time supporter of Crane. The magazine featured, in symposium format, position papers prepared by experts. Its standards were high. "It would be difficult to find a better exposition of the more serious interests of the American mind in the decade of 1886 to 1896 than is afforded by the first twenty volumes of the *Forum* . . . . The progress of science and industry, education in its many phases, religious controversy, and movements in literature and the fine arts gave variety to *Forum* content" (Mott 1957, 4:512–13). Its list of contributors was also distinguished; college presidents and U.S. senators were favorites.

In 1891, Walter Hines Page became the *Forum's* second editor. Responding to the lively science versus pseudo-science debate about the status of psychical research, Page contacted William James. James's *The Principles of Psychology,* although published only two years earlier, had already become the standard psychology textbook. In 1892, to capitalize on the textbook market, James and Holt released an abridged one-volume *Psychology, Briefer Course.* For several decades thereafter, virtually all psychology courses in American colleges used either *The Principles of Psychology* (called "*James*") or *Psychology, Briefer Course* (called "*Jimmie*"). In *James,* James argued that psychology was not speculation, nor was it a branch of metaphysics, but it had become an empirical science. However, for James, "empirical" was an elastic notion; during the twelve years when he was writing *James,* he continued his long-standing interest in psychical phenomena. For example, he became a member of the English Society for Psychial Research in 1884 just two years after its founding. By 1890, when he was vice president of the society, *Scribner's* published his "The Hidden Self," an argument for the existence of a self beyond ordinary awareness. James also actively promoted the organization of the American Society for Psychial Research, serving as its president in 1895–96.[29]

When Page approached James for an assessment of the findings of psychical research, the result was a lengthy essay, "What Psychical Research Has Accomplished," published in the *Forum* of October 1892. The quality of this article can be gleaned from the fact that the core of James's 1886 "Address of the President before the Society for Psychical Research," published in the Proceedings of the English Psychical Society (and later in *The Will to Believe*), was simply lifted from his *Forum* article.

Page resigned from *Forum* in 1895 to become associate editor of *Atlantic Monthly*, where he continued to take the initiative and contact authors to request material. For example, on March 2, 1896 he wrote to Crane: "I beg to ask, on behalf of the *Atlantic Monthly*, whether you have or are likely to have, a piece of fiction, preferably not longer than 'The Red Badge of Courage', ready for publication during the last two or three months of the year? If you have, we shall be glad to communicate further with you" (*Correspondence* #211).

Page's successor at *Forum* was Alfred Ernest Keet, author of a slim volume, *Stephen Crane: In Memoriam*. Apparently Barry and Page had discussed Crane in the *Forum's* offices, for even if Keet's sense of Crane, the man, is off-target, his grasp of Crane's work is impressive. "He was a student at first-hand of the seamy side of life, and analyst of life's tragedies among the poor. He pierced through artificialities to the heart and grim reality of things—and he was a faithful, vivid reporter of things as they were. With extraordinary condensation and clarity he flashes the episodes before you; and his phrases and paragraphs have all the sudden and startling distinctness of a film picture.... His main theme...was the submerged tenth" (Keet n.p.).

The story of Crane's dealings with magazines comes full circle with *Century*, which appealed to him more than the other magazines. His first attempt to interest a commercial publisher for *Maggie* was to send the book to Richard Watson Gilder and *Century*. As editor, Gilder's greatest accomplishment at *Century Magazine* was "Battles and Leaders," the famous Civil War series initially planned as a group of articles by leading generals on both sides about battles in which each man had been involved.[30] Former generals Grant, McClellan, Johnson, Hill, Longstreet, Beauregard, and others were enlisted. Initial response was so positive that the series was expanded several times and eventually had 230 contributors. *Century*'s circulation in 1884, before the series, was 127,000; it had soared to 225,000 by the series's end in 1887. The book that resulted from the series, *Battles and Leaders of the Civil War*, earned the Century Company more than $1 million.

In the spring of 1893, Crane had poured over "Battles and Leaders," lounging on an old sofa at K. C. Linson's studio. He was researching the battle of Chancellorsville for *The Red Badge of Courage*.[31] In addition to articles on the Civil War, readers of *Century* found a mix of articles similar to *Cosmopolitan*'s: travel articles on China and Japan, John Muir's "Yosemite," Remington on Dakota, Theodore Roosevelt's Badlands Ranch, biographies of Lincoln, Jefferson Davis, and Columbus, and sports articles on golf, the revived Olympic games,[32] and Walter Camp on football. *Century* also gave generous space to problems of inner cities; for example, "How Shall We Educate the Children of the Dependent Poor?" appeared in January 1893.

More than the other polite magazines, *Century* covered theoretical matters, especially the philosophical issue of science versus religion: "Does the Bible Contain Scientific Errors?" (November 1892), "The Effect of Scientific Study upon Religious Beliefs" (December 1892), and "What Has Science to Do with Religion?" (December 1894). *Century* took the lead in raising ethical and social issues involved in scientific and medical experimentation. For example, it regularly ran items on the morality of vivisection, and the May 1896 issue featured an elaborate treatment of x-rays, "Photography of the Unseen: A Symposium on the Roentgen Ray."

After Gilder had rejected *Maggie*, Crane waited nearly four years before he tried *Century* again. Meanwhile, *The Red Badge of Courage* had made him famous. In part because of Theodore Roosevelt's enthusiastic response to the manuscript version, Crane also submitted "A Man and Some Others" to Gilder. *Century*, too, was impressed but worried about the sheepherder's language, especially "B'Gawd." But by then Crane no longer dealt with magazine editors; his literary agent Paul Revere Reynolds negotiated with Gilder and the haughty *Century* about the offending swear words.[33]

"Searching for Stephen Crane"[34]

The subtitle of Alfred Keet's *Stephen Crane: In Memoriam* is *A New York Poet Who Through Starvation Achieved Success—but Too Late.*

The caricature of Crane as the starving genius in a garret, friendless and wracked with ill health, has, thankfully, lost favor. There is, of course, no doubt that Crane struggled and suffered and that the wildfire fame of *The Red Badge of Courage* all too soon vanished. Nonetheless, any balanced picture of Crane must note his health, energy, and creative vigor. It must also acknowledge the support of his many loyal friends.

Standard biographies stress Crane's athletic talent as a young ball player, but they also dwell on his cough-ridden, consumptive end. The truth is that his health was fragile, and he was also a gifted athlete. Not many five-foot-six, one hundred-thirty pounders are catchers on college baseball teams. A correct observation of Crane's energy and physical prowess looks beyond baseball to his ability and passion for riding—for pleasure at the Crane camp at Hartwood, in the West, in Mexico, and at Brede Place in England—and for work as a war correspondent in Cuba and Greece. With no baseball in England, Crane took up handball. Edwin Pugh played with him at Ravensbrook and Brede Place. "His hands were miracles of strength and cleverness. He could play hand-ball like a machine-gun. He would fire the ball at me from every conceivable angle, in that green old damp garden of his, with a sort of wild-cat fury" (Pugh 163). Cora and Stephen Crane had many visitors like Pugh at Brede. Many of the callers upon the baron of Brede Place were hangers-on and fame seekers, but many faithful and loyal friends also came to visit. Thus, a balanced picture of Crane cannot lose sight of his capacity for long-term friendships.

Crane and his old newspaper colleagues did not forget each other. For example, he and Post Wheeler were friends until Crane's death. From Brede, Crane telegraphed Wheeler that he had seconded his nomination for membership in the Authors Club. Crane's follow-up note, "What the hell your reasons were for joining the club I can't see!" (*Correspondence* #637) had difficulty reaching Wheeler in Alaska: "I was some thousands of miles away, in the upper Yukon, and with a man strangely like him in genius and history. That was Jack London. Both had the undying thirst to taste all experiences" (Wheeler 101).

Another caller at Brede was Curtis Brown, who had been editor of the Sunday edition of the New York *Press*, where one of Crane's earliest and most noted pieces of experiential reporting, "An Experiment in Misery," appeared on April 22, 1894. Crane gave his young friend Brown an inscribed copy of *The Black Riders* in 1895. Later, when Brown moved to London to be a literary agent, he visited Brede Place and received an inscribed copy of *Active Service* in 1900.[35]

Above all others, Crane's dealings with Edward Marshall indicate true friendship. Marshall's interview with Howells, along with his own commentary, helped *Maggie.* In addition, a week before the *Press* published "An Experiment in Misery," it carried a promotional note likely written by either Marshall or Curtis Brown. After their early New York City Press Row days, Marshall and Crane stayed in close contact. Both were members of the Lantern Club, and they covered many of the same events as journalists.

As a foreign correspondent for William Randolph Hearst's New York *Journal,* Marshall telegraphed the news of Crane's safe arrival on shore after the *Commodore* sank. In Cuba some months later, when Marshall was seriously wounded, Crane helped him to a field hospital and then walked to the cable office at Sibony to telegraph Marshall's *Journal* dispatch. Because Crane was a correspondent for Joseph Pulitzer's *World,* the *Journal*'s rival, he was fired for his act of disloyalty to his employer; his loyalty to Marshall, his friend, was never in doubt.[36]

A balanced and judicious picture of Crane plainly acknowledges the contradictory tensions of his life. He was a writer, and he prized an active outdoor life.[37] He thirsted after experience, and much of his best writing was the vicarious product of his imagination. His education was brief and gap-ridden, and he was a voracious reader. His health was frail, and he was a gifted athlete. He was prolific and famous, and he was poorly paid. He was a loner, and he had the support of many friends. He was an ideosyncratic genius, and he was immersed in the political, cultural, and intellectual ferment of his day. On this last point, as the remaining chapters will indicate, Crane was also philosophically astute and aware of the intellectual developments of the late-nineteenth century.

CHAPTER 2

Metaphysics and Epistemology: Exploring the Epiphanies of Experience

The mould on the biscuit in the store-room of a man-of-war vegetates in absolute indifference to the nationality of the flag, the direction of the voyage, the weather, and the human dramas that may go on on board.

William James, "Great Men and Their Environment"

It was a great moment! . . . It seemed made to prove that the emphatic time of history is not the emphatic time of the common man, who throughout the changing of nations feels an itch on his shin.

"'God Rest Ye, Merry Gentlemen'"

The central claim of the philosophy of William James is that what we regard as "the world" is but a selection among the superabundant, unselected resources of our experience.[1] Further, because all facts are theory-laden, any appeal to reality or facts involves a theoretical context. For example, I cannot begin to count the things on my desk until "thing" is defined. Shall I count the pen in my hand as one thing, or should I consider the parts of the pen? Perhaps I should consider molecules or atoms, for they are real things. Shall I define "thing" or "real" with reference to scientific theory, or should I use a much older but indispensable theory, common sense?

Even within common sense and ordinary experience, we confront selection and choice. Consider James's example: "A Beethoven string-quartet is truly . . . a scraping of horses' tails on cats' bowels, and may be exhaustively described in such terms; but the application of this description in no way precludes the simultaneous applicability of an entirely different [esthetic] description" ("The Sentiment of Rationality" 66). In his first lectures on pluralism and pragmatism, James had difficulty getting audiences to confront the multiple dimensions of reality. Most people, he found, assume that behind the veil of appearances is a monastic "block world." Most also believe "that typical idol of the tribe, the notion of *the* Truth" (*Pragmatism* 115).

James might have recommended to his audiences Stephen Crane's tale "An Eloquence of Grief." Crane does not explain that the meaning and significance of events depends upon one's point of view. Instead, he maneuvers his reader into experiential contact with richness, novelty, and surprise. "This girl's scream . . . was so graphic of grief, that it slit with a dagger's sweep the curtain of common-place" (863). Crane's strategy is to disorient and weaken readers' confidence in the ordinary and conventional account of things and then to suggest compelling alternative points of view.[2] Often he directly states two points of view:

> The roll of musketry was tremendous. From a distance it was like tearing a cloth; nearer, it sounded like rain on a tin roof and close up it was just a long crash after crash. It was a beautiful sound—beautiful as I had never dreamed. It was more impressive than the roar of Niagara and finer than thunder or avalanche—because it had the wonder of human tragedy in it. It was the most beautiful sound of my experience, barring no symphony. The crash of it was ideal.
>
> This is one point of view. Another might be taken from the men who died there.
>
> The slaughter of the Turks was enormous. . . . The insane, wicked squadrons were practically annihilated. Scattered fragments slid slowly back, leaving the plain black with the wounded and dead men and horses. ("Crane at Velestino" 935)

Distance is an important factor in point of view; however, the fundamental constituent of the meaning and significance of experience is the involvement of the experiencer. Is he or she an observer or a participant? The incompatibility of the worlds of the participant and the observer is a key insight in Crane's views of reality and human experience.

Participant or Observer—and the Difference It Makes

Participant Becomes Observer

In "An Episode of War," Crane explores the consequences of a stray bullet that strikes the right arm of a lieutenant as he uses his sword to divide the company's ration of coffee beans equally. After Crane deftly captures how the injury turns the routine matter of sheathing a sword into "a desperate struggle," he fixes attention on the spell the wound casts. "A wound gives strange dignity to him who bears it. Well men shy from this new and terrible majesty" (672).

The story's import lies in the complexity and mystery of human experience. A judicious, competent, and experienced combat veteran is shocked by his own ignorance of the reality of war. "As the wounded officer passed from the line of battle, he was enabled to see many things which as a participant in the fight were unknown to him" (672). Upon leaving his battle station, the lieutenant sees war through the eyes of the general and his field staff, then he studies, with the artillery corps, distant explosions and puffs of smoke. Away from the action, he asks some stragglers how to find the field hospital. "They described its exact location. In fact these men, no longer having part in the battle, knew more of it than others. They told of the performance of every corps, every division, the opinion of every general. The lieutenant, carrying his wounded arm rearward, looked upon them with wonder" (673).

Passing a brigade making coffee and "buzzing with talk like a girls' boarding-school" (673), hospital tents, and two ambulance drivers who, oblivious to the moans of their wounded passengers, blame each other for their vehicles' interlocked wheels, the lieutenant makes his way through scores of men resting under trees and nursing heads, arms, or legs. When the busy surgeon finally notices the lieutenant's wounded arm, he tends to it in an old schoolhouse.

As the lieutenant is transformed from combatant to spectator, he is forced to consider which of several views of the situation is reliable.[3] It is not at all clear whether any or all of the ongoing episodes constitutes the reality of war. Crane presses the point by showing how ambiguity extends even to deeply personal experiences like war wounds and death.

Can anyone understand death or pain better than victims themselves? Crane suggests that onlookers might have superior insight. Just before the lieutenant is treated, he sees "sitting with his back against a tree a man with a face as grey as a new army blanket . . . serenely smoking a corn-cob pipe. The lieutenant wished to rush forward and inform him that he was dying" (674). Is the man is aware of his state? Is his serenity the appropriate attitude? Crane leaves the question open.[4]

Who best comprehends the reality of a war wound? Crane makes one wince as he contrasts the responses of a sister, a mother, and a wife, who "sobbed for a long time at the sight of the flat sleeve," with the lieutenant's reply. "'Oh, well,' he said, standing shamefaced amid these tears, 'I don't suppose it matters so much as all that'" (675).

Observer Becomes Participant

In "Death and the Child," Crane reverses the conversion by having a journalist-observer, Peza, become a soldier-participant. Crane brings terrific complexity to the tale. Layer upon layer of observers—journalists, peasants, children, a bird, and the mountain—and layer upon layer of participants—new recruits and veterans, fresh replacements, and retreating wounded, infantry and artillery, field and executive officers—all experience the "same" thing, "the battle, the great carnival of woe" (946).

From a distance Peza views a ceremony, a promenade, a blank canvas, and a picture. From the generals, he overhears discussions of drama, theory, business, opportunity, and practice. Among the soldiers, he experiences boredom and anxiety, hatred and indifference, confidence and fear, leisure and hard work. With the fleeing peasants, he again experiences terror, confusion, agony, wonder, and awe. Moved by patriotism, Peza asks to join the fighting. An officer equips him with a rifle that had belonged to a dead man, which seems to Peza to squirm in his hands like a serpent, and a bandoleer of cartridges that Peza feels to be the dead man's arms throttling him. On his way to the front, Peza is overcome by the sight of badly maimed soldiers. He bolts and runs. When he stops running, he finds himself near the top of a mountain, where a child asks him, "Are you a man?" (963).

The child, somehow left behind by his parents, has also been watching the battle. He has taken the events below to be a sort of herding game and so has occupied himself by duplicating with sticks and stones, "any movements which he accounted rational to his theory of sheep-herding, the business of men, the traditional and exalted living of his father" (951). Later, having watched the battle all day, the child, along with Peza, "was beginning to be astonished. . . . It was mystery" (962).

Crane's most aloof spectator-participant is nature. At the top of the mountain, where the birds see the world, "one felt the existence of the universe scornfully defining the pain in ten thousand minds. . . . The sea, the sky, and the hills combined in their grandeur to term this misery inconsequent" (943).

For Crane, neither the spectator's nor the participant's perspective deserves preeminence or authority. The point of view of every participant is selective and limited, as are the various observers' perspectives. Still, the admission of a variety of perspectives is not equivalent to claiming that each is veracious. Instead, the nature of a "true report" needs to be explicated carefully.

Like the philosophers who were his contemporaries, William James and C. S. Peirce, Crane is not skeptical about humanity's ability to know the world.[5] However, no single world exists. Accordingly, no single record of it can claim truth. On the contrary, because a multitude of worlds can be experienced, a plurality of true descriptions is both a realistic goal and a reasonable expectation. The search for relatively true accounts of the worlds of experience does not amount to a surrender to subjectivism because equal value is not attributed to every interpretative report.[6]

Relatively true accounts are either better or worse. The measure of their value is faithfulness to the perspective, purposes, and information available to the knower. This contextual theory of knowledge aims at reconstructing and appreciating the lived worlds of various experiencers. The pragmatic dimension of this epistemology stipulates the conditions that must be satisfied for a description to count as successful, that is, practically true.

Reality is too rich and powerfully dynamic to be captured in all its completeness. Whenever we act, our thinking is guided by concepts that abbreviate and summarize important elements in past experience. (Language, as a conceptual shorthand, ignores and shunts aside massive quantities of experience.) In the thinking process, we temporarily treat a truncated, highly selective sample of reality as the whole. Eventually, through its successes and failures, our conduct establishes the value of our concepts. Faulty concepts misfire and mislead; reliable ones aid and guide. On this analysis, truth and falsity are relatively assigned according to success and failure and specific contexts and purposes.

Crane understood the limited and contextual nature of human knowledge. For example, as soon as the reader grasps the mind set and point of view of a child—a central theme of the Whilomville stories—another interpretation of events becomes understandable. In Crane's view, a child's grasp of a situation is often as satisfactory as an adult's. For example, in "Death and the Child," the child's understanding of events is ironically akin to the understanding had by "the experts," who are high-ranking officers in the field. Both see the battle as a kind of a game.

Highly selective attention to a few details is neither a liability nor a limitation. It is a practical necessity. An overdetailed, exhaustive report is worthless. Tom Larpent, in "Moonlight on the Snow," explains that "a man was shot and killed in my gambling house. . . . The details are not interesting" (844). In "An Excursion Ticket," Crane gives a sketchy, fragmented, and distilled account of Billie, who hops trains from Denver to Omaha. Near the end of the sketch Crane captures the requirements of a workable, coherent account as he abruptly breaks off. "The rest of the trip is incoherent, like the detailed accounts of great battles" (686).

Crane is eager for readers to be explicitly aware that the price paid for isolating "significant" details of an event is suppression of the richness and texture of lived experience. For example, referring to the sense of time and chronological sequence, he observes that he watched the Battle of Velestino for a long time. "War takes a long time. The swiftness of chronological order of battle is not correct. A man has time to get shaved, or to lunch or to take a bath often in battles the descriptions of which read like a whirlwind" (936). He understood well that in the search for intelligibility we devalue much of the content of experience. At the same time, we notice particular details and invest them with significance.[7] Crane makes readers become participants, helping them learn to read the clues that are crucial to the experiencer.

Reader Becomes Participant

Crane's third kind of observer-participant problematic actively involves the reader. Sometimes he provides the data and correct inference. In "The Price of the Harness," he sets the scene. Soldiers who have worked all day with shovels and picks to remake a path into a road look back toward camp at dusk, "the tiny ruby of light ahead meant that the ammunition guard were cooking their supper" (1016). In "The Kicking Twelfth," he switches, supplying the correct conclusion and then citing the evidence. "The enemy was indicated by a long noisy line of gossamer smoke, although there could be seen a toy battery with tiny men employed at the guns" (1268). Crane occasionally mixes data and correct interpretation. In "The Clan of No-Name," he explains the behavior of the sentries, who "began to fire from all four sides of the blockhouse from the simple data apparently that the enemy were in the vicinity" (1034–35).

Telling both what can be seen and how to see it, Crane begins "The Pace of Youth" with a beach scene in which, at the edge of the ocean, far in the distance, "a girl in a red dress was crawling slowly like some kind of a spider on the fabric of nature" (465). "An Impression of the 'Concert'" also begins with an insect image, "a scouting torpedo boat as small as a gnat crawling on an enormous decorated wall came from the obscurity of the shore" (9:5). Crane then shows how distance can both disclose and conceal. After the torpedo boat "returned to the obscurity . . . a man with a glass discovered a tan-colored crease on one of the steep hillsides, and afterwards it could be seen to be an earthwork" (9:5–6). "Twigs" appear, first turning into masts and then "before the steady ploughing advance of the steamer these twigs grew into the top-gear of warships, stacks of tan, of white, of black, and fighting masts and the blaze of signal flags"

(9:6–7). At the end of the sketch, distance and darkness bring nonexistence, "for a long time the tall tan stacks of the *Camperdown* and the long grey hull of the *Kaiserin Augusta* remain distinct, but eventually in the twilight the fleet was only a great black thing, and afterward it was nothing" (9:12). Similarly, in "A Fragment of Velestino" the enemy disappears by wearing "the black velvet mask of distance" (9:40).

Crane makes demands upon his reader, hinting at correct interpretations while the reader puzzles over data as they become available to the participants. Gradually, we vicariously acquire the experiences needed to gain the skilled seeing of knowledgable, expert witnesses.[8] In "The Open Boat," the captain points while telling the correspondent what to look for, "the correspondent did as he was bid, and this time his eyes chanced on a small still thing on the edge of the swaying horizon. It was precisely like the point of a pin. It took an anxious eye to find a light-house so tiny" (889). Elsewhere, in "With the Blockade on the Cuban Coast," Crane begins with an officer pointing out the torpedo ship *Porter*, "although how he could identify this vacillating uncertain form is known only to seamen" (9:110); "the extremes of the coast line were misty, but an officer defined a certain depression in the hills as indicating the position of Havana" (9:111). Crane explains how he learned how to look: "see that yellow band on her forward funnel? Well, that is the easiest way to distinguish her from the *Dupont*"; and the markings "on the sides of the hills . . . two long, straight yellow scars, [were] modern batteries" (9:112). After Crane observes that the blockade fleet went further out to sea, we learn that all that could be seen were "two dim points on the horizon" (9:112). His dispatch ends in counterpoint. In reality, not much had happened; it had been a peaceful, dull scene, "in fact it was more peaceful that peace, because one's sights were adjusted for war" (9:112).

Crane insures sustained involvement by providing indefinite images and incomplete sensory information that are indicated by such expressions as "a thin line of black figures," "a bit of dirty, white jacket," "a long black winding thing," "an inky square," "a long racing line," "long animal-like things," "three dots," "tiny black figures," "a black puzzle," "a handful of black dots," "three tumbled and silent forms," and "a patch of dirty brown." Once the reader has been made to interpret the data, the narration reverts to raw, uninterpreted information. Midway through "The Shrapnel of Their Friends," we learn that "suddenly an exciting thing happened. To the left and ahead was a pounding Spitzbergen battery, and a toy suddenly appeared on the slope behind the guns. The toy was a man with a flag" (1273)—a signal flag. For the rest of the story no mention is made of signalmen or signal flags, only that "the toy" wigwagged or that it spoke.

Crane draws readers into the drama, preparing them to be alert for more information. In "The Revenge of the *Adolphus*," we are told that the cruiser moves very slowly toward the shore because "the wooded shore was likely to suddenly develop new factors" (1085). It is artillery fire we are to expect. Crane does not say how far away the shore is; there are more effective way to convey distances: "to the watchers at sea, it [the gun battery] was smaller than a needle" (1085).

Sometimes Crane so arranges information that the reader, as a vicarious participant, sizes up situations before the story's participants do. In "The Pace of Youth," it is clear from the start that the young man and Stimpson's daughter are in love. Stimpson, however, does not read the clues of "this silent courtship . . . the swift, eloquent glances" (467). Closest to the scene, he belatedly "came into possession of these obvious facts. 'Well, of all the nerves'" (469).

Conflicting Participant-Observer Perspectives

Crane's most ambitious and complex treatment of observer-participant perspective occurs in "The Clan of No-Name." First, we are made to see that, according to degree of involvement, participants on the same side of the conflict experience different realities. For example, the Cuban insurgents' general is a detached, spectatorlike participant who sits comfortably under a tree, so far away from the fray that he needs binoculars. "The General watched them through his glasses. It was strange to note how soon they were dim to the unaided eye. The little patches of brown in the green grass did not look like men at all" (1037).

For the general, engaging the enemy is a matter for thoughtful strategy. He sends a patrol of thirty men "to worry and rag at the blockhouse" (1037). But the men, who follow the general's order, face death "in all this flashing and flying and snarling and din" (1044). The lieutenant sent to tell the patrol to hold off the Spanish guerrillas for at least twenty minutes finds little strategy or thoughtfulness in the skirmish; "three or four bullets cut so close to him that all his flesh tingled" (1045).

Crane also contrasts the Cuban insurgents. The general is safe but restless, nervous, and agitated; "besides the obvious mental worry, his face bore an expression of intense physical strain, and he even bent his shoulders" (1038). The men who face near-certain death are calm and casual, however, "singularly reposeful, unworried, veteran-like" (1036).

Beyond exploiting the different experiences of the soldiers on the same side of the conflict, Crane's stunning achievement in "The Clan of No-Name" is to challenge readers to understand (as he does) both sides of the conflict through the eyes of its combatants. He provides separate, parallel accounts, first from the guerrillas' block-house[9] and then from the insurgents' position in the pampas grass. Midway through the story it becomes clear that he has used two accounts of the same battle. For example, the guerrillas' blue and white uniforms remind the insurgents of bed ticking; the guerrillas see the insurgents' linen clothing as dirty brown rags. As the story proceeds, the reader must reconstruct events of the battle from the sort of information available to the participants who "suddenly blazed away at the bed-ticking figure in the cupola and at the open door where they could see vague outlines" (1038), or who "were driving their bullets low through the smoke at sight of a flame, a movement of the grass or sight of a patch of dirty brown coat" (1044).

The battle is finally over, but there is still doubt about what actually happened. The Cuban general's strategy worked. The guerrillas were occupied long enough for the insurgents to transport fifty boxes of guns and fifty boxes of ammunition through enemy lines. There were, however, heavy casualties. The Spanish colonel has driven off the insurgents but he has not intercepted the supplies. He is "immensely proud, and yet in a rage of disappointment. . . . As a matter of truth, he was not sure whether to be wholly delighted or wholly angry" (1046). Ambiguity about the battle's significance persists, for political issues were involved beyond the concerns of the soldiers and officers. In fact, the battle's "importance lay not so much in the truthful account of the action as it did in the heroic prose of the official report" (1046).

In his New York *Herald* dispatch, "Spanish Deserters among the Refugees at El Caney," Crane offers another sort of conflicting participant-observer perspective, that of soldiers and their wives. First come the wounded and worn-down insurgents, "one saw in this great, gaunt assemblage of the true horror of war. The sick, the lame, the halt and the blind were there . . . tottering upon the verge of death, plodded doggedly onward" (9:167). Then the wives, eager and full of energy welcome them, "in sharp contrast . . . now and then, women radiant with joy. These were the kindred of the insurgents . . . with glad cries, in the great gathering of the troops they came upon the ones they sought. This, indeed, was another side of war" (9:167).

The Legitimacy of Multiple Points of View

The thoughtful reader must wonder whether Crane believes that a truthful account can be given. Because the occurrence and meaning of events depend upon perspective, and because several points of view are legitimate, it appears impossible to claim universality and truth for any single account. The involvement of the experiencer, as spectator or as participant, radically alters the meaning and significance of events. Crane does not explain that perspective is constitutive of the reality of an experience, rather, he provides a point of view and the sensory, perceptual data necessary to enable a vicarious experience of another's world. Crane's exceptional ability to enter other worlds is best indicated by the range of perspectives he explores.

For Crane, position makes all the difference. We are made to feel, for example, the difference between the haves ("An Experiment in Luxury") and the have-nots ("An Experiment in Misery")—and then both stations at once ("The Men in the Storm"). Poverty and plenty join when the crowd of hungry, frozen men who mill around in the blizzard, waiting for "the doors of charity" to open, notice a stout, well-clothed, bewhiskered man looking down at them through the window of a dry-goods store. The men in the storm shout insults to the man, to whom "it seemed that the sight operated inversely, and enabled him to more clearly regard his own environment, delightfully relatively" (581). In other sketches and tales, Crane describes the worlds of insiders and outsiders, beginners and old-timers, natives and immigrants, easterners and westerners, children and adults.

Nonhuman perspectives also fascinate Crane. Among others, he dramatized the worlds of snakes in "The Snake"—"the dull vibration perhaps informed him and he flung his body to face the danger . . . he knew that his implacable enemies were approaching" (8:66) and bears in "A Tent in Agony"—"then he grew not very angry, for a bear on a spree is not a black-haired pirate. He is merely a hoodlum" (510). Above all, Crane gives careful consideration to dogs and horses. He clearly understood dogs. People who comment upon Crane's work regularly note that the characters in The Third Violet are wooden and uninteresting. There is, however, a memorable and vibrant exception—Hawker's dog, Stanley.

> Down at the farmhouse, in the black quiet of the night, a dog lay curled on the door mat. Of a sudden the tail of this dog began to thump-thump on the boards. It began as a lazy movement, but it passed into a state of gentle enthusiasm and then into one of curiously loud and joyful celebration. At last the gate clicked. The dog uncurled and went to the

edge of the steps to greet his master. He gave adoring, tremulous welcome with his clear eyes shining in the darkness. "Well, Stan, old boy,"
said Hawker, stooping to stroke the dog's head. (334)[10]

In "The Dogs of War," the Battle of Velestino is no more than an an-
noying intrusion. "The pup's interest was always in the thing directly under his nose. He was really in the battle of Velestino, but what
he wanted to do was to waddle in his curious way among the stones
of the roadway and smell at them . . . once a cavalryman with orders
galloped past him . . . he didn't care. . . . He was busy with his geolog-
ical survey" (9:49–50). And in "A Dark-Brown Dog," Crane conjures
up canine nightmares, "at night . . . [he] would raise from some black
corner a wild, wailful cry, a song of infinite lowliness and despair,
that would go shuddering and sobbing among the buildings of the
block and cause people to swear" (535).

Crane was also fond of horses and was a skilled rider. Perhaps on
that account he finds sharp and unsettling differences between human and equine sensibilities. "A Mystery of Heroism" describes a
line of passive and dumb spectators, artillery horses:

> it is the business of battery horses to stand with their noses to the fight
> awaiting the command to drag their guns out of the destruction or into
> it or wheresoever these incomprehensible humans demanded with
> whip and spur . . . in this rank of brute-soldiers there had been relent-
> less and hideous carnage. From the ruck of bleeding and prostrate hors-
> es, the men of the infantry could see one animal raising its stricken
> body with its fore-legs and turning its nose with mystic and profound
> eloquence toward the sky. (625)

In "One Dash—Horses," Richardson (Crane), poised for a predawn
getaway, "was wondering, calculating, hoping about his horse" (739).
Would he sense that the affair was critical? "Who could tell if some
wretched instance of equine perversity was not about to develop.
Maybe the little fellow would not feel like smoking over the plain at
express speed this morning, and so he would rebel and kick and be
wicked. Maybe he would be without feeling of interest, and run list-
lessly. All men who have had to hurry in the saddle know what is to
be on a horse who does not understand the dramatic situation. Riding
a lame sheep is bliss to it" (739).

Crane also explores, although not so systematically, the world of
plants and things. The point is, if it were possible to imagine—with
Crane's help—what an experience *might mean* to a building or to a
machine, many human enterprises appear odd. Gaining distance from
ordinary human perspectives is Crane's intention when he personifies

apartment houses, saloons, train stations, merry-go-rounds, and fire-men's pumpers. Taking the machine's view of things, Crane devastat-ingly captures the wonder of coal miners who debilitate mules and destroy their own health in order to feed a coal crusher. "Great teeth on revolving cylinders caught them and chewed them. . . . With terri-ble appetite this huge and hideous monster sat imperturbably munch-ing coal, grinding its mammoth jaws with unearthly and monotonous uproar" ("In the Depths of a Coal Mine" 606).

Sometimes Crane imagines machines as obnoxious children, in need of the care and correction of parents. Consider two glimpses into the world of howitzers. The first is from a newspaper account of a battle, "A Fragment of Velestino":

> These little howitzers remind one somehow of children. When one exploded it threw itself backward in a wild paroxysm as does some angry and outraged child. And then the men ran to it and set it on its pins again, and straightened it out and soothed it. The men were very attentive and anxious. One of these howitzers would remain quiet then for a time, and all the trouble would be over. Then suddenly it would have another fit, and necessitate the scampering of a whole squad to set it right again. They were foolish little guns, peevish, in-tolerable as to their dispositions. It was a wonder the men would take so much trouble with them. (9:33)

And in his fictional reconstruction of the same battle, "Death and the Child," the howitzer-children have to be disciplined to behave properly. "The guns were herded and cajoled and bullied intermina-bly. One by one, in relentless program, they were dragged forward to contribute a profound vibration of steel and wood, a flash and a roar, to the important happiness of man" (959).

Success in making a variety of unusual perspectives reasonable and believable is an essential step in establishing a contextual epis-temology. In understanding the world of a child, or a howitzer, or a peasant, or a soldier, or a general, one gains initial qualification to assess interpretations of a variety of experiences.

Crane's first goal, shared with William James, is to lead readers away from habitual ways of seeing things, freeing them to the possi-bility of multiple worlds.[11] Crane's second goal is for readers to ap-preciate the appropriateness and merit of alternative views. For ex-ample, when he understands the child's herding-game interpretation of battle, Peza understands the battle in a novel and insightful way. Third, Crane argues that a true report seeks neither exhaustive de-tail nor a total picture. Rather, one expects from a report useful and significant information with reference to the purposes and intentions of the inquirer.

A direct way of explicating Crane's contextual epistemology is to call attention to his frequent use of the language of games.[12] The key notion is that in order to understand what is going on, what counts as winning and losing, which performances are superior or substandard, which events are important and which trivial, one needs to know the intentions of the players and the rules of the game. Competent analysts isolate crucial developments because they know what is happening. They also know which details are insignificant or extraneous.

Crane's knowledgeable witnesses are often quasi-observer, quasi-participant journalists like Little Nell in "'God Rest Ye, Merry Gentlemen.'" Unlike the other journalists, Little Nell understands the invasion, including the fact that, "in reality it was the great moment—the moment for which men, ships, islands and continents had been waiting for months—but somehow it did not look it. It was very calm; . . . But nothing lessened Little Nell's frenzy. He knew that the army was landing—he could see it; and little did he care if the great moment did not look its part—it was his virtue as a correspondent to recognize the great moment in any disguise" (1060).

Crane was a knowledgable observer. Highly respected by other correspondents, he modestly understated his qualifications, "I know nothing about war, of course, and pretend nothing, but I have been enabled from time to time to see brush fighting" ("Stephen Crane at the Front for the *World*" 997).[13] Note that Crane separated knowing about war from actually experiencing it. He nearly duplicated a distinction worked out by William James in *The Principles of Psychology*, that between "knowledge about" and "knowledge by acquaintance."[14]

Crane agrees with his philosophical contemporaries that epistemological competence requires a blend of experiential and theoretical knowledge. Reliable witnesses are neither too aloof nor too engrossed, neither too far away nor too close, neither too clinical nor too empathetic. Further, attentive, balanced witnesses, like Crane, show how the openness to experience can revise long-held views and considered opinions. In the effective "In the Depths of a Coal Mine," he delicately and convincingly demonstrates tractability and sensitivity when he relates how his appreciation of nature changes radically in the mine's depths. The sketch begins with a graphic description of the land around the mine—nature ruined and degraded. "The breakers squatted upon the hillsides and in the valley like enormous preying monsters eating of the sunshine, the grass, the green leaves. The smoke from their nostrils had ravaged the air of coolness and fragrance. All that remained of the vegetation looked dark, miserable, half-strangled. Along the summit-line of the mountain, a few unhappy trees were etched upon the clouds. Overhead stretched a sky of imperial blue, incredibly far away from the sombre land" (605).

At the end of the sketch, as Crane rides up the shaft in the elevator, he wonders about "the new world that I was to behold in a moment" (614). Reborn, the ravaged and ugly land around the coal mine now seems beautiful, wholesome, and natural. "Of a sudden the fleeting walls became flecked with light. It increased to a downpour of sunbeams. The high sun was afloat in a splendor of spotless blue. The distant hills were arrayed in purple and stood like monarchs. A glory of gold was upon the near-by earth. The cool fresh air was wine" (614).

Neither spectators nor participants are automatically qualified to render a reliable account; indeed, at times Crane shows the obvious incompetence of both. Those most intimately involved and those with most at stake often behave bizarrely because they are too wrapped up in—too frightened, overwhelmed, and confused about—what is going on. Fires are especially disorienting. In "The Veteran," the Swede, who has caused the barn fire, babbles incessantly, running to and fro as "he carried an empty milk-pail, to which he clung with an unconscious fierce enthusiasm" (669). In "Manacled," when a fire breaks out in a theater and panics the audience into a stampede, "most of the people who were killed on the stairs still clutched their play-bills in their hands as if they had resolved to save them at all costs" (1291). In "The Fire," a woman carries a bamboo easel out of her burning house yet forgets her baby.

Mortal danger does not blot out prosaic concerns. In "Ol' Bennet and the Indians," Bennet interrupts the forced march to his own death to insist that his Indian captors return the button accidentally pulled from his coat.[15] The child in "Death and the Child" has been left by his parents. "Terror had operated on these runaway people in its sinister fashion, elevating details to enormous heights, causing a man to remember a button while he forgot a coat, overpowering every one with recollections of a broken coffee-cup, deluging them with fears for the safety of an old pipe, and causing them to forget their first-born. Meanwhile the child played soberly with his trinkets" (950). In "Three Miraculous Soldiers," a girl seeks to aid three Confederate soldiers. Held in the barn, their escape involves tunneling under the side wall of the building. Hypnotized at the sight of the first man, squirming on his back under the floor joists, and neglecting her lookout duties, "the girl thought of the dirt in his hair" (6:40).

At the other extreme, observers too detached, distant, naive, or with little experience also can fail to understand what it is they "see." In "The Kicking Twelfth," soldiers notice, far in the distance, movement in another regiment; what "looked like a causal stroll . . . small black groups of men . . . walking meditatively" (1268) is, in reality, a bloody, desperate charge. The onlookers in "The Fire" crowd closer to get a better view, only to be driven back by policemen. They fail to understand the fire, either up close or from afar. They feel only "indefinite regret and sorrow, as if they were not quite sure of the reason of their mourning" (597). Nor do they understand what the firemen are trying to do. They sense only "with their new nerves . . . the thrill and dash of these attacks . . . upon the common enemy, the loosened flame" (599).

Almost any page of Crane, selected at random, notes observers who experience odd sounds or unusual shapes and colors because they are too far away or too close to the action. Crane insists that readers appreciate that sound and color depend upon distance and light. He practically forces them to investigate the distances he has described. In "The Revenge of the *Adolphus*," the American cruiser *Chancellorville* nearly rams the gunboat *Adolphus*, "swept by . . . so close that one could have thrown a walnut on board" (1080). In "The Five White Mice," at midnight the little Mexican street is "as dark as a whale's throat at deep sea," so dark that "the projecting balconies could make no shadows" (765). In "A Fragment of Velestino," Crane takes up both color and distance. He explains that the Turks had charged the Greek lines. How close did Turks get? No measurement is given, but "there were no Turks in front save a great number of dead ones, and none of these lay close enough for one to see that the fez was red" (9:43).

Such concrete and vivid illustration of requirements for competent witnessing can be made systematic with a framework that William James proposes. James argues that experiential access to the world is not a passive, photographlike reflection of what is out there. Rather, cognitive contact with the world is an interested selection. Because, for example, color varies with light, background, and distance, we select as the "true" color of a brick, the color perceived in a medium light, at close range. A similar selection occurs with sounds, sizes, and shapes. In perception, "part of what we perceive comes through our senses from the object before us, another part (and it may be the larger part) always comes out of our own head" (*The*

Principles of Psychology 2:103). In experience, the mind's ever-present contribution is not by way of addition, but involves selective attention to certain aspects of the given. A true perception is not a mental duplicate of the given, it is a judicious selection of relevant aspects.

It is an error to attend to too many or too few aspects of the given. With anxiety, too much "comes out of our head," and we suffer the illusion of seeing what is not there.[16] In "The Open Boat," the men in the dingey anxiously and falsely interpret every movement on the beach as a rescue effort. Anxiety-inspired misapprehension intrigued Crane throughout his life. At fourteen, in his first piece, "Uncle Jake and the Bell Handle," he described the powerfully distortive influence of fear. Later, the fear-driven, overactive imagination of "the little man" dominates the Sullivan County tales, and, finally, one of his very last sketches, "The Upturned Face," depicts soldiers' fear of sharpshooters' fire as well as their dread of the face of the corpse they must bury.

James's account of consciousness's interested selection provides a theoretical structure for understanding humanity's awareness of the world. Equipped with his theoretical "knowledge about" conscious awareness, we can better appreciate Crane's uncanny "knowledge by acquaintance" of the texture of human experience. Could anything better capture James's doctrine of interested selection than Crane's description of the melancholy and self-pity of an Irish fisherman: "the old man is one of the home types, bent, pallid, hungry, disheartened, with a vision that magnifies with a microscopic glance any fly-wing of misfortune and heroically and conscientiously invents disasters for the future" ("A Fishing Village" 981). In "The Clan of No-Name" Crane is also on target. As Margharita walks in the moonlit garden, her demeanor and mood evince "a peculiar muscular exhibition, *not discernible to indifferent eyes*" (1033, emphasis added). The phrase precisely captures the balance, insight, and credentials that make up the skill with which a competent witness sees events.

Although the competent witness must appreciate the situation being observed and must tolerate the legitimacy of multiple points of view, he or she need not endorse the point of view thus mastered. Crane maintains journalistic distance in his stories.[17] Although he clearly enters the world of other experiencers, he retains an external reference point for value appraisal. For example, duty and honor, about which he is so enthusiastic, require the context of war. Crane well-appreciated the significance of war but was not blind to its absurdity. To put the point differently, Crane's flexibility in comprehending various points of view allowed him to critique, often ironically, those same points of view. For example, he both endorses and challenges bravery in war. In "A Mystery of Heroism," the puzzle comes down to how ideas like honor or abstractions like the flag and fatherland can impel such extraordinary behavior. All grand causes aside, could one be brave while getting a bucket of water? Collins is thirsty. To his question, "Captain, I want t' git permission to git some water from that there well over yonder!" the captain replies, "Look here, my lad. . . . Don't you think that's taking pretty big risks for a little drink of water?" (626–27). Collins, it turns out, has doubts too. "It seemed to him supernaturally strange that he had allowed his mind to maneuver his body into such a situation" (628).

Crane uses doubts about the sense of Collins's actions to question the rationality of war in general. He overlays any consideration of the sanity of war with a more fundamental, human context as he describes Collins doubling back to give a drink to a dying officer. Then, when Collins finally returns to the cheers of his regiment, Crane adds another twist; two officers, quarreling over who should get the first drink, spill the bucket of water on the ground.

If actions are given definition and significance by a context, then deprived of their context they become inconsequential, even incomprehensible. Crane probes to find out which events war invests with significance—and how significance itself varies. War produces pain, injury, and death. In "A Fragment of Velestino," war is a machine in which "the noise of the battle, the roar and rumble of an enormous factory" are hard at work on a product. "This was the product, not so well finished as some, but sufficient to express the plan of the machine. This wounded soldier explained the distant roar. He defined it. This—this and worse—was what was going on. This explained the meaning of all that racket" (9:29). Away from the front, aboard the ambulance steamer *St. Mariana*, "Stephen Crane Tells of War's Horrors" describes the pain and agony of the wounded. Then, in a rare editorial aside, he explains, "there is more of this sort of thing in war than glory and heroic death, flags, banners, shouting and victory" (942). Ever alert, Crane captures still another view of the pain and trauma manufactured by the war machine. "The hospital was simply packed . . . through the door of the hospital could be seen a white-clothed surgeon, erect, serene, but swift-fingered. He was calm enough to be sinister and terrible in this scene of blood. He had every necessary casual mannerism of a surgeon facing his patients, but it was ghoulish anyhow. This thing was a banquet for him" ("My Talk with Soldiers Six" 9:63).

Thus war involves casualties. Are all casualties equivalent? No, given the soldier's viewpoint. Some deaths are wasteful. "The battalion had suffered heavy losses, and these losses had been hard to bear, for a soldier always reasons that men lost during a period of inaction are men badly lost" ("The Price of the Harness" 1028). In "The Little Regiment," Crane observes that "veterans detest being killed when they are not busy" (660). Collins is busy getting the bucket of water. Had he had been killed, would his death have been meaningful? Crane poses yet another dilemma.

Because war is an exceptional event, it offers dispensation from some rules that regulate ordinary conduct. "Which rules?" asks Crane. For example, in "A Grey Sleeve" and "Death and the Child," he shrewdly examines mores as he displays both the fittingness and the oddity of civility and proper manners in the middle of the barbarity of war.

With regard to the conduct of war, Crane raises issues about the objective of soldiering. He observes that "the profession of arms lost much of its point unless a man shot at people and had people shoot at him" ("The Kicking Twelfth" 1262) and remarks that the central objective is, naturally, victory. With that in mind, Crane considers the tactics of guerrillas. In "Stephen Crane's Vivid Story of the Battle of San Juan," he notes, "Red Cross men, wounded men, sick men, correspondents and attachés were all one to the guerilla . . . viewed simply as a bit of tactics, the scheme was admirable" (1005–6). But in the wider context of civilized behavior, the guerrillas, who "successfully rewounded some prostrate men in a hospital and killed an ambulance driver off his seat as he was taking his silent, suffering charges to the base," are judged vile barbarians by "humane and gentle hearted men in the army" (1006). Of course. But in wider contexts, war is all three: inhumane, vile, and reprehensible.

Crane uses nature to put human concerns into low relief. In nature's eye, individual human lives, which had enjoyed such prominence and even sanctity, fade into triviality: "in this wide conflict, his life was an insignificant fact, and. . . his death would be an insignificant fact" ("The Little Regiment" 651); "he reflected that the accidental destruction of an individual, Peza by name, would perhaps be nothing at all" ("Death and the Child" 948); or "the sea always makes me feel that I am a trivial object" ("Coney Island's Failing Days" 585).

Thus, for Crane, the conditions of meaningfulness and significance are context-dependent. First, events acquire status and importance in a context. Next, a context is required to assess the appropriateness of responses, actions, and interpretations. Third, the admissibility of several perspectives forces notice of how drastically meaning and significance wax and wane whenever one says, as Crane so often does, "but, from another point of view."

The nagging relativity and context-dependence of Crane's epistemology suggest the advantages of evaluation from the widest possible context. For example, in the case of an omniscient narrator, truth would be judged with reference to a single intention and a fixed goal. Then, too, the relative standing of other points of view could be assigned.

Truth, Reality, and the Widest Possible Context

On the theoretical, structural level, an omniscient narrator, God with a comprehensive view of things and total grasp of reality, would resolve the ambiguities contained in a pluralistic worldview. On a personal and practical level, God speaks to deep-seated and persistent human needs. Much in Crane is congenial to traditional religion (its concerns, if not its solutions),[18] especially its attempt to address questions of ultimate meaning, purpose, and the role of humans in the scheme of things.

God figures prominently in Crane's poetry, and he explicitly invokes the authority of an omniscient narrator in many tales.[19] His statement, "but it was known that the lieutenant-colonel who had been in command was dead" (1024), in "The Price of the Harness," is typical. Further, whenever Crane's characters become aware of the limitations of their perspective, they automatically trust that someone must understand the situation. The soldiers in "The Kicking Twelfth" believe "that a superior intelligence was anxious over their behavior and welfare" (1266), and the enlisted men in "The Little Regiment" are "in possession of a simple but perfectly immovable faith that somebody understood the jumble" (654).

Theistic tendencies notwithstanding, it is clear that Crane does not subscribe to the existence of Truth or Reality. He urges progressive revision toward wider contexts, more comprehensive understandings, and more expansive evaluations, but he modestly acknowledges that our insights and accomplishments are subject to revision, addition, correction, and improvement.

The reader's confidence in any sort of finality in Crane's work is undercut by the fallibility of his would-be omniscient narrators. Not only do ordinary soldiers have confidence that someone understands what is going on, but, in the tales cited, the men also believe that their officers have the answers. However, in both cases, the officers' grasp of the situation is not better, only different.

Crane uses several symbols of omniscience. Birds circling over-head are his usual expression of comprehensive knowledge. But what the birds know is not communicated to the men below, or else the message from the birds concerns the inconsequence of human lives. Crane ironically notes that when the Rough Riders landed in Cuba they took the cooing of Cuban wood doves as a sign that they were safe. They misunderstood and were ambushed, for "the beautiful coo of the Cuban wood-dove—ah, the wood-dove! [was] the Spanish-gue-rilla wood-dove which had presaged the death of gallant marines" ("Stephen Crane at the Front for the *World*" 998).

The most distinctive symbol of omniscience in Crane's tales is a balloon used to gather military intelligence in "The Price of the Har-ness." The trouble is, the war balloon gives away the point of attack, and once the enemy is engaged, any "intelligence" from the balloon is lost. It is shot down; "the balloon was dying, dying a gigantic and public death before the eyes of two armies" (1022).[20]

Peza, in "Death and the Child," suffers most from the illusion of omniscience. Near the climax of the story, he climbs to the top of a hill and for the first time sees the lay of the land, the lines of troops, and the placement of artillery. He can see clearly and has all neces-sary information. "Peza, breathless, pale, felt that he had been set upon a pillar and was surveying mankind, the world" (958). Unfortu-nately, his infallible pronouncements must be postponed because "in the meantime dust had got in his eye. He took his handkerchief and mechanically administered to it" (958).

Crane's misgivings about any single account capturing Truth are not based upon epistemological reservations about the ability to know. Instead, his pluralistic worldview is confirmed by his experi-ence of experience, notably the fact that realities—not Reality—are revealed. Readers are forced to consider the natures of truth and real-ity. For example, in "An Episode of War," the lieutenant wishes to inform the man "with a face as grey as a new army blanket . . . se-renely smoking a corn-cob pipe" (674) that he is dying. It is, of course, a fact that the man is dying. But dying is not a simple biological fact. As a personal experience, the meaning and significance of death for the grey-faced man are inaccessible to the lieutenant. Thus is it Crane's contention that, for personal events, the experiencer is in an authoritative position to comprehend "the facts"? By now, we should expect a counterpoint, and Crane readily supplies several.

In "The Price of the Harness," Martin, shot in the arm like the lieutenant in "An Episode of War," walks to the rear of the battle line. Like the lieutenant, he sees many wounded men and is bewildered by all the events and conflicting points of view that make up "the same" battle. At the front, Nolan is mortally wounded as his regiment charges the enemy position. When his comrades find him, he is lucid and calm but also thirsty and cold, "I'm chilly—lyin' on this damp ground" (1030). Nolan is told that the ground is not damp, but insists that his comrades feel under his back for themselves. "Grierson seemed to be afraid of Nolan's agitation, and so he slipped a hand under the prostrate man, and presently withdrew it covered with blood. 'Yes,' he said, hiding his hand carefully from Nolan's eyes, 'you were right, Jimmie'" (1031). Crane ends his counterpoint by debunking Nolan's claim that he, the experiencer, not the onlookers, is in the authoritative position to know "the facts." Nolan remarks, "this hillside holds water like a swamp. . . .Guess I ought to know. I'm flat here on it, and you fellers are standing up" (1031). Crane leaves the conflict to his readers. "He did not know he was dying. He thought he was holding an argument on the condition of the turf" (1031).

In Crane's pluralistic universe, reality is the totality of conflicting, ongoing, interpenetrating experiences. From various vantage points, time-frames, intentions, roles, purposes, and levels, all sorts of things are, at once, real and unreal, existing and nonexisting, important and trivial, essential and accidental. Recall the epigraphs at the beginning of this chapter. The mould on the biscuit is one of reality's epiphanies, so, too, the battle between the warships. Both have importance within their own levels of reality, although with respect to each other, they exist in absolute indifference. A similar internal importance and external triviality holds for the itch on the shin and for the great moment in history. Likewise, "An Impression of the 'Concert,'" a dispatch from on board the French steamer *Guardiana*, is structured as two parallel descriptions. One concerns the awesome international peacekeeping armada, "the fleet of the Powers; the Concert—the Concert, mind you, this most terrible creature which the world has known. . . . It was a limb of Europe displayed, actual, animate" (9:7). The other concerns an infant passenger, "at times from the cabin arose the thin wail of a baby that objected without pause from Marseilles to the roll and heave of the ship" (9:6). Throughout the dispatch, along with information on the mighty ships, Crane notes that "the babe. . . continued to cry in the cabin" (9:7). The dispatch ends not with the Concert, but with the baby, "the mother of the sick child had come on deck and to inquiries of some good-natured passengers she replied gratefully that it was rather better" (9:12). Thus Crane's persistent message is that alongside individual persons and the world of humankind, a multiplicity of simultaneously existing worlds, large and small, has standing and significance.

Crane's metaphysics is also attentive to the fact of process. For him, reality is fluid and episodic; ephemeral processes and events are as real as substances and discrete things. In "The Little Regiment," the rendition of an infantry charge provides a paradigmatic description for process metaphysics. The brigade hurls itself against enemy fire. "The men, panting, perspiring, with crazed faces, tried to push against it; but it was as if they had come to a wall. The wave halted, shuddered in an agony from the quick struggle of its two desires, then toppled and broke into a fragmentary thing which has no name" (661). As a wave, it is a real thing; when it loses energy and configuration, it ceases to exist. Like the infantry charge, the life of a plant, the life of an animal, the breeze in the trees, the life of a human being, or the unity of a team, an army, or a family has analogous reality and significance as well as analogous impermanence and insignificance (chapter 5).

Crane's sensitivity to the utter multiplicity of real things echoes themes in the writings of the man who originated the term *pluralistic universe*, William James. Crane shares James's doubts that any statement could capture, even from the widest possible context, all of reality. James argues that capturing "the Truth" is a task beyond human capacities.

> We have no organ or faculty to appreciate the simply given order. The real world as it is given objectively at this moment is the sum total of all its beings and events now. But can we think of such a sum? Can we realize for an instant what a cross-section of all existence at a definite point of time would be? While I talk and the flies buzz, a sea-gull catches a fish at the mouth of the Amazon, a tree falls in the Adirondack wilderness, a man sneezes in Germany, a horse dies in Tartary, and twins are born in France. ("Reflex Action and Theism" 95–96)

James concludes that because the real world is an indefinitely large collection of contemporaneous events, we are forced to use selective attention to break reality into whatever manageable units can serve our purposes and interests. Crane, agreeing about the partial and selective nature of human consciousness, is especially attuned to the phenomenon of focus as we selectively attend to reality's various epiphanies.

Keeping an event in focus means, for Crane, sustaining attention to the context that constitutes reality for the experiencer. When attention lapses, awareness shifts to another level or context, and we are jarred by the intrusion of unexpected, sometimes strange, realities. In "The Five White Mice," the New York Kid (Crane) at the very instant of his showdown with a Mexican, grips his revolver. His attention wanders, and he muses about the decorative carving on his pistol grip. "He recalled that upon its black handle was stamped a hunting scene in which a sportsman in fine leggings and a peaked cap was taking aim at a stag less than one eighth of an inch away" (767). His lapse of attention leads him to confuse several levels of reality, including his conflation of the hunting scene as a representation and the physical details of his pistol grip. In his inattention to context, he intertwines the literal and symbolic levels of reality.

By adjusting the focus of consciousness, we can attend to several worlds in rapid succession. As awareness ranges over several worlds, items from one world become incongruous in another. For example, a bodily change can either be a simple muscular movement or it can be an action. Slight, even trivial, occurrences can have profound consequences. In "The Fire," a policeman runs to a fire box and sets off an alarm, bringing the firemen "in clamor and riot of hoofs and wheels" (597). As the firemen and firewagons converge, "Other roars, other clangings, were to be heard from all directions. It was extraordinary, the loud rumblings of wheels and the pealings of gongs aroused by a movement of the policeman's fingers" (598). Considered on the physical level, the cause and the effect are grossly disproportionate. However, a physical movement can be a highly charged action. With actions as the frame of reference, the firemen's vigor is an appropriate response to an emergency call.

In "The Fire," Crane perceptively displays how, in two worlds at once, "a movement of the policeman's fingers" is both trivial and momentous. He also describes, in "The Kicking Twelfth," similar disproportion between cause and effect. "Whereupon, Major-General Richie, commanding a force of 7,500 men of His Majesty of Spitzbergen, set in motion with a few simple words the machinery which would launch his army at the enemy" (1264). The supreme commander gives the order. It is also true that what had happened was that a someone had made a few sounds. Crane's analysis precisely recalls William James's point that a beautiful violin melody is also just noise, horsehair rubbing on catgut.

Crane was among several nineteenth-century American thinkers who explored connections between events and meanings. The pistol-grip example indicates a sensitivity to questions about the meaning of meaning and the relationships among signs, tokens, and symbols. At the same time as Crane was writing his stories, C. S. Peirce, with James's encouragement and financial support, was developing his semiotics and, later, a general theory of signs.

Peirce argued that although humans can approach truth, even our closest approximation, the settled opinion of a community of experienced and expert inquirers, remains subject to correction, revision, and reinterpretation. Crane concurs. Although the four men in "The Open Boat" have struggled together and experienced, in the face of nature's flat indifference, self-worth and human solidarity, Crane does not conclude that they had discovered the truth. Like his contemporaries, the American pragmatic philosophers, he is content with a modest statement of the epistemological accomplishments the three survivors: "they felt that they could then be interpreters" (909).

CHAPTER 3

Humanism: Brotherhood in an Indifferent Universe

The wind blows because it is the wind, the rain beats because it is the rain. Who can fathom the ways of nature?

"Stephen Crane in Texas"

The sidewalk soon became completely blocked by the bodies of the men. They pressed close to one another like sheep in a winter's gale, keeping one another warm by the heat of their bodies.

"The Men in the Storm"

"How did you get along?"
"Don't git along, stranger. Who the hell told you I did get along?"
In the meantime, they depend upon their endurance, their capacity to help each other, and their steadfast and unyielding courage.

"Nebraska's Bitter Fight for Life"

Stephen Crane's dozen productive years began with his Asbury Park dispatches for the news bureau run by his brother Townley and ended with his deathbed dictation of *The O'Ruddy*. Using his short story "Uncle Jake and the Bell-Handle" as a beginning extends his writing career to a mere sixteen years. Understandably, then, Crane had little opportunity to evolve as an observer, recorder, and interpreter of life's experiences, and the positions he took on epistemological, metaphysical, and ethical issues remained essentially unchanged. However, Crane subtly revised his humanism. He did not alter his view of an indifferent universe as the arena for human action, but he did reassess the efficacy of actions and the possibility of human solidarity.

Much has been written about environmental determinism in Crane, especially on his focus upon powerless, inept, isolated humans of his early Bowery tales, *Maggie* and *George's Mother* as well as his early New York City newspaper work.[1] Later, his acclaimed short story "The Open Boat" celebrated both effective effort and human solidarity. Understanding Crane's espousal of both views requires close attention to his intervening treatment of the resourceful and competent protagonists in the western and Mexican tales.

Crane expresses his fully developed judgment about human existence in "The Open Boat." He readily admits that thirty hours at sea in an open boat profoundly influenced his assessment of the worth of human actions and the feasibility of community. In addition, however, other biographical, cultural, literary, and philosophical factors predisposed him toward a melioristic, progressive, and communal view of human existence, so that gradually Crane's humanism developed from estrangement in *Maggie* to brotherhood in "The Open Boat."

A standard topic in American thought is city versus nature.[2] So, too, for Crane. Nature invigorates and enables the correspondent in "The Open Boat," Richardson in "One Dash—Horses," and the young stranger of "A Man and Some Others." But also, "an impenetrable mystery, this city" (*George's Mother* 235) enervates young Kelcey, the Bowery slum crushes Maggie, and the "roar of the city" (548) confuses and defeats the aimless outcasts of "An Experiment in Misery." Closely related to city versus nature is east versus west.

Crane's philosophical account of human activity makes that opposition a matter of attitude, posture, and the dynamics of effort. In an eastern city during a February snow storm "those on the walks huddled their necks closely in the collars of their coats and went along stooping like a race of aged people" ("The Men in the Storm" 577). Out west, correspondent Crane, caught in a February blizzard in Eddyville, Nebraska, reports that "the thermometer at this time registers eighteen degrees below zero. The temperature of the room which is the writer's bedchamber is precisely one and a half degrees below zero" (694); nonetheless the Nebraska farmers remained "strong, fine, sturdy men, not bended like the Eastern farmer but erect and agile" (696). Why? And why in the face of difficult challenges, either natural or made, do some persons retrench and resign themselves while other persist and struggle? Crane explores cooperative effort, probing to see if it produces solidarity even when falling short. Or, to put matter in the terminology of Immanual Kant's philosophy, Crane investigates the conditions of the possibility of meaningful human action.

Humans amid Indifference, Sullivan County and New York City

"The Open Boat" contains Crane's famous declaration of the universe's indifference: "the serenity of nature amid the struggles of the individual . . . she was indifferent, flatly indifferent" (905). This, however, is only one of Crane's affirmations of the unconcern of the universe. Staple features of his humanism are actions in a neutral, indifferent arena. In the chapel scene of *The Red Badge of Courage*, Henry Fleming throws a pinecone at a squirrel to measure nature's reaction to human affairs. Nature's response gives Fleming little insight or encouragement. When Crane's other protoganists look to nature for confirmation, encouragement, or comfort, they also discover an unaligned universe.

The little man of the Sullivan County sketches suspects that nature is menacing and predatory. [3] After his fears have run their course, he finds he had made typical human errors. For example, he had supposed that the universe was ordered for humans, but "this country may have been formed by a very reckless and distracted giant. . . . Not admiring the results of his labors he set off several earthquakes under it and tried to wreck it." The result is perfect for wild animals, "here the wild hogs were in a country which just suited them. Its tangled forests, tumbled rocks and intricate swamps were for them admirable places of residence" ("Hunting Wild Hogs" 483, 484). Or, although a dangerous place for human travel, the little man learns that the "entangled, disordered and intricate Sullivan County" (8:207) is a haven for "The Last Panther."

In addition, Crane's little man mistakenly personifies nature: "the music of the wind in the trees is songs of loneliness, hymns of abandonment" ("A Ghoul's Accountant" 498); "he battled with hordes of ignorant bushes on his way to knolls and solitary trees which invited him . . . the peak swayed and tottered and was ever about to smite with a granite arm" ("The Mesmeric Mountain" 513, 515). He explores a cave when "its black mouth had gaped at him . . . traitorous rocks rolled from beneath the little man's feet" ("Four Men in a Cave" 489, 490); when he fishes, he struggles "with a hook and line entangled in the hordes of vindictive weeds and sticks on the bottom" ("The Octopush" 495); and, late at night, "the camp-fire spluttered valiantly for a time, opposing its music to the dismal crooning of the trees that accented the absence of things congenial and alive" ("The Cry of a Huckleberry Pudding" 8:255).

Fear pays the tuition for the little man as he learns that the "octopush" is actually a wet stump; that "the song of the spectral dog" is not a mystical omen, but that "the damn dog was hungry" ("The Black Dog" 505); and "a bear on a spree is not a black-haired pirate. He is merely a hoodlum" ("A Tent in Agony" 510). He also discovers that the mountain has no eyes nor is it following him; when he reaches the summit, the little man sees that "the mountain under his feet was motionless" ("The Mesmeric Mountain" 515). Thus the

little man of Crane's early Sullivan County sketches learns that nature proceeds on its own way, pursuing its own purposes. Nature is
neither threatening nor anti-human, but rather uninterested, aloof,
and unconcerned about human enterprises.

After the Sullivan County sketches Crane turned to life in the
city and found that—despite the presence of people—it, too, was a
place of disinterest, as in "Mr. Binks' Day Off," in which "the sense
of a city is battle" (562). Many other stories depict the city as a bat-
tleground. Crane uses the language of war to describe much of city
life. For instance, in rush-hour traffic, "In the Broadway Cable
Cars," "sometimes the conductor breaks the bell-strap when he
pulls it under these conditions. Then as the car goes on he moves
forward and bullies some person who had nothing to do with the affair. . . . From the forward end you hear the gripman uttering shrill
whoops and running over citizens . . . . The interior of the car resembles the scene of the battle of Wounded Knee . . . that war is grim"
(8:374, 376). There are also pitched battles in restaurants: "whenever I come into a place of this sort I am reminded of the Battle of
Gettysburg, remarked the stranger" (591), who narrates "In a Park
Row Restaurant." The waiters dash about attacking the patrons;
"they served customers with such speed and violence that it often
resembled a personal assault . . . . A waiter struck two blows at the
table and left there a knife and a fork" (592). The command center
for the restaurant battle is out of sight but within earshot. "From
afar back, at the places of communication to the kitchen, there
came the sound of a continual roaring altercation, hoarse and vehement, like the cries of the officers of a regiment under attack" (592).
The beer hall in *Maggie* is so crowded that it needs "a battalion of
waiters" (30).

Elsewhere in the city, squads of soldiers fight skirmishes over ter-
ritory. There are novice warriors: "a baby was wandering in a strange
country. . . . His dress . . . was soiled and showed the marks of many
conflicts like a chain-shirt of a warrior . . . . He braced his legs apart
in an attitude of earnest attention . . . he clenched his thin hands
and advanced with a formidable gesture. He looked like some wee
battler in a war" ("An Ominous Baby" 527, 529). There are apprentice warriors: "a very little boy stood upon a heap of gravel for the
honor of Rum Alley. . . . Tattered gamins on the right made a furious
assault on the gravel heap. On their small, convulsed faces there
shone the grins of true assassins" (*Maggie* 7). Of course, in time ap-
prentices become journeymen, although some of Crane's full-
fledged warriors are remarkably young. In *Maggie*, Pete is "a lad of

sixteen years, although the chronic sneer of an ideal manhood already sat on his lips . . . swinging his shoulders in a manner which denoted that he held victory in his fists" (8). In young Jimmie, "the inexperienced fibres of the boy's eyes were hardened at an early age. He became a young man of leather . . . . He maintained a belligerent attitude. . . . He became a truck driver" (20–21) who respects only fire engines. When Jimmie brings Pete to the Johnson "home," Maggie thinks "his patent-leather shoes looked like murder-fitted weapons" (25). In the masterful chapter 11 of *Maggie*, Bowery-warriors Pete, Jimmie, and a friend "edged for positions like frigates contemplating battle" (49). In the battle royal that follows, only a club-wielding policeman saves the saloon from destruction.

Another of Crane's New York City sketches, "The Duel That Was Not Fought," follows Patsy Tulligan and two friends who "had been away up on Eighth avenue, far out of their country." Upon their return they frequent several taverns and on lower Sixth enter "a better saloon than they were in the habit of seeing, but they did not mind it" (8:353). A Cuban prize fighter takes offense at Patsy's careless and loud comments. In the tense moments that follow it looks like the peacemakers who rise from nearby tables will have the opposite effect: "the interference and intolerable discussion brought the three of them forward, battleful and fierce" (8:356). But tempers cool, wasting adrenaline, and the peacemakers prevail.

The city has women warriors, too. Long before Jimmie Johnson fights for the honor of Rum Alley, he watches fights in and around the tenement and, close up, at home. The first look into the Johnson home in *Maggie* reveals "a lighted room in which a large woman was rampant" (12). Mary Johnson walks with "a chieftain-like stride" (13) that befits her battles with her husband and son and her frequent altercations with her neighbor, Mary Murphy, and assorted bartenders and street urchins.

Near the Johnson's apartment lives *George's Mother*, Mrs. Kelcey. Although thin and frail, with her weapons of broom and dustpan, mops, and rags, she, too, is a warrior. Resting at the window she "was planning skirmishes, charges, campaigns" (220). Against the "dust demons" (219) in her apartment she is well matched. "The little intent warrior never hesitated or faltered. She fought with a strong and relentless will" (220–21). One on one against George she also has a good record and invariably wins the daily battle: "each morning his mother went to his room, and fought a battle to arouse him. She was like a soldier. Despite his pleadings, his threats, she remained at her post, imperturbable and unyielding" (265).

George, and his mother, soon measure a grander opponent, the city.[4] George "had begun to look at the great world revolving near to his nose. He had a vast curiosity concerning this city in whose complexities he was buried. It was an impenetrable mystery, this city. It was a blend of many enticing colors. He longed to comprehend it completely, that he might walk understandingly in its greatest marvels, its mightiest march of life, its sin" (235). Mrs. Kelcey sizes up her fighting, cursing, howling neighbors in the alleyways. From her window, she studies "in the distance an enormous brewery [that] towered over other buildings. Great gilt letters advertised a brand of beer. . . . It vaguely interested her, for a moment, as a stupendous affair, a machine of great strength" (220).

Neither George nor his mother lack auxiliaries in their fights with the city. His mother's ally is "the little chapel [that] sat humbly between two towering apartment-houses" (255); his alliance is with Bleecker's drinking club.[5] Each ally agrees that personal vindictiveness and animosity must be overcome. George's city-as-conspirator theory is reinforced in the private room in the rear of the saloon where he joins Bleecker's gang. In this refuge "they began to fraternize in jovial fashion. It was understood that they were true and tender spirits. They had come away from a grinding world filled with men who were harsh" (228). For its part, the tiny chapel braces George's mother against the intrigue and treachery of worldly evil; "a roar of wheels and a clangor of bells [was] . . . emblematic of the life of the city. It seemed somehow to affront this solemn and austere little edifice. It suggested an approaching barbaric invasion" (255).

Kelcey's effort to conquer the city ends when he is fired. George's mother understands better than he; "she continued to sob in a dull, shaking way. In the pose of her head there was an expression of her conviction that comprehension of her pain was impossible to the universe" (267). When George seeks out his saloon allies, he realizes his isolation; "in them all he saw that something had been reversed" (271).

As the little man of Sullivan County, George and his mother had to confront indifference. In the city there is no grand plan, only multiple purposes; no unified project, only countless conflicting claims and claimants. The city notices individuals but without concern for their well-being. For example, the street urchins' battle in the opening scene of *Maggie* is widely observed; "from a window . . . there leaned a curious woman. Some laborers . . . paused for a moment and regarded the fight. The engineer of a passive tugboat hung lazily to a railing and watched" (7). But no one moves to intervene. The city is like the warm, well-fed, dry-goods proprietor at the window in "The Men in the Storm," who "stood in an attitude of magnificent reflection. He slowly stroked his moustache with a certain grandeur of manner, and looked down at the snow-encrusted mob" (581). Elsewhere, dozens pass by, as in the "The Broken-Down Van." Some few pause to look. Most rush on as the unnoticed van driver searches for the lost hub nut while "the ever-forward flowing tide of the growlers flowed on" (524).

From time to time the city's interest is piqued by the troubles of others, but help is rarely forthcoming. Bystanders at "The Fire" are briefly thrilled at the fire and the firemen. But soon their interest in the flames and the fate of the victims wanes; "men had already begun to turn toward each other in that indefinite regret and sorrow, as if they were not quite sure of the reason of their mourning" (597). In "When a Man Falls, a Crowd Gathers," the crowd is aggressively attentive to "the marvel of this mystery of life or death [that] held them chained" (601). Morbid curiosity hampers the feeble effort to find out what ails the fallen old man, while fascination blocks any late arrival who muscles forward; "from the rear, a man came thrusting his way impetuously, satisfied that there was a horror to be seen and apparently insane to get a view of it. Less curious persons swore at these men when they trod upon their toes" (601).

In "An Experiment in Luxury" and "An Experiment in Misery," the fate of the rich and the poor and the city's attitudes toward individuals are reduced to formulas, "the eternal mystery of social condition" (552) and simply "social position" (547). While social position is an obvious matter to the youth, he is unsure whether the gap between the haves and the have-nots is morally indictable. When he observes the rich, the youth wonders "if incomprehensible justice were the sister of open wrong" (552), and he recalls that "there had been times in his life when little voices called to him continually from the darkness; he heard them now as an idle, half-smothered babble on the horizon edge" (552–53). Lounging in the comfortable room of his wealthy friend, the youth thinks, for the time being, "there was the horizon, he said, and, of course, there should be a babble of pain on it. Thus it was written; it was a law, he thought. And, anyway, perhaps it was not so bad as those who babbled tried to tell" (553).

The same pattern occurs in "An Experiment in Misery." Initial moral outrage is followed by bewilderment at the obdurate status quo. During his night in the flop house the youth hears the cry of the poor:

The sound, in its high piercing beginnings that dwindled to final melancholy moans, expressed a red and grim tragedy of the unfathomable
possibilities of the man's dreams. But to the youth these were not
merely the shrieks of a vision pierced man. They were an utterance of
the meaning of the room and its occupants. It was to him the protest
of the wretch who feels the touch of the imperturbable granite wheels
and who then cries with an impersonal eloquence, with a strength not
from him, giving voice to the wail of a whole section, a class, a people.
(543)

But with approaching dawn, light "made the room comparatively
commonplace and uninteresting" (544). During the day, the "is"
rather than the "ought" of city life holds sway. Resting on a park
bench, the youth studies the distance between the rich and the poor
as he notes the pace and intensity of "the people of the street hurrying . . . in their good clothes as upon important missions" (547) and
the lassitude of the loafers. The busy pedestrians pay him no attention, neither does the city heed its outcasts. Those on the margin do
not understand "the roar of the city"; to them, it is like the babble
the youth heard in the room of his rich friend, "the confusion of
strange tongues, babbling heedlessly" (548). The city has a clear
voice—"the clink of coin" (548)—but gives little hope to the mar-
ginalized.

Regarding social position and justice, Crane sees only a coinci-
dental connection between the forces that govern city life and ele-
mental human needs, although he does find that the unconcern, animosity, and intransigence of city life throttle individual hopes. He
suggests that although the artificial environment of the city is, like
nature, indifferent to aspirations, nature's rhythms and laws have a
neutrality amenable to human effort.

"Mr. Binks' Day Off" calls attention to the restorative power of
nature. Binks's notice of new green grass in the little park gives him
spring fever. "It cried to him that nature was still supreme; he had
begun to think that the banking business to be the pivot on which the
universe turned" (558). Accordingly, the Binks family takes a day trip
to a New Jersey village. The country "cooled their nerves . . . . The
tranquillity of the scene contained a meaning of peace and virtue that
was incredibly monotonous to the warriors from the metropo-
lis . . . they heard the song of the universal religion, the mighty and
mystic hymn of nature" (560, 562). In this sketch, published by the
New York *Press* on July 8, 1894, Crane offers a diagnosis of—and
prescibes an antidote to—urban life. If "the sense of a city is battle"
(562), perhaps life away from the city is not. Notice that Crane recom-

mends, as a remedy, not pristine nature but a half-way station. The Binkses find relief in the cultivated, humanized, "improved" surroundings of lawns, orchards, fields, and gardens.

For Crane, in obvious and useful ways, nature is congenial and manageable. In several New York City sketches, he reiterates the prescription of "Mr. Binks' Day Off"—the natural as a tonic and a relief. In "Stories Told by an Artist," when "Purple Sanderson went to his home in St. Lawrence county to enjoy some county air," Little Pennoyer becomes even more depressed. "It is bad to be imprisoned in brick and dust and cobbles when your ear can hear in the distance the harmony of the summer sunlight upon leaf and blade of green" (574). "The Roof Gardens and Gardeners of New York" tells of city dwellers' search for fresh air and open spaces. Unable to leave the city as do the Binks, they go to the roofs; "just above their heads is what might be called a country of unoccupied land . . . as lonely as a desert . . . as untrodden as the corners of Arizona" (8:381). Although not a lasting solution, roof-top nature provides relief; "an evening upon a tenement roof . . . is not so bad if you have never seen the mountains nor heard, to your heart, the slow sad sound of the pines" (8:381).

Crane's Sullivan County and New York City sketches depict the indifference of nature and city to human aspirations. Nature's indifference also has a neutrality that provides respite to the Binkses or relief to the roof-top gardeners. In 1895, some eighteen months before Crane wrote of roof-top gardens, he had encountered in the West and in Mexico a pristine, primitive, and unpeopled nature. The space and opportunity he found offered relief, encouraged initiative, and repaid effort. Nature led him to innovate and improvise as he discovered that, as the author of his own script, real success and real failure were possible. Genuine courage, not merely a badge of courage, was within reach.[6]

Clearly, Crane believed in human freedom before his western trip, still, the West significantly altered his view of human action and his opinion about individual initiative. Previously, the Sullivan County tales and New York city newspaper sketches portrayed confused and ineffectual actions. After the western trip, competence and optimism surfaced in his writings. Both east versus west and city versus nature are involved in the evolution of Crane's view of human action. Why the East and the city enervate while the West and nature energize is a complex matter.[7] For example, in the West, Crane discovered a demanding world, an environment in some ways harsher than the Bowery's.[8] Why should a winter storm make the population of an eastern city passive and reclusive whereas a January blizzard summons the ingenuity and combative instincts of Nebraska farmers? Crane suggests that the constructed world is fraught with whim and caprice, whereas events in the natural world have both regularity and sufficient loose-play that human actions can make a difference.

Human Initiative in the Indifferent Nature of the West and the Brotherhood of Joint Effort

What can be finer than a fine frosty morning, a runaway horse, and only the still hills to watch.

Crane to Willis Brooks Hawkins, October 24, 1895

Dark mesquit spread from horizon to horizon. There was no house or horsemen from which a mind could evolve a city or a crowd. The world was declared to be a desert and unpeopled.

"A Man and Some Others"

It would be difficult to describe the subtle brotherhood of men that was here established on the seas. No one said that it was so. No one mentioned it. But it dwelt in the boat, and each man felt it warn him. . . . there was this comradeship that the correspondent, for instance, who had been taught to be cynical of men, knew even at the time was the best experience of his life.

"The Open Boat"

Even though the civilized world had penetrated the natural world of the "Old West," vast stretches of uncontaminated nature remained. In "One Dash—Horses," Crane retells a night and a morning of his own life. Richardson (Crane) and his companion, José, leave the desert for an evening meal and a place to sleep. After a bowl of tortillas, he "decided to smoke a cigarette, and then changed his mind. It would be much finer to go to sleep" (733). Hours later he is awakened by a drunken gang who threaten him. Richardson sits up, draws his revolver, and stares down the "fat, round-faced Mexican, whose little snake-like mustache was as black as his eyes, and whose eyes were black as jet. He was insane with the wild rage of a man whose liquor is dully burning at his brain" (735). But Richardson does not use his revolver. Courageous reactions notwithstanding, luck saves him, "Come, the girls are here! . . . Laughing, his comrades hustled him toward the door" (736–37). Later, in a predawn ride, Richardson's vigilance and expert horsemanship lead to his rescue away from the village.[9] "The houses of the village glided past in a moment, and the great, clear, silent plain appeared like a pale blue sea of mist and wet bushes. Above the mountains the colors of the sunlight were like the first tones, the opening chords of the mighty hymn of the morning" (739).

In Crane's adventure stories, the natural environment of the West can be congenial and invigorating, as in "One Dash—Horses," or reassuring and safe, as in "A Man and Some Others," when, after a showdown and gunfight, the stranger walks away into the "stillness and the peace of the wilderness" (786).[10] But nature can also threaten. In "The Blue Hotel," a Nebraska blizzard is "a turmoiling sea of snow. The huge arms of the wind were making attempts—mighty, circular, futile—to embrace the flakes as they sped. . . . When the party rounded the corner they were fairly blinded by the pelting of the snow. It burned their faces like fire" (801, 819).

Crane often set his adventure tales in the desert. What is significant is not so much the paucity of people as the fact that so much space exists that humans have been unable to tranform either the natural setting or "the vast vacancy of the plains" ("An Excursion Ticket" 682–83). Awed by its immensity, Crane sought to measure the scale of the West. "Stephen Crane in Mexico (II)" traces the two-and-a-half-day, thousand-mile train ride he took from San Antonio, Texas, to Mexico City. The endless land is not empty; nature is abundant—mesquite, brown and sage colored bushes, cactus, pines, and maguey plants.

> The brown wilderness of mesquite drifted steadily and for hours past the car-windows. Occasionally a little ranch appeared half-buried in the bushes . . . as the train went on over the astonishing brown sea of mesquite . . . over this lonely wilderness vast silence hung, a speckless sky, ignorant of bird or cloud . . . . The train again invaded a wilderness of mesquite. It was amazing . . . . Infrequently horsemen, shepherds, hovels appeared in the mesquite. Once, upon a small hillock a graveyard came into view and over each grave was a black cross. These somber emblems, lined against the pale sky, were . . . new in this lonely land of brown bushes . . . . The sage-bushes became scarce and the cactus began to grow with a greater courage . . . all the afternoon the cactus continued to improve in sizes. . . . These hills were grown thickly with pines, fragrant, gently waving in the cool breeze . . . . the maguey plant . . . flourished its lance-point leaves in long rows. (718, 719, 721, 724, 726, 727)

Humans and their habitations are inversely noteworthy, sporadic interruptions. Ironically, human knowledge, skill, and determination are potent in this barely altered, undomesticated, nonhumanized landscape.

The concepts of the pristine West as a tonic and outdoor living to build a robust self were not new with Crane.[11] Sixty years earlier, Washington Irving had declared that "we send our youth abroad to grow luxurious and effeminate in Europe, it appears to me, that a previous tour on the prairies would be more likely to produce. . . manliness, simplicity and self-dependence" (43). Like others before him, Crane was able to develop independence and confidence in the West as he discovered that the natural world provided an opportunity for self-actualization.

Crane's view of human action evolved as he experienced the open, natural arena. There he discovered that human beings are not given extra consideration or extended special dispensation. Individuals of the human or any other species are neither helped nor handicapped. Nature is neutral and unbiased toward results. "Finally, when the great moon climbed the heavens and cast its ghastly radiance upon the bushes, it made a new and more brilliant crimson of the camp-fire, where the flames capered merrily through its mesquit branches, filling the silence with the fire chorus, an ancient melody which surely bears a message of the inconsequence of individual tragedy—a message that is in the boom of the sea, the sliver of the wind through the grass-blades, the silken clash of hemlock boughs" ("A Man and Some Others" 779).

Second, and significantly, Crane's western stories and his Mexican sketches explain that even though individual tragedies might be inconsequential against the backdrop of an indifferent nature, human courage and human efforts remain indispensable. In the West Crane was impressed with the value of courage and the worth of trying, whether or not effort produced success. Indeed, "Nebraska's Bitter Fight for Life," "The Five White Mice," and "A Man and Some Others" focus on struggles in which steadfastness, courage, and initiative are crucial to outcomes.

Sometimes the outcome of the tales is left unsettled, and sometimes the protagonists fail, partially succeed, or are surprised. Most interesting, however, are stories like "The Five White Mice," in which Crane alleges that "nothing had happened" (771). Still, whether or not anything happened depends upon the perspectives of both participants and observers. In "The Five White Mice," very little happens for Benson and the Frisco Kid—only a brief interruption in the New York Kid's escorting them home. For the New York Kid, the brief interruption is a showdown. He has been alone in space with the face of the Mexican, "a yellow mask smiling in eager cruelty, in satisfaction, and above all it was lit with sinister decision"

(766). In a few seconds his mind's eye has witnessed a complete drama, "these views were perfectly stereopticon, flashing in and away from his thought with an inconceivable rapidity" (768) while he feels "some of the eels of despair lay wet and cold against his back" (769. When he effortlessly draws his revolver, "the fulsome grandee sprang backward with a low cry. The man who had been facing the 'Frisco Kid took a quick step away. The beautiful array of Mexicans was suddenly disorganized" (769–70). Much happens to the New York Kid. He discovers that he can act with courage and self-assurance. He also discovers that others are "all human beings. They were unanimous in not wishing for too bloody combat. . . . he was bursting with rage because these men had not previously confided to him that they were vulnerable" (770). When his opponent asks, "Well, señor, is it finished?" the Kid realizes the elasticity of time. "After a moment he answered: 'I am willing.' He found it strange that he should be able to speak after this silence of years" (770). The reader has been shown the elasticity of events—nothing has happened and everything has happened.

Crane's tales with mixed, unresolved outcomes also examine the indispensability of human courage. In the poignant "A Man and Some Others," eight Mexicans twice ambush Bill and the stranger. As a result, the stranger's (and Bill's) capacity for courage and self-assertion are actualized. The stranger also experiences "the inconsequence of human tragedy" (781) as he confronts the two faces of death: killing, "he had killed a man . . . it was easy to kill a man," and dying, "Bill was dying, and the dignity of last defeat, the superiority of him who stands in his grave, was in the pose of the lost sheep-herder" (785).

If the outcome of "Nebraska's Bitter Fight for Life" is uncertain, Crane's admiration for the resolute farmers is not. When the drought comes, "Some few despaired at once and went to make new homes in the north, in the south, in the east, in the west. But the greater proportion of the people of this stricken district were men who loved their homes, their farms, their neighborhoods, their counties. . . . They are a fearless folk, completely American. Their absolute types are now sitting about New England dinner tables. They summoned their strength for a long war with cold and hunger" (690). With the onset of winter, a farmer leaves his wife and child to search for work. "The woman lived alone with her baby until the provisions were gone. . . . The nearest neighbor was three miles away. She put her baby in its little ramshackle carriage and traveled the three miles. The family there shared as long as they could—two or three days. Then she went on to the next house. There, too, with the quality of mercy which comes with incredible suffering, they shared with her" (695). Near the end of the sketch Crane expresses admiration for the courageous and compassionate farmers and marvels at their faith in nature. "They have a determination to wait until nature, with her mystic processes, restores to them the prosperity and bounty of former years" (698). "In the meanwhile," Crane concludes, "they depend on their endurance, their capacity to help each other, and their steadfast and unyielding courage" (699).

Crane's western experiences prepared the way for the mature philosophy of human action of his greatest short story, "The Open Boat," which reaffirms the value of the resourceful human efforts characteristic of the western tales. It also offers the possibility of real success and genuine community born of joint effort.

Crane's January 6, 1897 newspaper dispatch, "Stephen Crane's Own Story," sets out the facts retold six months later in a *Scribner's Magazine* story, "The Open Boat," subtitled "A tale intended to be after the fact. Being the experience of four men from the sunk steamer *Commodore.*" The four men are the cook, the oiler, the correspondent, and the injured captain. Crane was dispatched by the Bacheller newspaper syndicate to slip into Cuba to report on the Cuban revolution in late December 1896. The *Commodore,* loaded with munitions and Cuban insurgents—and with Crane on board as an able seaman—struck a sandbar when leaving the port of Jacksonville. Damaged while being towed off the sandbar, the ship took on water and two days later sank at sea. All the lifeboats were launched, leaving Crane and three others with a small dingy. The story retells some thirty hours of exposure, rowing, and suffering before the small dingy capsized on the breakers, forcing the four to swim a half mile to shore at Daytona Beach.[12] As in his western stories, the setting for "The Open Boat" is natural—the ocean. However in place of a solitary or unorchestrated efforts, four men struggle in unison. They find that their shared trial discloses human solidarity as each encounters an efficacious, social self:

> They were a captain, an oiler, a cook and a correspondent, and they were friends, friends in a more curiously iron-bound degree than may be common. The hurt captain, lying against the water-jar in the bow, spoke always in a low voice and calmly, but he could never command a more ready and swiftly obedient crew than the motley three of the dingey. It was more than a mere recognition of what was best for the common safety. There was surely in it a quality that was personal and heartfelt. (890)

In their ordeal, solidarity instead of rancor and mistrust flourishes because their survival test is neither impossible nor routine. It is a stern but fair trial of wits and determination.

The existential[13] disinterest of nature is only apparent after painful struggle. Initially, the correspondent finds the dingy to be overmatched by waves that are "most wrongfully and barbarously abrupt and tall" (885). He soon discovers that any particular wave mastered is not "the final outburst of the ocean, the last effort of the grim water" (886). It is only a wave, soon there will be another. "A singular disadvantage of the sea lies in the fact that after successfully surmounting one wave you discover that there is another behind it just as important and just as nervously anxious to do something effective in the way of swamping boats" (886). The four are silent in the struggle; neither optimism nor hopelessness is expressed.

They see a lighthouse, then the land, then the beach, and they conclude that they will be safe in an hour. It had turned out to be an easy contest, so they celebrate. Three dry matches and four good cigars are produced, and "the four waifs rode impudently in their little boat . . . puffed at the big cigars and judged well and ill of all men. Everybody took a drink of water" (892–93). But no one on shore sees them; they are not rescued. The slowly setting sun brings anger but not despair. The men are bitter because no one recognizes their plight or appreciates their efforts.

> As for the reflections of the men, there was a great deal of rage in them. Perchance they might be formulated thus: "If I am going to be drowned—if I am going to be drowned—if I am going to be drowned, why, in the name of the seven mad gods who rule the sea, was I allowed to come thus far and contemplate sand and trees? Was I brought here merely to have my nose dragged away as I was about to nibble the sacred cheese of life? It is preposterous. If this old ninny-woman, Fate, cannot do better than this, she should be deprived of the management of men's fortunes. She is an old hen who knows not her intention. If she has decided to drown me, why did she not do it in the beginning and save all this trouble. The whole affair is absurd." (894)

Finally, a man on the beach waves to them. He is then joined by a crowd from the resort hotel, and all the people on land wave merrily to the four "fishermen" in the tiny boat. The people do not recognize the men's plight, and, with nightfall, both the lighthouse and the shore disappear.

Through the long, painful night the men spell each other at rowing. Crane uses the seriousness of the task to point up the precariousness of human existence. The small boat has two fragile oars, each was "a thin little oar and it seemed often ready to snap" (885). They cannot let the boat drift, so they row continually. Crane skillfully exploits the hazards of taking turns at the oars.

> The very ticklish part of the business was when the time came for the reclining one in the stern was to take his turn at the oars. By the very last star of truth, it is easier to steal eggs from under a hen than it was to change seats in the dingey. First the man in the stern slid his hand along the thwart and moved with care, as if he were of Sèvres. Then the man in the rowing seat slid his hand along the other thwart. It was all done with the most extraordinary care. As the two sidled past each other, the whole party kept watchful eyes on the coming wave, and the captain cried: "Look out now! Steady there!" (889)

They row and row. During most of the night, a great shark circles their boat. Finally, at dawn, still alive and still forced to struggle, the correspondent realizes humanity's situation in nature. Shipwrecks are merely natural events, "*apropos* of nothing" (891); they are less than "the breaking of a pencil's point" (903). The correspondent learns that nature places no special significance or insignificance upon individual lives. "When it occurs to a man that nature does not regard him as important, and that she feels she would not maim the universe by disposing of him, he at first wishes to throw bricks at the temple, and he hates deeply the fact that there are no bricks and no temples" (902). In the early morning light, the wind-tower reappears. "This tower was a giant, standing with its back to the plight of the ants. It represented in a degree, to the correspondent, the serenity of nature amid the struggles of the individual—nature in the wind, and nature in the vision of men. She did not seem cruel to him then, nor beneficent, nor treacherous, nor wise. But she was indifferent, flatly indifferent" (905).

The four decide to risk a run through the breakers onto the beach. A half-mile from shore, the dingy capsizes, and they must swim. Later, after a wave tosses the correspondent over the up-turned boat, he finds himself in waist-deep water. A man on shore drags the cook, the captain, and the correspondent to safety. Billie, the oiler, drowns.

The stern ordeal over, the three survivors understand the serene indifference of nature. That night, they stand on the beach. Amid the perpetual sea wind and the ceaseless waves, as they meditated upon nature's abiding message, "they felt that they could then be interpreters" (909). Through their confrontation with the indifferent universe the survivors understand both the limits and possibilities of human effort and human community.[14] Their sense of community, however, is a sharp contrast to the bogus brotherhoods of battlefield and barroom.

The Bogus Brotherhoods of Battlefield and Barroom

> He suddenly lost concern for himself, and forgot to look at a menacing fate. He became not a man but a member.
> He felt the subtle battle brotherhood . . . it was a mysterious fraternity born of the smoke and danger of death.
>
> *The Red Badge of Courage*

> They began to fraternize in jovial fashion. It was understood that they were true and tender spirits. They had come away from a grinding world filled with men who were harsh.
> Afterward a general hand-shaking was inaugurated. Brotherly sentiments flew about the room. There was an uproar of fraternal feeling.
>
> *George's Mother*

That Crane should use the term *subtle* to describe both the calm communion of "The Open Boat" and the frenzy of Fleming's battle brotherhood is startling. But then he also points out several similarities between the heartful, unstated affection that dwelt in the open boat and the bold and brassy comradery of the back barroom of the Bleecker drinking club.

It is, observes Crane, often difficult to distinguish genuine from sham brotherhood. During Kelcey's first meeting with Bleecker, "he began to feel that he was passing the happiest evening of his life" (*George's Mother* 227). In "The Open Boat," "there was this comradeship that the correspondent, for instance, who had been taught to be cynical of men, knew even at the time was the best experience of his life" (890). Surface similarities aside, Crane fixes upon the significant difference with epistemologically precise language: Kelcey "felt" while the correspondent "knows." When he leaves the bar that night, "the cold air of the street filled Kelcey with vague surprise. It made his head feel hot. As for his legs, they were like willow-twigs" (230). Nonetheless, as he falls asleep, "he felt that he had spent the most delightful evening of his life" (230). After a night of clear-headed reflection, as the shark circles the dingy, the correspondent "knows the pathos of his situation . . . [and he] was moved by a profound and perfectly impersonal comprehension" (902–3).

Actually, there are numerous differences between the Bleecker bar brotherhood and the open boat comradeship. Kelcey is naive, in-experienced, and easily impressed; the correspondent is well-trav-eled, hardened, and jaded. As significant as the contrast between so-briety and drunkenness are the attitudes and self-images of the members of the two groups. Different backgrounds, the city and na-ture, also inform the experiencers.

The Bleecker brotherhood requires an artificial environment: "a gas-jet with a colored globe shed a crimson radiance. The polished wood of walls and furniture gleamed with faint rose-colored reflec-tions. Upon the floor sawdust was thickly sprinkled" (227). In the smoke-filled back room, the brothers of brew have elaborate greet-ing ceremonies, great shows of courtesy, and fervent expressions of concern for each other. "Jones began to develop qualities of great el-oquence and wit. . . . He grew earnest and impassioned. He delivered speeches on various subjects. His lectures were to him very impos-ing. The force of his words thrilled him. Sometimes he was over-come. The others agreed with him in all things" (228). As each takes his turn at oratory, they discover that no one's talents have been rec-ognized by the cruel world. "When one of them chose to divulge some place where the world had pierced him, there was a chorus of violent sympathy. They rejoiced at their temporary isolation and safety. . . . Each man explained, in his way, that he was totally out of place in the before-mentioned world. They were possessed of vari-ous virtues which were unappreciated by those with whom they were commonly obliged to mingle" (228–29).

Each self-disclosure is met with sympathy and support: "they ex-changed compliments . . . arose and shook hands emotionally. . . ."(229). Leave-taking is painful that night, and farewells deeply felt, "on the sidewalk the men took fervid leave. They clutched hands with ex-traordinary force and proclaimed, for the last time, ardent and ad-miring friendships" (230).

Later, Maggie Johnson becomes the personification of Kelcey's ro-mantic dreams of "an indefinite woman . . . consumed by a wild, torrential passion . . . beseeching for affection as a pet animal" (236). Her cold unresponsiveness fills George with self-pity; he "could now perceive that the universe hated him" (240). Thereafter, an in-vitation to a party at Bleecker's presents an opportunity to "taste the delicious revenge of a partial self-destruction. The universe would regret its position when it saw him drunk" (240). That evening, the diffidence, courtesy, and fellow-feeling of the back barroom are im-measurably increased in Bleecker's apartment. Kelcey arrives to find glasses, beer keg, whiskey bottles, cigars, and smoking tobacco.

"Old Bleecker had arranged them so deftly that they resembled a primitive bar" (241). Again, Kelcey "felt that there was something fine and thrilling in this affair isolated from a stern world . . . he knew that old sentiment of brotherly regard for those about him . . . he rejoiced at their faces . . . he was capable of heroisms" (245).

The aftermath of Kelcey's beer brotherhood is that "the grim truthfulness of the day showed disaster and death" (249). When George loses his job and his mother falls ill, he seeks out his bar brothers only to discover "that he was below them in social position. Old Bleecker said gloomily that he did not see how he could lend money at that time" (271). Neither can Jones or O'Connor.

On the contrary, the brotherhood of "The Open Boat" does not pale with the dawn. After a night at sea, the correspondent understands the indifference of nature and genuine brotherhood. Hours later, at dusk and on land, the survivors hear "the sound of the great sea's voice to the men on shore" (909). It tells of the value of joint effort and the worth of each man in his willingness to do his part. Each man tends his role: the captain navigates, the cook bails, and the correspondent and the oiler row. Preparing to make a run for the shore, they face their situation squarely and realistically; "there were no hurried words, no pallor, no plain agitation" (906).

The open boat is a quiet place, very little is said, "speech was devoted to the business of the boat" (902). Absent are the showy reassurances and the boisterousness of Bleeker brotherhood. In the open boat, brotherhood is not talked about. "No one said that it was so. No one mentioned it" (890). The open boat is a sanctuary of competence, honesty, and devotion. "The men in the dingy had not discussed these matters. . . . The men were silent" (902, 906).

A serious challenge requiring intelligence and hard work can produce the certifiable brotherhood of "The Open Boat." Crisis situations in battle also prompt actions and promote a sense of brotherhood, but Crane finds the frenzy and fraternity of the front-line wanting. He views the semiconscious, reflex actions of combat as remarkably akin to barroom behavior. Fleming's superior officer acts inebriated; "the lieutenant was crowing. He seemed drunk with fighting" (174). Fleming himself, like the drunken Kelcey, has trouble walking. The former "lost the habit of balance and fell heavily" (173), and the latter "stumbled . . . in his voyage across the floor" (230).

When battle mania seizes Fleming in his first encounter with the enemy, his reactions are rote and mechanical as he "fired a first wild shot. Directly he was working at his weapon like an automatic affair" (112). During his battlefield seizure he does not act; he reacts, responds, and behaves. "He became not a man but a member. He felt that something of which he was a part—a regiment, an army, a cause, or a country—was in a crisis. He was welded into a common personality which was dominated by a single desire. For some moments he could not flee no more than a little finger can commit a revolution from a hand" (112). After the first charge, the men celebrate, like the brothers of Bleecker's club, with "some handshakings and deep speeches" (117). Their merriment is interrupted by the enemy's second charge. Then a different sort of hypnotic trance overtakes Fleming, and he panics "like a proverbial chicken" (119).[15]

Crane also perceptively notes unusual, not obvious, traits shared by bar and battlefield drunkenness. First are the same sensations and physical reactions. Fleming finds that the "mysterious fraternity born of the smoke and danger of death" (113) gives him novel sensations, "a blistering sweat, a sensation that his eyeballs were about to crack like hot stones. A burning roar filled his ears" (113). He acquires new reflexes, "following this came a red rage. He developed the acute exasperation of a pestered animal, a well-meaning cow worried by dogs" (113).[16] Nothing unique here. After his first bout with Bleecker, Kelcey is battle-sore. His eyes "felt as if they had been baked. When he moved his eyelids there was a sensation that they were cracking. In his mouth there was a singular taste. It seemed to him that he had been sucking the end of a wooden spoon. Moreover, his temper was rampant within him. It sought something to devour" (231).

The participants at the bar and the battle are also quasi-spectators of their own conduct. Each suffers the frustration of being blocked from articulating perceptive and profound insights. At the party in Bleecker's apartment, Kelcey, flat on the floor, hears the din of the party above him, "the sound of the many voices was to him like the roar of a distant river. Still, he felt that if he could only annul the force of these million winding fingers that gripped his senses, he was capable of most brilliant and entertaining things" (246). Fleming, rationalizing after his desertion at the front, convinces himself that "his actions had been sagacious things" (124). Sadly, because he is forced to serve with dull and stupid fellows, his keen intellect is wasted: "overturned and crushed by their lack of sense in holding the position, when intelligent deliberation would have convinced them that it was impossible. He, the enlightened man who looks afar in the dark, had fled because of his superior perceptions and knowledge. He felt a great anger against his comrades. He knew it could be proved that they had been fools. . . . [But] their density would not enable them to understand his sharper point of view" (124).

Crane's assessment of Fleming's battlefield "heroism" is that it is neither worthier—nor much different—from running away. Both are conditioned, involuntary responses. His fighting during the first charge is "an automatic affair" (112); he is aware only of "a mass of blurred shapes" (113). So, too, when he deserts, "he lost the direction of safety . . . . he ran like a blind man" (119–20). Then, the next day when he rejoins his regiment and eventually leads the attack as the flag bearer, another kind of trance takes hold of him, "the youth was not conscious that he was erect upon his feet. He did not know the direction of the ground" (173). He is seized by "a mad enthusiasm . . . [and] the delirium that encounters despair and death, and is heedless and blind to the odds. It is a temporary but sublime absence of selfishness" (183). Note that "It" refers to the delirium and the frenzy, not to courage, bravery, or heroism.

Crane, then, criticizes the bogus brotherhoods of battlefield and barroom. In *George's Mother*, Kelcey solves nothing, and Crane's critique is direct. The joys of Bleecker and bar brotherhood notwithstanding, George wakes to "the grim truthfulness of the day" (249). Without a job, he joins the others on the streets; "they were all too clever to work" (262). As his contempt for life grows, so does his inability to deal with it. He is left staring at the wallpaper: "the pattern was clusters of brown roses. He felt them like hideous crabs crawling upon his brain" (276).

Besides the subhuman qualities of "mad enthusiasm" (183) and battlefield delirium, Crane objects to battlefield brotherhood's faulty grasp of reality. Granted a trancelike state, Fleming is enabled to reconstruct, as from a painting, details of battles. Nevertheless, he has no grasp of the big picture. Thanks to his photographic recall, all is "explained to him, save why he himself was there" (183). Battlefield and barroom brotherhood are specious. Their grasps of situations are unreliable, and they result in temporary, destructive states far different from the communities and activities that Crane's humanism endorses.

Tolerance for Escape, Admiration for Competence, and Awareness of Limits

The native, filled with pulque, seldom wishes to fight. Usually he prefers to adore his friends. They will hang together in front of a bar, three or four of them, their legs bending, their arms about each other's necks, their faces lit with an expression of the most ideal affections and supreme brotherly regard.

"A Jag of Pulque Is Heavy"

The man who does the work . . . occupies a position for which the exercise of temperance, of courage, of honesty, has no equal at the altitude of prime-ministers. . . This driver was worth contemplation. . . .[He] is the finest type of man that is grown. He is the pick of the earth . . . for outright performance carried on constantly, coolly, and without elation by a temperate, honest and clear-minded man.

"The Scotch Express"

The combination of his family background—his father was a well-known Methodist clergyman and his mother an activist in church and reform causes, including holding office in the New Jersey Women's Christian Temperance Union—and Crane's own free-spirited, unconventional approach to life are reflected in his humanism. He sees room for both the genial and the strenuous moods.[17]

As for the genial mood of relaxation, his treatment of "A Lovely Jag in a Crowded Car" is a tender, sympathetic treatment of alcohol as a way of dealing with reality. The focus of Crane's sketch is the way the drunk's amiability softens "the atmosphere of the car [which] was as decorous as that of the most frigid of drawing rooms" (8:361). Once aboard, the tipsy man "put his hands on his knees and beamed about him in absolute unalloyed happiness" (8:362). Although he has been on a solitary spree, now he asks the other passengers to join his celebration; "presently his excited spirits overflowed to such an extent that he was obliged to sing" (8:362). But his glad song is rudely and unnecessarily interrupted by the conductor; "he had been on the best of terms with each single atom in space, and now here suddenly appeared a creature who gruffly stated a dampening fact" (8:362). Near the end of the streetcar's run, and after the women shoppers depart for the department stores, the drunken man shares the car with one passenger, a man in the corner. Becoming jovial again, he returns to his song; "he rejoiced that the world was to him one vast landscape of pure rose color" (8:364). When the celebrator gets off, the man in the corner remarks to the conductor, "well, he was a peach" (8:364), and they both reflect upon the drunk's rosy sense of reality, "the pearl-hued joys of life as seen through a pair of strange, oblique, temporary spectacles" (8:364).

For the McClure syndicate, on May 17, 1896, Crane reported that opium produced a similar, temporary adjustment of reality.[18] "Opium's Varied Dreams" explains that "the influence of 'dope' is evidently a fine languor, a complete mental rest. The problems of life no longer appear. Existence is peace. . . . The universe is re-adjusted" (857–58). So far so good, remarks Crane, "wrong departs, injustice vanishes; there is nothing but a quiet, a soothing harmony of all things—until the next morning" (858). There is no denying that chemically induced escapes are short–lived and that ordinary reality reasserts itself. Still, the feeling of peace that occurs is a real fact. Indeed, when this feeling of peace leads to brotherhood, Crane rises to defend it.

On the train ride from Texas to Mexico Crane sees acres and acres of maguey plants. Once in Mexico city, he discovers the need for the "thousands of acres planted in nothing but the maguey" ("A Jag of Pulque Is Heavy" 8:458). Maguey is used to make pulque. "To the Mexican, pulque is a delirium of joy. The lower classes dream of pulque" (8:457). Pulque shops are everywhere, "on every corner in some quarters of the city" (8:457). Crane explains that "the lower classes can purchase pulque, the national beverage, at a rate of 3 cents per glass. Five glasses seem to be sufficient to floor the average citizen of the republic" ("Free Silver Down in Mexico" 8:446). Pulque, unless mixed with other drinks, does not bring aggressive anger, but rather peace and contentment. Under the influence of pulque, the native "prefers to adore his friends. . . their whole souls are completely absorbed in this beatific fraternal tenderness" ("A Jag of Pulque Is Heavy" 8:459).

Crane refuses to pass a negative judgment upon "The Mexican Lower Classes" who love pulque. He argues that "the stranger [who] finds the occupations of foreign peoples to be trivial and inconsequent" (728) has either been unable to "comprehend the new point of view" (728) or else has not recognized "the arrogance of the man who has not yet solved himself and discovered his own actual futility" (728). Crane defends the Mexican peasant way of life. Although they are satisfied with a cheap drink like pulque, content to carry bundles or sit in a doorway while they ponder the sun, and "their clothing is scant and thin" (731), Crane senses their peace and contentment.

He carefully singles out another sort of contentment that comes from successfully dealing with reality—the calm competence of ordinary people doing ordinary jobs, "the pageantry of the accomplishment of naked duty. One cannot speak of it—the spectacle of the common man serenely doing his work, his appointed work" ("War Memories" 6:249). He enthusiastically applauds the engineer of the

Scottish express train, the operator of the elevators in "In the Depths of the Coal Mine," Admiral Sampson's poised, unhurried efficient "plain, pure, unsauced accomplishment" ("War Memories" 6:240), the steady work of relief worker L. P. Ludden, the inconspicuous bravery of the average enlisted man, "the soldier of the regular army is the best man standing on two feet on God's green earth" ("Regulars Get No Glory" 1013), and the resolute and steadfast farmers in Nebraska.

Crane's humanism endorses both genial and strenuous moods. As for the former, he is tolerant of temporary escapes when the result is peace. Further, he defends altered perceptions of reality when brotherhood is produced. To be sure, Crane is forthright that these palliatives are temporary; ordinary experience will reassert itself. As for the latter, he praises, without reservation, men and women who have the energy and confidence to assert themselves as they adjust reality in harmony with human needs and aspirations. "The Open Boat" celebrates a joint effort that both overcomes a fatal danger and produces genuine human brotherhood. In ordinary times against mundane challenges Crane holds up as models those who cooperate to make the world a gentler, less hostile, less indifferent place.

A world indifferent to human aspirations is the common setting for Crane's philosophical explorations of human actions. Inadequate human responses, and eventually failure, occur when the universe's indifference is perceived as a threat or special obstacle. Successful human responses, including those with the potential to create flourishing communities, regard the universe's indifference as an opportunity and an invitation to take creative, responsible action.

Neither pessimistic nor optimistic, the fundamental orientation of Crane's humanism affirms the centrality of human effort. He endorsed the dominant American outlook of the 1890s, meliorism.[19] Meliorists hold that humans have sufficient freedom and their actions sufficient power to alter the ongoing course of reality. Neither final defeat nor final victory is fated. Rather, the significant determinant in the world's decline or improvement is human action. This is not to say that the actions of a single individual can radically alter the existing state of affairs or prevailing drift of world events. Crane agreed with the meliorists that the status quo is obdurate and that existing social forces have considerable inertia. He also agreed that the best efforts of highly motivated, properly unified humans can make a world of difference.

In June 1896, the summer of the open-boat ordeal, America's celebrated and influential philosopher, the pragmatist William James,

In this flight toward Scotland one seldom encountered a grade crossing. In nine cases out of ten there was either a bridge or a tunnel. The platforms of even the remote country stations were all of ponderous masonry in contrast to our constructions of planking. There was always to be seen as we thundered toward a station of this kind, a number of porters in uniform who requested the retreat of anyone who had not the wit to give us plenty of room. And then as the shrill warning of the whistle pierced even the uproar that was about us, came the wild joy of the rush past the station. It was something in the nature of a triumphal procession conducted at thrilling speed. Perhaps there was a curve of infinite grace, a sudden hollow explosive effect made by the passing of a signal box that was close to the track, and then the deadly lunge to shave the edge of a long platform. There was always a number of people standing afar with their eyes riveted upon this projectile and to be on the engine was to feel their interest and admiration in the terror and grandeur of this sweep. A boy allowed to ride with the driver of the band-wagon as a circus parade winds through one of our village streets could not exceed for egotism the temper of a new man in the cab of a train like this one. This valkyric journey on the back of the vermillion engine, with the shouting of the wind, the deep mighty panting of the steed, the grey blur at the track side, the flowing quicksilver ribbon of the other rails, the sudden clash as a switch intersected, all the din and fury of this ride was of a splendor that caused one to look abroad at the quiet green landscape and believe that it was of a phlegm beyond patience. It should have been dark, rain-shot and windy; thunder should have rolled across its sky.

It seemed somehow that if the driver should for a moment take his hands from his engine it might swerve from the track as a horse from the road. Once indeed as he stood wiping his fingers on a bit of waste there must have been something ludicrous in the way the solitary passenger regarded him. Without those finely firm hands on the bridle, the engine might rear and bolt for the pleasant farms lying in the sunshine at either side.

This driver was worthy contemplation. He was simply a quiet middle-aged man, bearded and with the little wrinkles of habitual geniality and kindliness spreading from the eyes towards the temple who stood at his post always gazing out through his round window while his hands went here to there over his levers. He seldom changed either attitude or expression. There surely is no engine-driver

Pages 6 and 7 of the manuscript of "The Scotch Express" (1898). From the Special Manuscripts Collection, Butler Library, Columbia University.

who does not feel the beauty of the business but the emotion lies deep and, mainly, inarticulate, as it does in the mind of a man who has experienced a good and beautiful wife for many years. This driver's face displayed nothing but the cool sanity of a man whose thought was buried intelligently in his business. If there was any fierce drama in it there was no sign upon him. He was so ~~buried~~ lost, in dreams of speed and signals and steam that one wondered if the wonder of his tempestuous charge and its career over England touched him, this impassive rider of a fiery thing.

It should be a well-known fact that, all over the world, the engine driver is the finest type of man that is grown. He is the pick of the earth. He is altogether more worthy than the soldier and better than the men who move on the sea in ships. He is not paid too much; nor his glories weight his brow but for outright performance carried on constantly, coolly, and without elation by a temperate, honest, clear-minded, ray he is the further point. And so the lone human at his station ~~guarding the shipping~~ in a cab, guarding money, lives and the honor of the road is a beautiful sight. The whole thing is aesthetic. The fireman presents this same charm but in a less degree in that he is bound to appear as an apprentice to the finished manhood of the driver. In his eyes turned always in question and confidence toward his superior one finds this quality but his aspirations are so direct that one sees the same type in evolution.

There may be a ~~sort of an~~ popular idea that the fireman's principle function is to hang his head out of the cab and sight interesting objects in the landscape. As a matter of fact he is ~~constantly at~~ always at work. The dragon is insahale. The fireman is continually swinging open the furnace door, whereat a red shine flows out upon the floor of the cab — and shoveling in immense mouthfuls of coal to a fire that is almost diabolical in its madness. This feeding, feeding, feeding goes on until ~~it becomes the~~ it appears as if it is the muscles of the fireman's arms that is speeding the long train. A engine running over sixty-five miles with five hundred tons to bring, has an appetite in proportion to this ~~labor~~ task.

View of the clear-shining English scenery is ~~enough~~ often interrupted ~~between~~ London and Crewe by long and short tunnels. The first one was disconcerting. Suddenly one knew that train was shooting proposed his controversial "The Will to Believe." James argued that, in the matter of beliefs about ourselves and reality, there is some loose play, enough slack to permit humans to choose a worldview that enhances dignity and bolsters the significance of individual contribution.

In selecting a suitable philosophy, James held that, beyond satisfying our practical nature and responding to the pressure of experience, an adequately rational philosophy must address three passional demands. First, its ultimate explanatory principle "must not be one that essentially baffles and disappoints our dearest desires and most cherished powers" (*The Will to Believe* 70). Second, we not only desire that our powers be stimulated but also that our choices and actions be made relevant. And third, an adequate philosophy must "banish uncertainty from the future" (*The Will to Believe* 67) by providing an appropriate guide for actions.

James, agreeing with Crane, found both optimism and pessimism inappropriate. In their place, he proposed the philosophy of meliorism: "a world not certain to be saved, a world the perfection of which shall be conditional merely, the condition being that each several agent does its own 'level best.' I offer you the chance of taking part in such a world. Its safety, you see, is unwarranted. It is a real adventure, with real danger, yet it may win through. It is a social scheme of co-operative work genuinely to be done. Will you join the procession? Will you trust yourself and trust the other agents enough to face the risk?" (*Pragmatism* 139).

The flatly indifferent universe of Crane's humanism, and the God with kind eyes of his poetry, are functionally equivalent to the finite God and the uncertified future of a Jamesian melioristic metaphysics. For James, even though God is first among equals, the best efforts of humans are needed and, conversely, the best-laid divine plans can be blocked by uncooperative, lazy, and vicious men and women. For Crane, too, human contributions significantly affect successes and failures.

The concerted, orchestrated actions of the four in the open boat and the subtle brotherhood that warms them vividly express Crane's melioristic view of human existence. His outlook is also practically and frankly realistic: Billie the oiler drowns, and before him, seven others go down with the *Commodore*. Billie Higgins, however, is the key. Why should the hardest working, most experienced, most skilled seaman in the open boat perish?[20] Only foolish, arrogant, or romantic humans believe we can fully dominate reality. What we must pay attention to is that three of four came ashore safely. Human actions, although efficacious, are limited; reality and the status quo have considerable resilience and potency.

In "In the Depths of a Coal Mine" and "Nebraska's Bitter Fight for Life," Crane broaches the possibility that the miners and farmers may have overreached in their dealings with natural reality. In the former sketch, he refers to "a grim, strange war that was being waged in the sunless depths of the earth" (605). The miners' work is a dangerous kind of stealing.

> Below was a curtain of ink-like blackness. It was like the opening of an old well, sinister from tales of crime. . . . Before us, there was always the curtain of an impenetrable night. . . . The sense of an abiding danger in the roof was always upon our foreheads. It expressed to us all the unmeasured, deadly tons above us. It was a superlative might that regarded with supreme calmness of almighty power the little men at its mercy. Sometimes we were obliged to bend low to avoid it. Always our hands rebelled vaguely from touching it, refusing to affront this gigantic mass. (607–8)

The miners pay a price for trespassing nature's unmarked boundary. Black lung disease if they live long enough, quick death otherwise. "It is war. It is the most savage part of all in the endless battle between man and nature. The miners are grimly in the van. They have carried the war into places where nature has the strength of a million giants. Sometimes their enemy becomes exasperated and snuffs out ten, twenty, thirty lives. Usually she remains calm, and takes one at a time with method and precision. She need not hurry. She possesses eternity" (611).

In the depths of a coal mine, "man is in the implacable grasp of nature" (613); so, too, the farmers in the sand-hill country of western Nebraska have perhaps ventured beyond the breaking point. If the dry and rainy years even out, the tough homesteaders will eventually prosper. Still, Crane senses danger. As the patrons of Scully's Blue Hotel know, nature is not always helpful and congenial. In western Nebraska, "the farmers helpless, with no weapon against this terrible and inscrutable wrath of nature, were spectators. . . .The earth from which they had wrested each morsel which they had put into their mouths had now abandoned them. Nature made light of her obligation under the toil of these men. . .upon these people came the weight of the strange and unspeakable punishment of nature. . . . They were soon driven to bay by nature, now the pitiless enemy" (689–90). The sketch ends with a cautious, measured hope: it is "probable" (698) that human enterprises will succeed in western Nebraska.

Crane and his pragmatic philosopher counterparts claim, then, that humans can sufficiently affect outcomes to satisfy appropriate desires and to answer reasonable aspirations—ones that have met the test of experience. Reality is neither menacingly hostile nor benevolently supportive. It is, for Crane, indifferent; for James, tolerant of human additions.

The hard-won success of three of the four in the open boat makes them qualified "interpreters" of humanity's place in reality. C. S. Peirce used similar moderation in describing our epistemological situation. The settled opinion arrived at by a community of competent inquirers is, for Peirce, truth. But although a highly reliable, pragmatically tested finding, the current experts' best judgment might be modified by further study and experience. We, then, cannot claim to possess absolute, unchanging, eternal Truth.

The evolution in Crane's humanism can be concisely summarized with reference to courage.[21] Crane realized that no human has total freedom but, within limits, all persons are free. Freedom imposes, on each, a fundamental obligation to take responsibility by being courageous. Because some environments are more constricting than others, different sorts of courage are morally appropriate. Crane's ideal of responsible conduct evolved through three stages: the courage to resist, the courage to initiate, and, finally, in the spirit of his contemporary, the American philosopher Josiah Royce, the courage to build community.[22]

Crane uses both positive and negative models to illustrate types of courage. For example, Jimmie, George, and the little man of the Sullivan County sketches fall prey to self-delusions or society's forces when additional resistance is required. Or, positively, Fleming, in the second half of *The Red Badge of Courage*, abandons his preconceived "Greeklike . . . Homeric" (83) ideals of glory in favor of actions suited to the battle front. To the question "Will you spell me?" both the correspondent and the oiler cheerfully respond, "Sure" (904); and L. P. Ludden endures the long hours and hard work but grows tired of the abuse. When he asks to resign, the governor tells him that "it would be impossible now to appoint a new man without some great and disastrous halt of the machinery. Ludden returned to his post and to the abuse" ("Nebraska's Bitter Fight for Life" 694).

Crane's third kind of courage, the courage to build community, rejects pessimism while responding to human need. In a letter to Nellie Crouse on January 12, 1896, he stated: "The final wall of the wise man's thought however is Human Kindness of course. If the road of disappointment, grief, pessimism, is followed far enough, it will arrive there. Pessimism itself is only a little, little way, and moreover it is ridiculously cheap. The cynical mind is an uneducated thing. Therefore do I strive to be as kind and as just as may be to those about me and in my meager success at it, I find the solitary pleasure of life" (*Correspondence* #184).

Crane's conclusions about the human situation are modestly but firmly stated. His considered opinions are neither casual beliefs nor the final truth, but rather careful experiential observations and thoughtful reflections on the worth of human effort in an indifferent universe. Finally, although Crane does not see the American as the New Adam or America as the New Eden, his western experiences and thirty hours in an open boat convinced him that natural world is an invaluable catalyst for releasing energy, inspiring effort, and creating subtle brotherhood.

A stanza of *War Is Kind* (#70, 1326) effectively captures the findings of Crane's humanism and sets the stage for his ethics.

> "The sea bids you teach, oh, pines
> "Sing low in the moonlight.
> "Teach the gold of patience
> "Cry gospel of gentle hands
> "Cry a brotherhood of hearts
> "The sea bids you teach, oh, pines."

CHAPTER 4

Ethics: Tolerance, Compassion, and Duty

"Have you ever made a just man?"
"Oh, I have made three," answered God
"But two of them are dead
"And the third—
"Listen! Listen!
"And you will hear the thud of his defeat."

War Is Kind

Stephen Crane was a serious man, even glum. Joseph Conrad said he heard him laugh only when playing with Conrad's children.[1] But he was also witty. Alert to irony in life, he was fond of tweaking dogmatists who had no qualms about their own rectitude or doubts about the error of another's ways.[2] Sensitive to ethical complication and uncertainty, and aware of the powerful qualifiers of context and motive, Crane was as earnest about morality as he was leary of moral pronouncement.[3]

Virtually all commentators mention the presence of moral concern in Crane's work. Still, treatments of his ethics have done little more than commend him for his moral seriousness, personal honesty, and deeply felt sincerity.[4] Crane's ethical deliberations deserve more. A careful examination of his stance on moral matters discloses subtle, persistent, and surprising challenges. For example, he characteristically stresses marginal ethical matters. At one end of the spectrum, he calls attention to the barely ethical responsibilities humans have to animals. At the other extreme, he repeatedly examines crisis situations that prompt heroic actions above and beyond the call of morality. "Ordinary" moral duties are more serious than our treatment of animals but less demanding than extraordinary and saintly behavior. About ordinary moral duties Crane offers positive declarations, but typically his comments are backhanded. "I will not declare upon how hard it is for a man to be honest. . . but I fully know that it is hard to throw a tomahawk" ("'Ol' Bennet' and the Indians" 8:148). Still, Crane's writing contains important stances on ordinary moral matters. More secure about premoral matters and more confident about actions beyond morality, Crane treats both quasi-moral realms at length. Then, with extramoral considerations as a background and warrant, he offers opinions on ordinary moral responsibilities.

Premoral Matters:
Compassionate Treatment of Animals

Crane's biographers have noted his fondness for animals, especially dogs and horses.[5] Crane, too, had a blind spot. Beer (1923: 119) reports that in Mexico he found bull fights disgusting. His objection was not the cruelty and slaughter of the bulls, but that horses were injured and sometimes killed in the ring.[6] Crane's understanding of an animal's world was distinctive, and his ability to empathize with nonhuman hopes, desires, pains, and pleasures was exceptional. In "A Dark-Brown Dog," the reader is persuasively initiated into the dog's consciousness, including canine nightmares, "sometimes . . . in his sleep, he would utter little yells, as from pain . . . when in his dreams he encountered huge flaming dogs who threatened him direfully" (536). Through his ability to lead readers to appreciate the hopes and disappointments, the joys and sorrows of other centers of consciousness, Crane fosters reflection on two little-noticed values. First, he argues that lives and desires beyond the human have integrity. Second, he insists that not all human lives and not every human desire merits peremptory status. Crane's poignant description of the relative standing of human and subhuman worlds is a significant contribution to moral philosophy.

What must be understood is the place of animals in Crane's value scheme. He is not a species egalitarian, nor does he deny the centrality of human welfare. Crane's interest is heightened ethical sensitivity. Anyone blind to the innocence and integrity of animal life or callous to animal suffering is liable to moral obtuseness. To put the matter a bit differently, many of Crane's contemporaries believed that etiquette and ethics correlate strongly and that good manners indicate moral responsiveness. Crane thought, however, that sensitivity to the well-being of animals and a sense of proportion about the merit of some human desires are better clues to moral development.[7]

"A Dark-Brown Dog" examines, from the dog's point of view, person-dog companionship, focusing upon the relative value of the desires of both partners. There is no shortage of suffering, human and animal, in the world according to Crane. Pain is a fact of life, and so, too, is the gratituous evil of abuse. A small child, already hardened by bullying parents and a threatening environment, is approached by a small, dark-brown dog. There is "an interchange of friendly pattings and waggles" (532). As the dog becomes more and more enthusiastic, the child strikes it on its head. The astonished dog rolls over on his back, and "with his ears and eyes he offered a small prayer to the child" (532).

When the dog follows the boy home, the boy repeatedly beats him with a stick, "proclaiming with childish gestures that he held him in contempt as an unimportant dog, with no value save for a moment" (533). Later, at the child's doorstep, the dog tries harder: "he performed a few gambols with such abandon that the child suddenly saw him to be a *valuable thing*" (533, emphasis added). When the child drags the dog up the steps, the whole family objects. His father, "in a particularly savage temper that evening" (534), decides he can infuriate everyone if the dog is kept, and so the dog stays.

The child has to be the dog's guardian, protecting him from the attacks of the rest of the family, although "sometimes, too, the child himself used to beat the dog. . . . The dog always accepted these thrashings with an air of admitted guilt. He was too much of a dog to try to look to be a martyr or to plot revenge" (535). He simply forgives the child. Although the boy cares for his dog, his own happiness remains paramount. He and the dog are friends, however, "the scene of their companionship was a kingdom governed by this terrible potentate, the child; [but the dog] was proud to be the retainer of so great a monarch" (536). The dog's interests and desires, when the child acknowledges them, are not afforded a priority. Nevertheless, the child grows to understand the goodness and worth of sensibilities, including his dog's subhuman and subordinate ones. The moral message of "A Dark-Brown Dog" lies in the shock of its ending.[8]

One day, however, the father of the family got quite exceptionally drunk. He came home and held carnival with the cooking utensils, the furniture and his wife. He was in the midst of this recreation when the child, followed by the dark-brown dog, entered the room. . . . It occurred to him that it would be a fine thing to throw the dog out of the window. . . . He swung him two or three times hilariously about his head, and then flung him with great accuracy through the window. . . . The dark-brown body crashed in a heap on the roof of a shed five stories below. From thence it rolled to the pavement of an alleyway. The child in the room far above burst into a long, dirgelike cry, and toddled hastily out of the room. . . . When they came for him later, they found him seated by the body of his dark-brown friend. (536–37)

Crane expertly focuses on the father's cruel disregard of the child's fondness for "his friend" and, even more, the father's total insensibility to animal pain. The drunken man trivializes what his son treasures. We should not be surprised, implies Crane, for when the father sees the world only in terms of his own desires, the dog is a mere thing, a dispensable object, a toy for sadistic enjoyment. Callousness to animal suffering is not far removed from ignorance and belittlement of human pain.

Crane's position on the ethical relevance of animals is precise and refined. He is not a sentimentalist about animal rights, he does not see animals as equal to humans, and he does not regard animal pain as an intrinsic evil. But he does recognize the seriousness of animal suffering. Animal pain can be necessary and unavoidable, or it can be a gratuitous and senseless evil. In formal moral language, for Crane, animals have ethical standing, their interests are morally considerable, and their lives have genuine value. Even though animal welfare is important, its priority is below human welfare, therefore differential treatment of humans and some weighting of human interests and welfare are morally appropriate.

How much less important are animal lives? How much more valuable are human desires? Crane does not offer formulas, but his poignant description of the sacrifices that animals make for people forces confrontation of a sometimes haughty species chauvinism. In "The Price of the Harness," Crane call attention to the devotion of horses: "some of the battery horses turned at the noise of the trampling feet and surveyed the men with eyes deep as wells, serene, mournful, generous eyes, lit heart-breakingly with something that was akin to a philosophy, a religion of self-sacrifice—oh, gallant, gallant horses!" (1021). For Crane, the sacrifice of the battery horses is undeniable, and their suffering is an evil. Whether the evil is justified depends upon whether the end served is good enough. In "The Mystery of Heroism," the battery horses go "wheresoever these incomprehensible humans demanded with whip and spur" (625). War and its demands are often "incomprehensible" to humans, too. Is the gain of war a sufficient recompense for so much suffering? Although Crane was not altogether clear about the good of war, its evil, the pain and suffering of men and animals, was obvious to him.

In another war, "the endless battle between man and nature" (611), Crane explores another sort of animal pain. He begins "In the Depths of a Coal Mine" by laying out the mine's awful working conditions. He skillfully contrasts the reluctant mine mules with the youngest boys, the slate pickers—eager to get deeper into the mine to become door boys—then mule boys, then laborers and helpers, and, finally, in the depths of the coal mine, "real miners" who make the blasts. The mules, who "resembled enormous rats" in their "stable . . . like a dungeon" (612, 611), are used to press the ethical point. Aghast at the conditions of the miners, Crane dramatically reserves his ethical condemnation of "the tragedy of it" for the lot of the animals.

> One had to wait to see the tragedy of it. . . . It is a common affair for mules to be imprisoned for years in the limitless night of the mines. . . when brought to the surface, these animals tremble at the earth, radiant in the sunshine. Later, they go almost mad with fantastic joy. The full splendor of the heavens, the grass, the trees, the breezes breaks upon them suddenly. They caper and career with extravagant mulish glee. . . .To those who have known the sun-light there may come the fragrant dream. Perhaps this is what they brood over when they stand solemnly in rows with slowly flapping ears. A recollection may appear to them, a recollection of pastures of a lost paradise. Perhaps they despair and thirst for this bloom that lies in an unknown direction and at impossible distances. (612–13)

Despite the fact that the imprisoned mules are needed to operate the mines, Crane's sensitivity for them effectively poses the ethical dilemma of justice involved in a glaring disparity between the gain in human enjoyment and the cost in animal (and also human) suffering.[9] Human welfare deserves clear priority, but, asks Crane, can this good adequately compensate for so much suffering? At least the miners, both men and boys, have a limited choice in the matter; the mules, like artillery horses, have no option.

An important dimension of Crane's ethical concern involves animals. He appreciates their pleasures; he values communication with them—in "Stephen Crane in Mexico (I)," he notices "the tender communion of two sympathetic spirits. The man pats affectionately the soft muzzle of the donkey" (8:440); he applauds kind treatment of livestock (as in "Nebraska's Bitter Fight for Life," where he cites the poor and suffering farmers "who would willingly give away their favorite horses if they could thus insure the animals warm barns and plenty of food" [696]); and he strongly responds to suffering animals. Crane's sensitivity to animals leads directly to his exploration of heroic actions on their behalf in "The Veteran."

Heroism

Unlike species egalitarians, Crane does not equate human and animal pain.[10] In fact, despite his moving description of the suffering of animals, Crane's moral prescriptions regarding the prevention of animal pain are fairly weak; he suggests that some sacrifices for animals are appropriate and commendable. His claim is not that we must or ought sacrifice to prevent animal pain, but only that it can be morally correct to do so. Moreover, serious sacrifices are optional and beyond the pale of morality. This will make dangerous efforts on animals' behalf extra-moral and heroic. In "The Veteran," Crane examines both morally correct and heroic actions with respect to animals. The central concern of this short story, published just three months after *The Red Badge of Courage* was released in book form, is heroism. As the story opens, Henry Fleming, now an old man recalling his war experiences, is asked if he was frightened. He readily admits "'you bet I was scared . . . . the trouble was . . . I thought they were all shooting at me . . . so I run!'" (666–67). His grandson Jimmie is astonished by this revelation, but the townspeople listening have no doubts about Fleming's bravery: "they knew that he had ranked as an orderly sergeant, and so their opinion of his heroism was fixed" (666).

The scene shifts to the Fleming farm, where one of the hired men, a Swede, returns home drunk and overturns a lantern, setting the barn on fire. Fleming enters the burning barn five times to lead out the work horses. Then he, his son, and the hired men save all but one of the cows from the barn's basement. Their "ordinary" efforts, involving acceptable risk, alleviate suffering; their response is morally correct, "they returned to the front of the barn and stood sadly, breathing like men who had reached the final point of *human* effort" (669, emphasis added).

When the Swede remembers the colts still in the barn, ordinary moral efforts are not enough. The onlookers describe the extent of sacrifice involved, "'why, its sure death,'" "'why, its suicide for a man to go in there!'" (670). Still, Fleming insists, "'I must try to get 'em out'" (670). Crane clearly states the extra-moral, nonrational, exceptional quality of the sacrifice. "Old Fleming staggered . . .[and] stared absent-mindedly. . . [then] he rushed into the barn" (670). The roof caves in. The story ends with a poetic and mystical description of Fleming's death, "a great funnel of smoke swarmed toward the sky, as if the old man's mighty spirit, released from its body—a little bottle—has swelled like the genie of the fable" (670).

From *The Red Badge of Courage* onward, Crane sought to understand the mental, emotional, and physical mechanisms of courage.[11] He carefully and clearly separated ordinary moral actions from heroic ones on behalf of animals in "The Veteran." In other stories depicting extraordinary actions beyond morality, Crane considers risks for humans. The heroic actions he examines are out of the ordinary in several ways. They involve exceptional risks, usually in wartime, inspired by motivations unclear to both observers and heroes. Indeed, these actions have little in common with ordinary, rationally motivated moral behavior.

In *The Red Badge of Courage,* heroism is a subhuman, animal reflex. During the second day of battle, after Fleming deserts, he returns to acquit himself in two separate battles, one as a rifleman and the other as the flag bearer. In both cases, Crane describes nonhuman, unconscious, savage, raging, vicious, wolflike behavior. As a rifleman, during the charge "there was the delirium . . . heedless and blind to the odds . . . a temporary but sublime absence of selfishness" (183). After the seizure relaxes and energy wanes, "they returned to caution. They were become men again" (183). As a flag bearer, Fleming is seized by "frenzy . . . sublime recklessness . . . the daring spirit of a savage, religion-mad . . . [and by] wild battle madness" (205).[12]

After *The Red Badge of Courage,* Crane locates courage outside the realm of ordinary actions by resorting to highly abstract motivation—pure devotion to duty. In "The Price of the Harness," the young staff officer's "ideal of duty" (1021) is out of step with ordinary concern for "the wails of the wounded," and it is immune from practical pressures, including "the persecution of legislators and the indifference of his country" (1020). In "The Clan of No-Name," Lieutenant Manolo Prat, ordered to take a message to the veteran officer Bas, runs five hundred yards through enemy fire. He does not want to do it, but "he thought that was what men of his kind would do in such a case. There was a standard and he must follow it, obey it, because it was a monarch, the Prince of Conduct" (1041). When he reaches an "established brave man," Bas, he is greeted with "you are one of the most desperate and careless officers I know" (1041). Later, "willingly" and knowingly, Prat walks into a trap. As a member of the clan of no-name, "something controlled him; something moved him inexorably in one direction; he perfectly understood" (1045). He has no difficulty knowing what he must do, even though "no man may give tongue to it" (1050). In "'God Rest Ye, Merry Gentlemen,'" an old army captain likewise responds out of devotion to principle. He cannot remain a spectator. Therefore, out of pure duty, "his sole honor was a new invitation to face death . . . he loved it for itself . . . the thing itself . . . the whirl, the unknown" (1068–69).

Crane's most revealing study of exceptional conduct, "A Mystery of Heroism," was published by the Bacheller syndicate eight months after it published the shortened, serialized version of *The Red Badge of Courage*. In the midst of a fierce battle, thirsty Fred Collins spots a well in the no-man's meadow between the armies. He talks so much about his thirst and boasts so loudly about his fearlessness that he backs himself into seeking permission to get water. Amid Collins's mixed motivations, his selfish desires, and the high probability of death in a trivial matter, Crane probes heroism. No one knows what to make of Collins's recklessness; "the colonel and the captain looked at each other then, for it had suddenly occurred that they could not for the life of them tell whether Collins wanted to go or whether he did not" (627). His fellow soldiers are amazed, "'That's foolishness'" (628). Collins cannot understand himself either; "he had blindly been lead by quaint emotions. . . . as a matter of truth he was sure of very little. He was mainly surprised" (628).

Heroism is thus made mystical in "The Veteran," reduced to subhuman behavior in *The Red Badge of Courage*, and made abstract in the Cuban war stories. In "The Mystery of Heroism," Crane proposes a religious explanation. He says of Collins, himself confused about why he had taken such a risk, "it seemed to him *supernaturally* strange that he had allowed his mind to maneuver his body into such a situation" (628, emphasis added). Primarily he is dazed and disappointed; if this is heroism, either "heroes were not much" (628) or "he was an intruder in the land of fine deeds" (629). Impelled by fear and inspired by pride, he takes great risk to satisfy purely personal and physical desires. On the way back, carrying a bucket (the canteens had taken too long to fill), he passes a wounded artillery officer pinned under a fallen horse. "'Say, young man, give me a drink of water, will you?'" (630). Collins charges on—"'I can't'" (631)—but then turns back. In so doing, a selfish, trivial, and reckless dare is transformed into a moral act.[13] Collins responds to a genuine need of another human being, "there was the faintest shadow of a smile on his lips as he looked at Collins. . . . Collins tried to hold the bucket steadily, but his shaking hand caused the water to splash all over the face of the dying man" (631). With both good consequences and an honorable intention, Collins has performed an unsullied ethical act of mercy.

Crane concludes the story by removing the confusion between false heroism and compassionate aid.[14] Some water is still in the bucket when Collins safely returns to his regiment. "The Captain waved the bucket away. 'Give it to the men!'" (631). But two young, skylarking lieutenants, fighting over the first drink, overturn the bucket and spill the water on the ground. No one but the wounded officer gets a drink, not even Collins, who left the well as soon as he fills the bucket. Despite several examinations, heroism remains enigmatic. But in "A Mystery of Heroism," Crane articulates a basic norm of his ethics. Morality consists of an unselfish response to a genuine human need.[15]

Morality and Models of Human Excellence

It is human agony and human agony is not pleasant.
"How They Leave Cuba"

Thus far, Crane's examination of morality takes a distinctly Socratic tenor; what morality is not is more obvious than what it is. However, negative knowledge is often useful. Such is the case in two challenging and memorable scenes wherein Crane elucidates morality by depicting genuine human needs left ignored: the tattered man in *The Red Badge of Courage* and the terrified Swede in "The Blue Hotel."

Having reached the limit of his desertion, Fleming rebounds and "began to run in the direction of the battle" (128), where he finds himself among the wounded, "a blood-stained crowd streaming to the rear" (129). Joining the retreat, he walks beside the tattered man. Feeling like "an invader" (129) and intolerably threatened by his gentle, pleading, and responsive companion, Fleming bolts when asked a second time, "'Where yeh hit?'" (132). A short flight brings him to the spectral soldier, his friend Jim Conklin. Later, when Fleming is rejoined by the tattered man, both try to help Conklin. As they watch his death dance, however, they are sent away, "'Leave me be—don't tech me—leave me be—'" (137).

The tattered man and Fleming continue down the road. The tattered man, wounded in both head and arm, is more concerned about Fleming, "'Ye'd better take keer of yer hurt. It don't do t'let sech things go. It might be inside mostly, an' them plays thunder. Where is it located?'" (139). Finally, when he asks a fourth time, "'where is your'n located?'" Henry bristles, "Oh, don't bother me. . . . Goodbye'" (140). As Fleming pulls away, the tattered man, now tottering and beginning slur his words, accosts Fleming, "'It ain't—right—it ain't—fer yeh t'go—trompin' off . . . ain't right'" (140). As Fleming climbs a fence and looks back, he sees the tattered man whom he has abandoned "wandering about helplessly in the fields" (141).

In the next chapter Fleming rationalizes. His self-defense is not about abandoning a man precisely when his efforts might have made a significant difference. Instead, he worries about the public specter of the desertion of his battle post. The more wounded men he sees, the more his envy of a badge of courage and "the black weight of his woe returned to him" (142–43). Shortly thereafter, he is accidentally "wounded" so that he can return to his regiment with "his self-pride . . . now entirely restored" (165). Later, his new self-esteem is, in part, warranted by his fierce fighting in the first wave of his regiment's attack and then by the "sublime recklessness" (205) of his charge as a flag bearer. He decides that his heroism on the second day of battle redeems his cowardice. "Later, he began to study his deeds, his failures, and his achievements. . . . At last they marched before him clearly. From this present view point he was enabled to look upon them in spectator fashion and to criticise them with some correctness . . . he felt gleeful and unregretting, for in it his public deeds were paraded in great and shining prominence. . . . He saw that he was good" (210).

Crane then skillfully draws a distinction. Fleming's heroism during the second day of battle easily atones for his cowardice, "the ghost of his flight from the first engagement appeared to him and danced" (210). These second-thought threats to his "pompous and veteranlike" (165) composure were merely faint and venial irritations, "small shoutings in his brain. . . for a moment, he blushed" (210–11). Quite another matter, the panic of his moral failure, ever bright and mortal, remains unredeemed. "A spectre of reproach came to him. There loomed the dogging memory of the tattered soldier— he who, gored by bullets and faint for blood, had fretted concerning an imagined wound in another; he who had loaned his last of strength and intellect for the tall soldier; he who, blind with weariness and pain, had been deserted in the field" (211).

Fleming's guilt persists, "whichever way his thoughts turned they were followed by the somber phantom of the desertion in the fields" (211). He finally convinces himself that his inner wound of moral failure is not evident to his companions. He becomes a man when he confronts "his vivid error . . . [and he] gradually mustered force to put the sin at a distance . . . he could look back upon the brass and bombast of his earlier gospels . . . he discovered that he now despised them" (212).

His growth to adulthood is not due to battlefield heroics and public deeds. Rather, his quiet manhood is the fruit of three separate moral realizations: his confrontation with a serious ethical choice, his acknowledgment that he had failed to respond morally, and his most difficult and humbling experience, the decision to forgive and accept himself.[16]

The opposite of the gentle and concerned tattered man is the obnoxious and pugnacious Swede in "The Blue Hotel." Unattractive,
even repugnant, the Swede is, nonetheless, a human being in need.
To aid him is the correct moral response, yet no one does. (Pat Scully, proprietor of the Palace Hotel tries to help the Swede, but his
motives are dictated by his role as owner-host and his aid, isolating
him from the other patrons and giving him whiskey, only exacer-
bates the Swede's paranoia.)[17]

Something is wrong with the "shaky and quick-eyed" (799) Swede.
At first he "said nothing . . . he resembled a badly frightened man"
(801), then three times he breaks the tense, artificial silence of the
hotel's front room with nervous laughs. Scully, his son Johnnie, the
old farmer (until he stalks out of the hotel), and the other two guests
"had begun to look at him askance, as if they wished to inquire what
ailed him" (802). Several shrill and blatant laughs later, the Swede
"explains" his dread that many men must have been killed in the
hotel. Johnnie and the cowboy do not understand. The Swede, for-
merly a tailor from New York City, naturally looks to the little easterner, but to no avail. He "encountered treachery from the only quar-
ter where he had expected sympathy if not help. "'Oh, I see you are
all against me'" (803) he concludes.

The fact that the manic Swede is himself the cause of much of his
own trouble makes the lack of response from Johnnie, the cowboy,
and the easterner understandable, but it does not change the nature
of their moral obligation to respond to another human being's
needs.[18] At first, despite Scully's "boisterous hospitality" (800), all
the newly arrived hotel guests remain cool and uninvolved: "they
reflected in silence of experienced men who tread carefully amid new
people" (800). Only the cowboy and the easterner reply to the old
farmer's questions, but even then their answers are minimal, merely
"short but adequate sentences" (800). The Swede is silent, and when
he does finally speak it is only to Scully at the noon meal. Gradually,
the cowboy and the easterner work themselves into the group with
Johnnie and the old farmer; the Swede "remained near the window,
aloof" (801), isolated and estranged. This natural grouping is also
quite understandable. The Swede is not likable, and it is uncomfortable to be with him.

Scully's patrons temporarily avoid relating directly to him by resorting to the ritual and regulation of a card game. Two details are
significant. Preestablished rules and responses take the place of the
give-and-take improvisation of normal human interaction, and a for-
malized code relieves tensions; "because of the absorbing play none

considered the strange ways of the Swede" (802). The situation remains under control, and the Swede's strangeness is concealed so
long as artificial rules replace direct and personal encounter. When
the card game's spell is broken and the Swede again feels threatened,
he goes upstairs to pack his valise. Scully intervenes by showing him
family pictures and giving him whiskey. This makes Scully the
Swede's confidant and protector. It also involves the Swede in another game with preset rules of conduct.

The Swede is strange enough that other human beings avoid inter-
acting with him on a personal, moral level. They play games with
him instead of responding to his human needs. When the Swede and
Scully are upstairs, the rest discuss him: "'he's clear frightened out
of his boots. . . . this man has been reading dime-novels'" (809). In
their arrangements they plan how to handle him, "'Yes,' said the
cowboy, 'this is a queer game'" (809). When the Swede and Scully
return, Scully ably performs the first go-around of the game. "The
five chairs were formed in a crescent about one side of the stove. The
Swede began to talk; he talked arrogantly, profanely, angrily. Johnnie,
the cowboy and the Easterner maintained a morose silence, while old
Scully appeared to be receptive and eager, breaking in constantly
with sympathetic ejaculations" (810).

After the six o'clock supper, at which the Swede "fizzed like a fire-
wheel . . . and in all his madness he was encouraged by old Scully . . . the Swede smote Scully ruthlessly" (811–12) on his tender
shoulder. Johnnie expects his father to explode, but instead "he
smiled a sickly smile and remained silent" (812). By now, because
Scully's players are privy to the game, his signal is clear; "the others
understood from his manner that he was admitting his responsibility for the Swede's new viewpoint" (812).

From an ethical point of view all that remains is to play out the
game. The home team has a decided advantage; the Swede's premo-
nitions are well founded: he is trapped. When he accuses Johnnie of
cheating, the game is moved outside to be played with fists instead
of words and cards. Scully acts as referee and the cowboy as enforc-
er. Twice the cowboy intervenes when the Swede gains brief advantage. First he pushes the Swede back to give Johnnie a chance to
compose himself. Later, when the Swede knocks Johnnie to the
ground, "the cowboy was barely in time to prevent the mad Swede
from flinging himself upon his prone adversary. 'No, you don't!'
said the cowboy, interposing an arm. 'Wait a second!'" (817–18).
Johnnie's stacked deck and Scully's one-sided refereeing notwithstanding, the Swede twice wins easily. Scully, laying aside his own-

er-host mantle, surrenders. "'Stranger,' he said, evenly, 'it's all up with our side'" (819).

The Swede is, from start to finish, a stranger in the Palace Hotel; seeking aid and if not companionship, at least acceptance, he receives only alienation. He finds a saloon, and once again his bluster and bravado do him in. Although it is quite understandable why the four men at the corner table shun him, a human being in need is immorally ignored.

The much-debated ninth section of "The Blue Hotel" reveals that Johnnie had been cheating and that the easterner knows it.[19] Crane thereby makes explicit his ethic of responding to human need. The easterner understands his moral failure, "'Johnnie was cheating. I saw him. I know it. I saw him. And I refused to stand up and be a man. I let the Swede fight it out alone . . . . We, five of us, have collaborated in the murder of this Swede'"(827). The cowboy is confused, "'Well, I didn't do anythin', did I?'" (828). The conclusion of "The Blue Hotel" reaffirms the moral position Crane took in *The Red Badge of Courage*. The Palace Hotel group refuses to acknowledge and aid a human being suffering from psychological injury; Fleming refuses to minister to the tattered man's physical trauma. Genuine needs are immorally and selfishlessly ignored in both cases.

Positive moral examples abound in Crane's writings. Their common denominator is recognition, followed by unselfish response, to other human beings. Most of Crane's illustrations of moral response lack the flair and drama of Fred Collins's aid to the wounded artillery officer. Quite the contrary, Crane was a master of brief, purposely understated, low-key sketches like "The Detail." In this lovely sketch, an old, frail, frightened woman looks to pedestrians among "the tempest of the Sixth Avenue shopping district" (8:111). No one will slow down to converse with her. Finally, she see two young, well-dressed girls looking at a shop window; "they seemed to have plenty of time; they leisurely scanned the goods in the window. Other people had made the tiny woman much afraid because, obviously, they were speeding to keep such tremendously important engagements" (8:112). She meekly asks the window shoppers if they can tell her where she might find work; "for an instant the two girls stared. Then they seemed about to exchange a smile but at the last moment they checked it" (8:112).

They listen as the woman explains that she needs money; she is not strong but she can sew, "'do you know any place where they would like me to come?'" (8:112). With sure mastery of both style and substance, Crane unobtrusively introduces a moral dimension; "the young women did then exchange a smile but it was a subtly tender smile, the verge of personal grief" (8:112). One girl is sorry, she does not know of anyone. Her companion asks for the old lady's address, just in case; "the tiny old lady dictated her address, bending over to watch the girl write on a visiting card with a little silver pencil" (8:112).

Numerous positive moral illustrations can be found in Crane's newspaper accounts on the care of wounded soldiers. Although he sometimes criticized and sometimes commended the courage of soldiers, Crane without fail celebrates, as genuine and moral, the heroism of ambulance drivers, medics, "the sure-handed, invaluable Red Cross men" ("Stephen Crane's Vivid Story of the Battle of San Juan" 1005), and nurses—"it is indeed a noble profession. It demands extreme tranquillity and faithfulness, steady nerves and . . . extraordinary deftness of touch" ("The European Letters" 8:716). He reserves his highest praise for the surgeons in the field; "this hospital was a spectacle of heroism. The doctors, gentle and calm, moved among the men without the commonsenseless bungling of the ordinary ward" ("Stephen Crane at the Front for the *World*" 1000).

The simple matter of a decent burial is the ethical message of "The Upturned Face" and "The Second Generation." "In the Tenderloin: A Duel Between an Alarm Clock and a Suicidal Purpose" is highly charged with the taboo topic of a drug overdose, but its moral theme is commonplace—one human being helping another recover from a mistake. In "The Open Boat," the correspondent and the oiler row and the cook bails in response to the orders of the injured captain, who "could never command a more ready and swiftly obedient crew than the motley three of the dingey" (890). In Crane's account, the actions of the men in the open boat go beyond self-preservation. Their actions acquire an ethical dimension due to consequences and motive: "it would be difficult to describe the subtle brotherhood of men that was here established on the seas . . . it was more than a mere recognition of what was best for the common safety. There was surely in it a quality that was personal and heartfelt" (890).

Crane's depictions of human excellence embrace a transcendent moral character. Although his ethical norm, the unselfish response to a human need, is orthodox and unoriginal, his firm grasp of the ethical dimension of situations is a significant contribution. The reader is compelled to respond with conviction, for example that Fleming's conduct in abandoning the tattered man is tawdry and contemptible; that, although it might be grudgingly admitted, it is obvious that the obnoxious and boisterous Swede is badly treated; and that there is a subtle but marked moral difference between window shoppers' first and second smiles at the old, frail woman. So far, it might appear that a clear and firm consensus about good and bad, right and wrong easily emerges from a study of Crane's ethics. That is not really the case, however; he was sensitive to ethical complexity and qualification.

Everyday Heroes and Variable Standards

> Bravery deals not so much in resolute action, as in healthy and assured rest. Its palmy state is staying at home, and compelling alliance in all directions.
>
> Henry David Thoreau, *Journal*

Crucial to Crane's general philosophy is his denial of the existence of Truth and Reality. His process metaphysics is pluralistic, holding that several contemporaneously existing, interpenetrating realities exist at once. His epistemology is contextual, with corrigible human truths approaching but not possessing Truth. His moral philosophy has an analogous modesty and reserve. Crane rejects Kantian categorical imperatives that command exceptionless obedience to universal maxims; Crane's interest is not in an ethic for all possible worlds and for every rational agent. His closest approach to a universal moral value is his appeal to the fundamental goodness of human needs. Nonetheless, because Crane is willing to entertain, and sometimes concede, that animal welfare can challenge human enjoyment, human needs have high but not peremptory status.

Crane rejects moral dogmatism because he clearly comprehends that value judgments, including the judgment of ethical good and evil or moral right and wrong, require an evaluative context. In the absence of a single context, moral absolutes are precluded.

If there are no moral absolutes, is there a reliable level of ethical generality? If so, conviction and consensus could be attributed to some ethical judgments. Crane would have had no qualms about general and reliable ethical norms if ordinary circumstances were the rule. But he was convinced not only of the great difference between ordinary, day-to-day life and emergency crisis situations, but also, paradoxically, that much of life is a sort of war. In other words, if emergencies and stress are the rule rather than the exception, dependable ethical maxims would have to be set aside on a routine basis.

Despite these complications and difficulties, Crane is neither a moral relativist nor an ethical subjectivist. He does not view ethical values as emotional states or subjective feelings. Ethical judgments, like all value judgments, require both a context and a criterion.[20] Crane's writings are full of instances wherein the reader can easily imagine that "water was the gold of the moment . . . . He asked for water . . . I tilted my canteen and poured into his cup almost a pint of my treasure" ("War Memories" 6:252–53); or that, in certain circumstances, anyone might "faint with joy at the sight of festive canned beef, hard-tack and coffee" ("Hunger Has Made Cubans Fatalists" 9:147); or that it is quite possible that "rations were scarce enough to make a little fat strip of bacon seem the size of a corner lot, and coffee grains were pearls" ("The Second Generation" 1121); or that "The breakfast was of canned tomatoes stewed with hard bread, more hard bread, and coffee. It was very good fare, almost royal" ("'God Rest Ye, Merry Gentlemen,'" 1069). The correctness of value judgments that water is gold or three meals are good is not tested by an appeal to subjective prejudices or personal food preferences. Instead, a rational and defensible process involving evaluative calculation is involved. Therefore Crane's regular reminders about the context dependence of value judgments are not the hedge of a subjectivist, but rather the prudence and caution of one who understands how value judgments are made. What eventually emerges is that the virtue of tolerance achieves paradigmatic status. Not surprisingly, the most convincing defense of tolerance is indirect—the condemnation of arrogance.

> Above all things, the stranger finds the occupations of foreign peoples to be trivial and inconsequent. The average mind utterly fails to comprehend the new point of view and that such and such a man should be satisfied to carry bundles or mayhap sit and ponder in the sun all his life in this faraway country seems an abnormally stupid thing. The visitor feels scorn. He swells with a knowledge of his geographical experience. . . .This is the arrogance of the man who has not yet solved himself and discovered his own actual futility. ("The Mexican Lower Classes" 728)

Crane's wide-spread travels gave him openness to other life-styles and impressed him with the need for sensitivity and patience in appreciating other points of view. On his way to Mexico, Crane stayed at Hot Springs. There he wrote that foreign visitors had instructed the natives of that Arkansas town, "this profound education had destroyed its curiosity and created a sort of wide sympathy, not tender, but tolerant" ("Seen at Hot Springs" 702).

Along with tolerance, Crane's later writings frequently praise competence in ordinary tasks. Just six months before his death, midway through "War Memories" he attempted to capture Admiral William Thomas Sampson, whom he viewed as the most interesting personality in the war in Cuba. "The quiet old man . . . a sailor and admiral" (6:239) seems at first bored with the war and indifferent to details. But once the action starts, "hidden in his indifferent, even apathetic, manner, there was the alert, sure, fine mind of the best sea-captain that America has produced since—since Farragut? I don't know. I think—since Hull" (6:239). Unimpressed with the common seaman's eager devotion and reverence, Admiral Sampson thinks not of glory, but "he considered the management of ships" (6:240). Crane's summary strikes, as it so often does, precisely the right note—Sampson's record is "just plain, pure, unsauced accomplishment" (6:240).

Other everyday heroes also received Crane's attention. In "In the Depths of a Coal Mine," he salutes the elevator operator. "Far above us in the engine-room, the engineer sat with his hand on a lever and his eye on the little model of the shaft wherein a miniature elevator was making the ascent even as our elevator was making it. . . . My mind was occupied with a mental picture of this faraway engineer, who sat in his high chair by his levers, a statue of responsibility and fidelity, cool-brained, clear-eyed, steady of hand" (614). In "Nebraska's Bitter Fight for Life," L. P. Ludden, secretary and general manager of the relief commission, "works early and late and always. . . . But he is the most unpopular man in the State of Nebraska. He is honest, conscientious and loyal; he is hard-working and has great executive ability" (693).

Crane's most effusive praise of ordinary competence is reserved for the railroad engineer in "The Scotch Express." The engineer's skills, indispensable although they be, are generally overlooked; "one often finds this apparent disregard for the man who. . .occupies a position which for the exercise of temperance, of courage, of honesty, has no equal at the altitude of prime-ministers" (8:743). The engineer's matter-of-fact attitude and the deceptive ordinariness of his tasks intrigued Crane. "He was simply a quiet, middle-aged man, bearded and with little wrinkles of habitual geniality and kindliness. . . . This driver's face displayed nothing but . . . cool sanity . . . the engine-driver is the finest type of man that is grown. He is the pick of the earth. He is not paid too much . . . but for outright performance carried on constantly, coolly, and without elation by a temperate, honest, clear-minded man he is the further point" (8:746).

Thus, subsequent to his examination of exceptional deeds beyond

morality—heroic acts and measures to alleviate animal pain—
Crane's ethics focus on the ordinary actions of ordinary people as
they address a central moral duty: an unselfish response to human
need.[21] Precisely which actions embody morally satisfactory responses to human needs requires a value judgment. In the absence of a single normative criterion operating in a single metaphysical context,
all value judgments involve proximate criteria and contexts. What
naturally follows, therefore, in Crane's ethics is the paramount value of compassion and tolerance. He also calls attention to the unex-
citing but nonetheless moral conduct of ordinary people in average
communities, and he celebrates the commonplace heroism involved
in a steady competence at mundane but essential tasks.[22] What
emerges is a common-sense morality in the service of the status quo.

Whether compassion, competence, and tolerance represent
Crane's final opinion on moral matters depends on how much weight
is placed on the *Whilomville Stories*, especially *The Monster*. As it
turns out, Crane's fixation with courage led him to reexamine criti-
cally his own version of common-sense morality. *The Monster* brings
together, in Henry Johnson's selfless dash into the fire to save Jimmie, the frenzy and abandon of Fleming's nonrational, animal courage; in Dr. Trescott's uncomplaining steadfastness and devotion to
duty, the quiet, competent heroism of the Scotch Express's engineer.
As Crane reexamines tolerance, compassion, and open-mindedness
in *The Monster*, he probes the appropriateness of ordinary moral
norms, cases in which, in the words of John Twelve, "this thing is *out
of the ordinary*" (446, emphasis added). What is at stake in *The Monster* is that if Trescott is a moral man, Crane has rejected common-
sense morality. If Trescott's actions are supererogatory and saintly,
however, he is to be applauded and admired, but the ordinary moral
behavior of average people and the competence of everyday heroes
will not have been impugned.

Good Doctor Trescott, or Ned Trescott, Martyr and Fool?

The Monster is a challenging work. In it, some critics have seen
Crane rethinking his standpoint as an author. They cite the clash
between his statements about being a writer—"I detest dogma" (*Correspondence* #204), and "I have been very careful not to let any theories or pet ideas of my own be seen in my writing. Preaching is fatal
to art in literature. I try to give readers a slice out of life; and if there
is any moral or lesson in it I do not point it out. I let the reader find it

for himself" (Crane to editor of *Demorest's Family Magazine, Correspondence* #240)—with what some consider a none too subtle moral indictment of the close-mindedness, narrowness, and intolerance of Waspish Whilomville.[23] With regard to ethics, if Trescott is not a saint but merely a good man, then Crane seems to be abandoning affirmation of the decency of ordinary people and his endorsement of the moral health of average societies.

In an explicit denial of environmental determinism, Crane states that the world is easy to change but human beliefs are not, "the majestic forces which are arrayed against man's true success—not the world—the world is silly, changeable, any of it's decisions can be reversed—but man's own colossal impulses more strong than chains" (Crane to Nellie Crouse, January 26, 1896, *Correspondence* #186). He did not underestimate the task of changing people's minds. In *The Monster*, John Twelve, speaking for the delegation of Whilomville's leading citizens, appeals to Trescott. "'You are doing yourself a great deal of harm. You have changed from being the leading doctor in town to about the last one. It is mainly because there are always a large number of people who are very thoughtless fools . . . . even if there are a lot of fools in the world, we can't see any reason why you should ruin yourself by opposing them. You can't teach them anything, you know'" (445–46). Trescott responds, "'I am not trying to teach them anything'" (446). Crane, however, is. If he can evoke a sympathetic endorsement of the ethical heroic actions of Dr. Trescott and if he can promote scrutiny of the shunning of Dr. and Mrs. Trescott, then without moral preaching, he will have accomplished its salutary effect: ethical reflection by his audience.

Crane has neither abandoned his stance on his role as an artist nor rejected ordinary morality. Instead, his literary skills are so successful in *The Monster* that some critics have been lead to confuse sainthood with ethical goodness, and many readers have misunderstood his moral prophecy (in the Old Testament sense of a call to conscience and conversion) for an ethical pontification.

Just as Crane depicts animal suffering in order to promote a heightened ethical sensitivity, his primary interest in *The Monster* is the story's impact upon the ethical sensibilities of his readers; he is not particularly concerned to maintain a neat separation of exceptional and ordinary moral conduct. However, if care is taken to distinguish exceptional from ordinary ethical duties, *The Monster* does not undercut the coherence or practical soundness of Crane's general moral position. Although he may have made it seem as if Dr. Trescott is good man and the conduct of his townspeople is reprehensible, Trescott is actually a moral martyr and the behavior of Whilo-mville is, in the main, excusable.

The morally considerable aspects of human behavior are the motive of the agent and the consequences of the action. When the fire breaks out in Dr. Trescott's laboratory, threatening Jimmie and his mother, several different people, differently motivated, respond. The would-be rescuers obey the basic moral maxim in Crane's ethics: an unselfish response to genuine human need. Considerable risks are involved in entering the burning house, but because comparable gains are foreseeable (unlike Collins's reckless dash for a bucket of water), a rescue attempt is morally justifiable. Whether the several rescue efforts are morally obligatory ("you *must*"), morally recommended ("you *ought*"), or morally permissible ("you *may*") depends upon the motives, personal ties, and social roles of the agents. In terms of consequences, the rescue is not heroic but well within the realm of morality.

First to reach the burning Trescott home is a neighbor, Edward Hannigan. He has already kicked in the locked door when the Trescotts' black stablehand, Henry Johnson, rushes past to hear Mrs. Trescott's plea, "'Jimmie! Save Jimmie!'" (403).[24] The ethically significant facts about Johnson are that he is employed by the Trescotts, and that he is Jimmie's pal and confidant "in regard to almost everything in life, they seemed to have minds precisely alike. . . . they were in complete but unexpressed understanding" (392–93).

On the strength of his personal ties with Jimmie and his formal ties with the Trescott family, Henry's response is correct but also little more than a reflex action. Crane is quite specific: "He now clutched Jimmie as unconsciously as when, running toward the house, he had clutched the hat with the bright silk band" (405). With the hallway blocked, Henry carries Jimmie, wrapped in a blanket, out the back way through Dr. Trescott's laboratory. There, overcome by the fire, Henry stumbles and falls. Jimmie, still wrapped in the blanket, rolls across the room under a window while Johnson lays at the base of an old desk upon which are stored Trescott's chemicals.

Upon Trescott's return from his evening house calls, he hears Mrs. Trescott again scream "'Jimmie! Save Jimmie'" (407), while she points to his second-story bedroom. Trescott sees that the hall is blocked and so leads the rescue party around to his laboratory. Crashing through the door, he enters to find "a form in a smouldering blanket near the window" (408), and Johnson prostrate, unconscious, and badly burned. His face has been monstrously disfigured by the chemicals, which had exploded and spilled over the edge of the desk, dripping onto his upturned face. Dr. Trescott first rescues his son and then returns to save Johnson, only to find that a young volunteer fireman has already brought him out and laid him on the grass. In just a few pages Crane manages to cover the gamut of relationships—mother, father, friend, neighbor, and volunteer—as well as a wide range of motivations that ethically sanction the risk involved in saving human lives.

During the night of the fire and the next day, Crane focuses attention on two additional, "ordinary" moral actions. Old Judge Denning Hagenthorpe, who lives across the street, "had thrown his door wide open to receive the afflicted family" (411). And Dr. Trescott and six of Whilomville's ten doctors care for Jimmie and Henry Johnson.

Later, when the paper tells of Henry Johnson's death, his girl friend Miss Bella Farragut reveals that she had been engaged to marry him, and the town widely admires his heroism. But Henry Johnson does not die. When Jimmie has recovered enough to visit his grandparents with Mrs. Trescott, Dr. Trescott stays behind at the Hagenthorpe home. "The doctor had remained to take care of his patients, but as a matter of truth he spent most of his time at Judge Hagenthorpe's house, where lay Henry Johnson. Here he slept and ate almost every meal in the long nights and days of his vigil" (413).

Early on, the judge expresses doubts about Trescott's efforts to save Johnson. "'Perhaps we may not talk with propriety of this kind of action, but I am induced to say that you are performing a questionable charity in preserving this negro's life. As near as I can understand, he will hereafter be a monster, a perfect monster, and probably with an affected brain. No man can observe you as I have observed you and not know that it was a matter of conscience with you, but I am afraid, my friend, that it is one of the blunders of virtue'" (413).

Trescott provides a predictable defense. As a doctor, his duty is to preserve life. Beyond that, "'He saved my boy's life'" (414). Nonetheless, Judge Hagenthorpe's probing forces Trescott to examine his own motivation and the consequences involved in his care of Henry Johnson.

Eventually the Trescott house is rebuilt, the family reunited, and Trescott resumes his medical practice. He arranges and pays for Henry to be kept at the home of Alex Williams on the outskirts of Whilomville. After a couple of months, Williams calls on Judge Hagenthorpe to complain that Henry has terribly disrupted his home, " 'my ol' 'ooman she cain't 'ceive no lady callahs, nohow'" [and] "the chillens . . . they—they cain't eat'" (418). When Hagenthorpe suggests that Trescott can find another place to board Henry, Williams seeks to renegotiate. If, instead of $5 a week, suppose "'I git six dollehs for bo'ding Hennery Johnson, I uhns it! I uhns it!'" (421).

As Whilomville returns to normal life, talk at the barbershop turns to Henry Johnson and Dr. Trescott. Although he may have created a monster, there is firm agreement that Trescott has done the right thing, "If I had been the doctor, I would have done the same thing.... It was the only thing he could do" (422–23). Still to be faced are the long-term effects of Trescott's action. As Crane examines the lasting consequences of the fire, he shifts attention from moral to heroic actions.

Johnson recovers and will not stay at the Williams's. During a jaunt back into town, his appearance demolishes a children's party, then, when he calls upon his "fiance" Miss Bella Faragut, "a monster making a low and sweeping bow . . . [causes] wreck of a family gathering" (429). Thereafter, he "stampeded" the whole town and is put in jail. With the town full of rumors about the monster and Jake Winter's threat to have Trescott arrested because his daughter has yet to recover from being frightened at the children's party, Trescott arranges Henry's release from jail and brings him to his new home.

Life at the Trescott's never returns to normal. Jimmie gradually gets used to the deformed Henry Johnson. Unfortunately, his fear turns into daredeviltry instead of compassion. He brings his friends home and makes a show of running up to touch the monster. "Jimmie seemed to reap all the joys of the owner and exhibitor of one of the world's marvels, while his audience remained at a distance— awed and entranced, fearful and envious" (435). The Hannigans, the neighbors first on the scene during the fire, plan to move across town. Trescott's medical practice falls off. Finally, when Mrs. Trescott receives callers at Wednesday tea, Mrs. Twelve comes, but no one else.

Why does Trescott continue to shelter Henry Johnson in his home? Heroism. Trescott's single-minded devotion to Johnson surpasses morality; his exemplary behavior is above and beyond the call of ethical duty.[25] It might even be argued that Trescott's service to Johnson, although praiseworthy, is not sufficiently meritorious to offset its costs. He devastates his practice, disrupts his family, and destroys the Trescotts' social life in the Whilomville community.

The moral barometers in *The Monster* are Judge Hagenthorpe and the wholesale grocer, John Twelve.[26] As leaders of the delegation of "active and influential citizens" (445), Twelve and Hagenthorpe understand Trescott's one-man crusade. They obviously respect him, and they are, if anything, too impressed with his heroism. Their counsel to him is prudentially sound and ethically correct. Trescott ought, morally and practically, "get Johnson a place somewhere off up the valley" (446). Trescott, of course, refuses. Then they offer another option, "'Well, then, a public institution.' 'No' said Trescott, 'public institutions are all very good, but he is not going to one'" (446).

The Twelve-Hagenthorpe delegation has the right answer but uses the wrong arguments. They should have directly appealed to moral considerations. (1) Trescott's care of Johnson is no longer medically necessary, no longer requiring his special attention and sacrifice. (2) It is not clear that Trescott's handling of Johnson's nonmedical needs is better than a public institution. Johnson lives alone above the carriage house and, because his brain has been affected, can never be an integral part of the Trescott family. (3) Finally, there are moral deficiencies in Trescott's arrangements for Johnson. Beyond the moral duties involved in Trescott's neglect of his medical practice and his disruption of family life, the noble doctor has been unable to prevent even his own son's callous and ungrateful treatment of Johnson.

From a moral point of view, the rescue of Jimmie and Johnson is correct, as are Trescott's initial medical care and financial support for Johnson at the Williams's. Shortly after the fire, Hagenthorpe offers the opinion that preserving Johnson's life is "a questionable charity. . . . one of the blunders of virtue" (413). The judge is mistaken about the moral duty to save Johnson's life, but his assessment precisely captures the questionable character of Trescott's heroic devotion after Johnson's life is no longer in danger.

John Twelve's analysis, on the other hand, blames Trescott's failing medical practice on the "large number of people who are very thoughtless fools" (445). Trescott does not speculate about whether the people of Whilomville are fools; he only comments on his own reasons, "Trescott smiled wearily. 'I—It is a matter of—well—'" (446). What Trescott leaves unsaid, Crane deftly captures. Trescott's ethical heroism forces the reader to reflect upon ordinary moral duties.

Although it has not seemed so to many readers, I find Crane remarkably nonjudgmental about the conduct of the average Whilomvillite. At the same time, his depiction of Trescott is even-handed, almost cool. Trescott either does not or cannot explain himself to his wife or son. He, like Private Collins and Lieutenant Manolo Prat, has entered into the mystery of heroism. Trescott's heroism echoes the to be virtuous. Inversely then, if he possesses this fair opportunity, he cannot rebel, he has no complaint. I am of the opinion that poverty of itself is no cause. It is something above and beyond. For example, there is Collis P. Huntington and William D. Rockefeller — as virtuous as these gentlemen are, I would not say that their virtue is any ways superior to mine for instance. Their opportunities are no greater. They can give more, deny themselves more in quantity but not relatively. We can each give all that we possess and there I am at once their equal.

I do not think however that they would be capable of sacrifices that would be possible to me. So then I envy them nothing. Far from having a grievance against them, I feel that they will confront an ultimate crisis that I through my opportunities may altogether avoid. There is in fact no advantage of importance which I can perceive them possessing over me.

It is for these reasons that I refuse to commit judgment upon these lower classes of Mexico. I even refuse to pity them. It is true that at night many of them sleep in heaps in doorways, and spend their days squatting upon the pavements. It is true that their clothing is scant and thin. All manner of things of this kind is true but yet their faces have almost always a certain smoothness, a certain lack of pain, a serene faith. I can feel the superiority of their contentment.

Stephen Crane

Concluding page of the manuscript of "Mexican Lower Classes" (1895). From the Special Manuscripts Collection, Butler Library, Columbia University.

old captain in "'God Rest Ye, Merry Gentlemen'": "he loved it for itself . . . the thing itself" (1069).

Putting aside Crane's fascination with the extra-moral obligations of heroism and his sensitivity to premoral treatment of animals, his central moral position firmly rests upon two norms: an unselfish response to genuine human need and a tolerant respect for others. Crane's insistence upon tolerance does not commit him to endorse the conduct of all persons, the value of every life-style, or the goodness of every culture.[27] Indeed, he was often critical at each of these levels. Still, Crane's maxim of tolerance requires patience, openness, and sensitivity to the meaning and context required for a correct ethical judgment. In *The Monster*, Crane's literary finesse illustrates the sort of measured ethical judgment he considers appropriate. Some years earlier, journalist Crane, in "The Mexican Lower Classes" had been direct, even blunt, on the same point.

> I measure their morality by what evidences of peace and contentment I can detect in the average countenance . . . . I refuse to commit judgment upon these lower classes of Mexico. I even refuse to pity them. It is true that at night many of them sleep in heaps in door-ways, and spend their days squatting upon the pavements. It is true that their clothing is scant and thin. All manner of things of this kind is true but yet their faces have almost always a certain smoothness, a certain lack of pain, a serene faith. I can feel the superiority of their contentment. (730–31)

CHAPTER 5

Philosopher-Poet

I detest dogma.
Crane to Nellie Crouse, February 1896

Personally, I like my little book of poems, "The Black Riders," better than I do "The Red Badge of Courage." The reason is, I suppose, that the former is the more ambitious effort. In it I aim to give my ideas of life as a whole, so far as I know it, and the latter is a mere episode,—an amplification.
Crane to the editor of *Demorest's Family Magazine*,
late April–early May 1896

The term *philosopher*, when used to refer to Crane's idea of life as a whole, is used in a nonspecialist's sense. It is, as a friend once wrote to me, "the sense of 'philosophy' you understood before you became a philosophy major." Or, as William James remarked in "The Sentiment of Rationality," when humans philosophize, "they desire to attain a conception of the frame of things which shall on the whole be more rational than that somewhat chaotic view which everyone by nature carries about with him under his hat" (*The Will to Believe* 57).

Inevitably, total views involve, even if by way of denial, reference to God. Crane's total view is no different. Although some have contended that his philosophy is nihilistic, agnostic, even atheistic, I argue that his stance is fundamentally theistic. Given Crane's heritage, God had to be faced, and he found interesting ways to involve God in his worldview. Initially, the religion poured into Crane came out sideways as swearing.

Crane and the Art of Fine Swearing

At his knees José was arguing, in a low, aggrieved tone, with the saints. José's moans and cries amounted to a university course in theology.
"One Dash—Horses"

Crane, the preacher's kid, was used to God-talk. Outside the parsonage he heard frequent references to God, too. He was fascinated by the vernacular of the streets and became proficient at it. At Syracuse

University, his profane performances were legendary.[1] Sorrentino (1984) even argues that Crane was "obsessed with profanity" (181). As evidence he cites accounts of Crane's daily swearing about the steepness of the hill to the Delta Upsilon fraternity house and an anecdote about how Crane's baseball teammates, hearing a game was canceled, waited for his arrival and reaction. The wait proved worthwhile—"that day Crane broke all his previous records in that line" (182).[2]

Apparently, however, some of his family were unaware of his swearing skills. On October 30, 1922, Thomas Beer, making final revisions of his biography of Crane, wrote a long letter to Edmund B. Crane. Among the several detailed questions that Beer asked of Stephen's elder brother was: "11. Do you remember that about 1894 he partly composed a dictionary of profanity. In a letter dated 1895 he says: 'Used to sit around last year on Ned's [Edmund B. Crane] kitchen steps and think up swear words for my dictionary.'"

Beer received this reply in a letter sent November 19, 1922: "Mother [Mrs. Cornelia Crane] and I [Miss Edith F. Crane] opened your letter to my father and we will answer the questions as best we can. My father, Edmund B. Crane, could have answered them more fully, if he had lived, but he passed away on September 20." Crane's sister-in-law and niece responded: "11. Uncle might have written such a thing in a letter as a joke and in planning a story such as Maggie or George's Mother he would need some practice. Mother never heard him swear and he did not even use slang very much she says. We girls certainly never heard him swear."[3] Family members notwithstanding, Crane both swore and appreciated unusual profanity.

Actually, Crane would not have had to practice for Maggie or his earlier New York City pieces. They contained only mild profanity because nothing stronger than "damn," "hell," and "gawd" was generally allowed in print. When Maggie was issued by a regular publishing house, he had to tone down the profanity even more, using the conventions of the day: "d—," "h—," and "g—." He wrote Appleton's editor Ripley Hitchcock, "I have dispensed with a goodly number of damns, . . . I have carefully plugged at the words which hurt" (Correspondence #199 and 203). Crane was, however, able to save some profanity by way of dialect, for example, "purtydamnsoon" and "damnquick" (26).

Crane's cultivated sense of the profane, his cursing connoisseurship, can be found in the portrayals of noted swearers and in the description of reactions to imaginative profanity. In The Red Badge of Courage, the lieutenant of the youth's company is a black-belt curser: "he began to swear so wondrously that a nervous laugh went along the regimental line" (108). What the swearer says is not often important: "he said more, but much of it could not be understood . . . . He stood then with his back to the enemy and delivered gigantic curses into the faces of the men. His body vibrated from the weight and force of his imprecations. And he could string oaths with the facility of a maiden who strings beads" (184). Despite being wounded in a lengthy battle, the lieutenant is able to maintain peak swearing efficiency. "The lieutenant, returning from a tour after a bandage, produced from a hidden receptacle of his mind new and portentous oaths suited to the emergency. Strings of expletives he swung lash-like over the backs of his men, and it was evident that his previous efforts had in no wise impaired his resources" (201). Near the end of the battle, the field commander finally slows; "the lieutenant, also, was unscathed in his position at the rear. He had continued to curse, but it was now with the air of a man who was using his last box of oaths" (203).

As Crane tells it, war is impossible without expletives.[4] In "The Fire-Tribe and the White-Face," he introduces "three soldiers whose duty it was to swear in a manner impartial and continuous" (10:167–68). These men are indispensable, for later we learn that the commanding officer "exhorted the three men detailed for impartial and continuous swearing to re-double their violence" (10:177). In "Three Miraculous Soldiers," Crane pauses to note "the unconscious and cheerful sentry at the door was swearing away in flaming sentences, heaping one gorgeous oath upon another, making a conflagration of his description of his troop horse" (6:36). As for inflammatory language, Crane found the Irish competent enough. Young Lord Streep in *The O'Ruddy* has the know-how: "he looked generous and kindly but just at the moment he was damning a waiter in language that would have set fire to a stone-bridge" (4:5).

In his western, Mexican, and Cuban travels Crane found that good swearers can close language barriers. "The Clan of No-Name" tells of a battle, first from the point of view of the Spaniards in the blockhouse and then from the position of the insurgents creeping through the pampas grass. Along with bullets, both sides exchange insults and profanities. "Whenever an insurgent was about to fire he ordinarily prefixed the affair with a speech. 'Do you want something to eat? Yes? All right.' Bang! 'Eat that.' The more common expressions of the incredibly foul Spanish tongue were trifles light as air in this badinage which was shrieked out from the grass during the spin of bullets and the dull rattle of the shooting" (1039).

Near the top of Crane's honor roll are Mexican cursers. "Stephen Crane in Mexico (I)" is a travel piece that informs visitors that "Mexican is a very capable language for the purposes of profanity. A good swearer here can bring rain in thirty minutes" (8:439). During his Mexican stay, Crane left Mexico City for the rural provinces to interview the infamous bandit Romon Colorado. One evening Crane and his guide José left the desert to spend the night at a cantine where, very late the same evening, Colorado's gang showed up for a party. "One Dash—Horses" begins with one of Colorado's men threatening to rob Crane and his guide. "The fat one posed in the manner of a grandee. Presently his hand dropped to his belt, and from his lips there spun an epithet—a hideous word which often foreshadows knife-blows, a word peculiarly of Mexico, where people have to dig deep to find an insult that has not lost its savor" (735).

As the Colorado gang moves across the room, Crane draws his revolver. When the women arrive, there are more interesting activities than a robbery. Several hours later, in a predawn getaway, Crane's horse smokes over the plain. José is not so fortunate; his horse does not want to run. With each jab of his spurs, José swears. The variety and range of his profanity is so outstanding that Crane reports that "José's moans and cries amounted to a university course in theology" (741).

It is Crane's sense that much of life, especially city life, is war. Because, war promotes profanity, a city is a fine place to serve an internship in cursing. In New York City swearing seminars can be found anytime a traffic jam occurs. "The Broken-Down Van" reports the aftermath of a lost hubnut. "'The nut is gone.' . . .'Yes, the damned nut is lost.' . . . Then the driver of the other van swore, and the two assistants swore, and the three car driver swore, and the three car conductors used some polite but profane expressions. Then a strange man, an unknown man and an outsider, with his trousers held up by a trunk-strap, who stood at hand, swore harder than any of the rest. The others turned and looked at him inquiringly and savagely. The man wriggled nervously" (523).

Policemen on the beat in New York City streets are excellent role models for the apprentice swearer; "owing to a curious dispensation, the majority of the policemen along the Boulevard were very stout and could swear most graphically in from two to five languages" ("New York's Bicycle Speedway" 861).

For advanced training, the sort that might turn an ordinary curser into a master, Crane recommends the Bowery. Bowery lessons add both polish and durability to a swearer's repertoire. The central character of "A Man and Some Others" is a one-time Bowery saloon bouncer, Bill, whom Crane finds tending sheep in Mexico. Bill senses an ambush. When he first spots movement in a nearby mesquite thicket, "he burst out violently and loud in the most extraordinary profanity, the oaths winging from him as sparks go from the funnel" (782). Bill and his companion withstand the first rush, and, as they wait for the second charge, Bill's Bowery education pays unexpected dividends: "he began to invent epithets and yell them at the thicket. He was something of a master of insult, and, moreover, he dived into his memory to bring forth imprecations tarnished with age, unused since fluent Bowery days. The occupation amused him, and sometimes he laughed so that it was uncomfortable for his chest to be against the ground" (784).

Crane's dedication to brevity is obvious in his revisions as he slowly moved from his first to final drafts. He did not seek brevity for its own sake. Instead, he prized a terseness that magnified the force of his distilled prose. Then, too, his deletions force readers to supply what has been left unsaid. The earlier works contain profanity, at least as much as he could slip by his editors. Later, Crane confidently directed the reader to imagine the curse words in a skillfully supervised supply-the-missing-expletive exercise. Ordinary profanity will not do. Crane's reader is challenged to create truly elegant and eloquent curses, including some that transcend language. One such sophisticated swearer appears in "The Blue Hotel." In the tiny western Nebraska town of Fort Romper, after a fist fight, "the cowboy was formulating new and unspellable blasphemies" (819).

From Crane's own prose, it turns out, it would be easy to compile a swearing dictionary of surprising variety and sparkling style. Beyond his sly, sometimes immature admiration for adept swearers, his treatment of swearing shows an appreciation of profanity as a performance on a purely linguistic level. More significant, however, is his ability to distance himself from his ancestors' dead-seriousness about God. His openness to experience and his tolerance of life-styles lends relief, especially in his treatment of swearing, lightness, and humor, about the place of God in his "idea of life as a whole." In Crane's poetry, he is wary of any single-answer solutions, even God, although God fulfills a significant role in a comprehensive scheme.

Crane's "Lines": Repudiations and Affirmations

Crane was uneasy about being thought of as a poet.[5] Elbert Hubbard's November 10, 1895 formal invitation for the dinner in his honor at

Buffalo, New York, began "recognizing in yourself and in your genius as a poet" (*Correspondence* #129). At the family camp in Hartwood on December 31, 1895, back in his corduroys two weeks after the dinner and with his formal dinner outfit returned, Crane wrote to Nellie Crouse and included a copy of Hubbard's formal invitation to the affair. He observed, "I knew little of the Philistines until they sent me this letter: I was very properly enraged at the word 'poet' which continually reminds me of long-hair and seems to me to be a most detestable form of insult" (*Correspondence* #166).[6]

Crane's next letter to Nellie Crouse, January 6, 1896, returns to his nervousness with the terms *poet* and *poetry*. "I am sorry you did not find the 'two poems'—mind you I never call them poems myself—in the *Philistine*" (*Correspondence* #173). Crane preferred to call his verses "lines"; the full title of his first book of poetry is *The Black Riders and Other Lines*. Shortly after it was published, he wrote to Linson, asking him to locate a box of manuscripts stored in Linson's studio. "There are some 'lines' among them which I should be very glad to get. . . . bundle them up and express them to me, C. O. D." (*Correspondence* #171). He also refered to his poems as "pills": "some of the pills are pretty darned dumb, anyhow. But I meant what I said" (quoted by Lowell, xxiii).

Crane's output of lines was not extensive, 136 poems in all. The largest group, sixty-eight, were published in *The Black Riders and Other Lines* in 1895. *War Is Kind*, containing thirty-seven, appeared in 1899, and he wrote thirty-one poems that were uncollected, only eight of them published while he was alive.

Many of the *Black Rider* poems are short, free-verse epigrams, more than half are ten lines or less, and only eleven of the sixty-eight are longer than sixteen lines. Copeland and Day published the *Black Riders* poems, one to a page, in capital letters throughout. Contemporary reaction fixed as much on the strange look of the poems as on what they contained. As Howells noted in a review in *Harper's Weekly*, "But, after all, how a man gives you his thought is not so important as what thought he gives you, and we can well be patient with Mr. Crane's form for as long as he can endure it himself" (*Critical Heritage* #19). Mark Anthony Howe, writing for *Atlantic Monthly*, found merit in both the brevity and condensed format of Crane's lines: "these small skeletons of poetry are printed entirely in capitals, and in the modern fashion which hangs a few lines by the shoulders to the top of the page, as if more had meant to come, but changed its mind. The virtue of these lines, however, is that they have often enough freshness of conception to set the reader thinking, and so perhaps the blank spaces are filled" (*Critical Heritage* #20).

Some of the poems in *War Is Kind* are also very short, twenty-three of the thirty poems have fifteen lines or fewer. The most widely remembered has but five.

> A man said to the universe:
> "Sir, I exist!"
> "However," replied the universe,
> "The fact has not created in me
> "A sense of obligation."
>
> (#89, 1335)[7]

Many of the poems in Crane's second volume, however, have conventional stanzas; several effectively use refrains and rhyme.

In the winter of 1893, wearing a suit borrowed from fellow freelance journalist John Northern Hilliard, Crane called upon William Dean Howells. Howells's reading to him several of Emily Dickinson's poems proved to be the catalyst for Crane's poetry. Within several months Crane "drew off" the cryptic lines that made up *The Black Riders*.[8] Early on, he showed his lines to John Barry, who was impressed enough to arrange for some of them to be read before a Manhattan literary group, the Uncut Leaves Society. Crane, terrified to read in front of a group, refused, and Barry read them in his absence.[9] Elbert Hubbard, however, even more than Barry, encouraged Crane's poetry.[10] He selected the more blasphemous of the *Black Riders* poems for the *Philistine*, remarking, "The 'Lines' in *The Black Riders* seem to me wonderful: charged with meaning like a storage battery. But there is a fine defy in the flavour that warns the reader not to take too much or it may strike in. Who wants a meal of horseradish?" (*Critical Heritage* #23).

Most of the *War Is Kind* poems were written after 1897, when Crane had moved to England. His uncollected poems cover a wide span, from "I'd Rather Have—" (#106), written in 1879 or 1880 at age eight or nine, to "Intrigue" (#96–105, 1338–45), written within two years of his death.

Most of the "pills" are tightly compressed epigrams or highly condensed parables. Crane often has the reader listen to the dialogue of a highly charged encounter.[11] A question is posed, and after the normal solution is rejected, a novel answer, or non-answer, is presented. Several commentators have remarked that much of Crane's prose is highly poetic. Conversely, as Howells first observed, many of Crane's poems are disguised prose. Howells sought to dispel the furor over the lack of poetic form in Crane's lines by treating them as prose. In his review of *The Black Riders* in the January 25, 1896 *Harper's Weekly*, he discussed one poem by first rearranging it.

I will print [it] as prose to prove that it owes nothing of its poetry to
the typographic mask of metre:
  "I was in the darkness. I could not see my words nor the wishes of
my heart. Then suddenly there was a great light—Let me into the darkness again!" (*Critical Heritage* #19)[12]

In his review of *War Is Kind* for the July 1899 *Bookman*, John Curtis
wrote, "Among the best things in the book are the epigrams. They
are obviously prose, nothing more. Stripped of the gray paper, the
black drawings, the printing of four solitary lines at the top of one
page, they stand for the thought in them, but the illusive glamour of
verse has fled. And the author seems naively conscious of this" (*Critical Heritage* #94).

Following Howells and Curtis, my examination of Crane's poetry
for philosophical statement will underplay the form of his lines. Second, his poems will be treated as a continuum. Unlike several commentators, I see not sharp philosophical shifts, but rather differences of degree between Crane's early and late poems.[13]

Crane, poet and lay philosopher-theologian, following a long line
of distinguished preachers comfortable with parables, adopted that
genre. Many of his parables are negative, renouncing orthodox no-
tions of Truth, Reality, and an all-powerful God. On the other hand,
his affirmations about God, realities, and truths are modest and tentative. Put in slightly different terms, his poetry rejects the religious
dogmas of his ancestors while he adopts the philosophical commitments of late-nineteenth-century American society: a finite god,
meliorism, solidarity, metaphysical plurality, and epistemological
relativity. Although God's nature and dealings with humans are the
high-profile topic in much of Crane's poetry, reflections on the nature of truth and reality are the constitutive elements of his "idea of
life as a whole."

Crane is unusually attentive to infra- and ultra-human forms of
consciousness; he is especially mindful of lives below and beyond
our own (chapter 3). The human world is important, perhaps paramount, in Crane's scheme, but we are not *the* constitutors of reality.
He argues, for instance, that human songs must be compared with
the melodies of birds.

> Three little birds in a row
> Sat musing.
> A man passed near that place
> Then did the little birds nudge each other.
>
> They said: "He thinks he can sing."
> They threw back their heads to laugh.

2'/4 in.

I.

Three little birds in a row
Sat musing.
A man passed near that place
Then did the little birds nudge each
                                    other.

They said: "He thinks he can sing."
They threw back their heads to laugh.
With quaint countenances
They regarded him.
They were very curious
Those three little birds in a row.

Holograph of "Three little birds in a row" (1893 or 1894). From the Special
Manuscripts Collection, Butler Library, Columbia University.

> With quaint countenances
> They regarded him.
> They were very curious
> Those three little birds in a row.
>
> (BR #2, 1299)

One of his uncollected poems refers to birds in another way, noting not only their song but also their *experience*.

> Little birds of the night
> Aye, they have much to tell
> Perching there in rows
> Blinking at me with their serious eyes
> Recounting of flowers they have seen and loved
> Of meadows and groves of the distance
> And pale sands at the foot to the sea
> And breezes that fly in the leaves.
> They are vast in experience
> These little birds that come in the night.
>
> (#108)

Plants, too, have important reality. For example, neither humans' point of view nor things' utilitarian value particularly interest Crane as he celebrates the integrity of grass,

> In Heaven,
> Some little blades of grass
> Stood before God.
> "What did you do?"
> Then all save one of the little blades
> Began eagerly to relate
> The merits of their lives.
> This one stayed a small way behind
> Ashamed.
> Presently God said:
> "And what did you do?"
> The little blade answered: "Oh, my lord,
> "Memory is bitter to me
> "For if I did good deeds
> "I know not of them."
> Then God in all His splendor
> Arose from his throne.
> "Oh, best little blade of grass," He said.
>
> (BR #18, 1304)

and the standing of trees,

> A man said: "Thou tree!"

The tree answered with the same scorn: "Thou man!
Thou art greater than I only in thy possibilities."

(#120, 1346)

In *War Is Kind,* Crane urges removing the "green spectacles" that block our appreciation of nature in its own right.

"I have heard the sunset song of the birches
"A white melody in the silence
"I have seen a quarrel of the pines.
"At nightfall
"The little grasses have rushed by me
"With the wind-men.
"These things have I lived," quoth the maniac,
"Possessing only eyes and ears.
"But, you—
"You don green spectacles before you look at roses."

(#75, 1328)

Humans fail to respect lives below their own, and an inflated sense of self-importance has us miss "the screams of cut trees . . . the chanting of flowers . . . the unknown appeals of brutes" (*WK* #82, 1332). The reality of animal suffering plays a critical role in both Crane's ethics and his poetry. Just as the moral message of "A Dark-Brown Dog" is the shock of the story's ending—when the family searches for the small boy after the drunken father has thrown the dog out the tenement window they find the boy "seated by the body of his dark-brown friend" (537)—the ethical message of "Fast Rode the Knight" is in neither chivalry nor courage but the abandoned, spent horse.

Fast rode the knight
With spurs, hot and reeking
Ever waving an eager sword.
"To save my lady!"
Fast rode the knight
And leaped from saddle to war.
Men of steel flickered and gleamed
Like riot of silver lights
And the gold of the knight's good banner
Still waved on a castle wall.

A horse
Blowing, staggering, bloody thing
Forgotten at foot of castle wall.
A horse
Dead at foot of castle wall.

(*WK* #76, 1329)

Holograph of "Fast rode the knight" (ca. 1896). From the Stephen Crane Collection, George Arents Library, Syracuse University.

Because a variety of realities having standing, an orthodox epistemology seeking comprehensive Truth is untenable. In its stead,
Crane's poetry works out, in three stages, an alternative theory of
knowledge. He begins negatively, repudiating the existence of the
Truth, then he attacks conventional truths baptized by religion or
sanctified by tradition and concludes by proposing an epistemology
of modesty, restraint, and self-reliance. Turning to the first stage,
fools who believe they know the Truth are scattered throughout
Crane's poetry.[14]

> A learned man came to me once.
> He said, "I know the way,—come."
> And I was overjoyed at this,
> Together we hastened.
> Soon, too soon, were we
> Where my eyes were useless,
> And I knew not the ways of my feet.
> I clung to the hand of my friend;
> But at last he cried, "I am lost."
>
>   (BR #20, 1305)

Others confuse gaining success with finding Truth.

> The successful man has thrust himself
> Through the water of the years,
> Reeking wet with mistakes,
> Bloody mistakes,
> Slimed with victories over the lesser
> A figure thankful on the shore of money. . . .
>
> He delivers his secrets to the riven multitude.
>   "Thus I defended: Thus I wrought."
> Complacent, smiling,
> He stands heavily on the dead.
> Erect on a pillar of skulls
> He declaims his trampling of babes;
> Smirking, fat, dripping,
> He makes speech in guiltless ignorance,
> Innocence.
>
>   (WK #85, 1333)

Yet others, believing that no one has been dogged enough in its pursuit, think Truth is still within reach.

> I saw a man pursuing the horizon;
> Round and round they sped.
> I was disturbed at this;

I accosted the man.
"It is futile," I said,
"You can never——"

"You lie," he cried,
And ran on.
                    (*BR* #24, 1306)

Crane next considers, at some length, the all-too human confusions of truth with strong personal belief, routine, familiarity, tradition, and patriotism. In both *The Black Riders* and *War Is Kind*, he excoriates the half-truths that newspapers offer. In the former, the poet comes upon a sage, reading and believing a newspaper. Crane's reflection, "Then I saw that I was greater, aye, greater than this sage" (*BR* #11, 1302), is reminiscent of the search that Socrates recounted as his defense in *The Apology*. Socrates related to the assembled men of Athens that the gods had told him that he was the wisest of men. He discovered in conversations with wise men of Greece that neither he nor they knew anything, but he, at least, was aware of his ignorance. In that way and in that measure, he was the wiser.[15] In a similar vein, with drenching sarcasm about both the newspaper and the "sage," Crane concludes with mock reassurance, "Old, old man, it is the wisdom of the age."[16] In *War Is Kind*, Crane's indictment of newspapers is blunt and heavy-handed: "A newspaper is a collection of half-injustices . . . [it] spreads its curious opinions . . . a newspaper is a court where every one is kindly and unfairly tried by the squalor of honest men. A newspaper is a market . . . a newspaper is a game . . . a newspaper is symbol . . . a collection of loud tales, concentrating eternal stupidities" (#80, 1330).

The fact that newspaper men and newspaper readers are "kindly" and "honest men" does not prevent error and harm; the same dangers face clergy and patriots. Elbert Hubbard sought out diatribes against organized religion, and Crane's poetry was a fertile resource. For example,

Two or three angels
Came near to the earth.
They saw a fat church.
Little black streams of people
Came and went in continually.
And the angels were puzzled
To know why the people went thus,
And why they stayed so long within.
                    (*BR* #32, 1309–10)

In Crane's poetry, angels and spirits as lives and consciousnesses above human awareness are the counterpart of the animals and plants discussed previously. For Crane, a whole spectrum of experiencers—subhuman, human, and suprahuman, both angels and God—constitute reality.

In "I stood upon a highway," Crane attacks the "many strange peddlers . . . holding forth little images, saying, 'This is my pattern of God'" (*BR* #34, 1311). In *War Is Kind*, he lambastes both organized religion and custom as purveyors of the truth.

> What! You define me God with these trinkets?
> Can my misery meal on an ordered walking
> Of surpliced numbskulls?
> And a fanfare of lights?
> Or even upon the measured pulpiting
> Of the familiar false and true?
> Is this God?
>
> (#72, 1327)

Tradition, normal expectation, majority opinion, experience, wealth, and patriotism are equally unreliable lodestones of the truth. (See also *BR* #45, 58, 64; *WK* #88; and uncollected poems #116 and 127.)

The positive side of Crane's epistemological poetry begins with the realization of error. This discovery is, strangely, not painful, but a surprising and welcome relief. As in "A learned man came to me once" (*BR* #20, 1305), in which both the "wise" man and the poet discover that they are lost, in *War Is Kind*, too, the realization of error could have been but was not devastating.

> When the prophet, a complacent fat man,
> Arrived at the mountain-top
> He cried: "Woe to my knowledge!"
> "I intended to see good white land
> "And bad black land—
> "But the scene is grey."
>
> (#90, 1335–36)

The discovery that there is no single Truth, and that the total picture is an infinite range of grays, does not relieve individuals of the burden of finding a way, or even several ways. This task, however, can be frightening,

> The wayfarer
> Perceiving the pathway to truth
> Was struck with astonishment.

> It was thickly grown with weeds.
> "Ha," he said,
> "I see that none has passed here
> "In a long time."
> Later he saw that each weed
> Was a singular knife.
> "Well," he mumbled at last,
> "Doubtless there are other roads."
>
> (#81, 1331)

or threatening,

> Mystic shadow, bending near me,
> Who art thou?
> Whence come ye?
> And—tell me—is it fair
> Or is the truth bitter as eaten fire?
> Tell me!
> Fear not that I should quaver,
> For I dare—I dare.
> Then, tell me!
>
> (BR #7, 1301)

or even deadly,

> There were many who went in huddled procession,
> They knew not whither;
> But, at any rate, success or calamity
> Would attend all in equality.
>
> There was one who sought a new road.
> He went into direful thickets,
> And ultimately he died thus, alone;
> But they say that he had courage.
>
> (#17, 1304)

Humans must lower their expectations, for their birthright is a modest, tentative, and quiet truth.

> "Truth," said a traveler,
> "Is a rock, a mighty fortress;
> "Often have I been to it,
> "Even to its highest tower,
> "From whence the world looks black."
>
> "Truth, said a traveler,
> "Is a breath, a wind,
> "A shadow, a phantom;

"Long have I pursued it,
"But never have I touched
"The hem of its garment."
(#28, 1308)

Crane sides with the second traveler as he insists upon two points about truth: simplicity—plain statement is better than eloquence— and realism. We do not inhabit a Garden of Eden, we live in a desert. As to the first:

There was a man with tongue of wood
Who essayed to sing
And in truth it was lamentable
But there was one who heard
The clip-clapper of this tongue of wood
And knew what the man
Wished to sing
And with that the singer was content.
(WK #84, 1332)

and for the second,

I walked in a desert.
And I cried,
"Ah, God, take me from this place!"
A voice said, "It is no desert.
I cried, "Well, but—
"The sand, the heat, the vacant horizon."
A voice said, "It is no desert."
(BR #42, 1314)

In the desert, Crane learns hard lessons from a beast: there are only truths and, therefore, the necessity of self-reliance.

In the desert
I saw a creature, naked, bestial,
Who, squatting upon the ground,
Held his heart in his hands,
And ate of it.
I said, "Is it good, friend?"
"It is bitter—bitter," he answered;
"But I like it
"Because it is bitter,
"And because it is my heart."
(#3, 1299)[17]

In our search for truth we are offered neither "a gardened castle" nor "a flowery kingdom," but "a hope" (*BR* #30, 1309). A point that goes to the center of Crane's poetry is that once humans seeking the truth have reached the top of the hill, God will meet them there, leaning forward to help.

> When a people reach the top of a hill
> Then does God lean toward them,
> Shortens tongues, lengthens arms.
>
> (#125, 1347)

The Redoubtable God and the God of Kind Eyes

God was a persistent concern for Stephen Crane, poet. The gospel according to Crane is the ascendancy of a quiet, gentle, forgiving God over an imperial, judgmental, awesome God. While the redoubtable God can serve as an explanatory principle in Crane's comprehensive theory, only the God of kind eyes, who is caring, can satisfy religious and emotional needs. Brutes and plants, too, cry out for a merciful God.

> A slant of sun on dull brown walls
> A forgotten sky of bashful blue.
> Toward God a mighty hymn
> A song of collisions and cries
> Rumbling wheels, hoof-beats, bells,
> Welcomes, farewells, love-calls, final moans,
> Voices of joy, idiocy, warning, despair,
> The unknown appeal of brutes,
> The chanting of flowers
> The screams of cut trees,
> The senseless babble of hens and wise men—
> A cluttered incoherence that says at the stars:
> "O, God, save us!"
>
> (*WK* #82, 1331–32)

Crane rejects the stern, Old Testament God of his great-uncle, Bishop Jesse Peck, and his mother and embraces the loving, New Testament God of his father, the Reverend Jonathan Crane. His father, after a Princeton education, left the Presbyterian church over the doctrine of infant damnation. He also refused to believe that God, as the agent of salvation and damnation, makes human effort inconsequential. Reverend Crane would have applauded his son's depiction of a compassionate God, but not his abandonment of organized religion.[18]

The harshness of the Old Testament God in Crane's poetry is out-
done only by Crane's harshness in denouncing that deity:

> "And the sins of the fathers shall be visited upon the
> heads of the children, even unto the third and fourth
> generation of them that hate me."
>
> Well, then, I hate Thee, unrighteous picture;
> Wicked image, I hate Thee;
> So, strike with Thy vengeance
> The heads of those little men
> Who come blindly
> It will be a brave thing.
>
> (*BR* #12, 1302)

and:

> A god in wrath
> Was beating a man;
> He cuffed him loudly
> With thunderous blows
> That rang and rolled over the earth.
> All people came running.
> The man screamed and struggled,
> And bit madly at the feet of the god.
> The people cried,
> "Ah, what a wicked man!"
> And—
> "Ah, what a redoubtable god!"
>
> (#19, 1304–5)

With Job-like defiance, Crane challenges the redoubtable God:

> Blustering god,
> Stamping across the sky
> With loud swagger,
> I fear you not.
> No, though from your highest heaven
> You plunge your spear at my heart,
> I fear you not.
> No, not if the blow
> Is as the lightning blasting a tree,
> I fear you not, puffing braggart.
>
> (#53, 1318)

In the second stanza, the poet tells the blustering God that, if He is
God, He can see that in the poet's heart there is no fear of Him, and

"why is it right" for the poet not to cower. In the third stanza, the poet, addressing the reader, explains "there is one whom I fear." Anticipating two responses, that the traditional God has been blasphemed and that the reader may doubt that there is another sort of God, Crane observes:

> Withal, there is one whom I fear;
> I fear to see grief upon that face.
> Perchance, friend, he is not your god;
> If so, spit upon him.
> By it you will do no profanity.
> But I—
> Ah, sooner would I die
> Than see tears in those eyes of my soul.
>
> (#53, 1318)

Before examining Crane's descriptions of the loving God, it is useful to consider two more poems in which he attacks the despotic, puffing God. "The livid lightnings flashed in the clouds" (BR #39, 1312) mirrors "'Truth,' said a traveller" (BR #28, 1308). In the latter, an arrogant, self-promoting Truth is contrasted with truth as "a breath, a wind, a shadow, a phantom." In the former, gentle melody supplants Thor-like rumbling.

> The livid lightnings flashed in the clouds;
> The leaden thunders crashed.
> A worshiper raised his arm.
> "Hearken! Hearken! The voice of God!"
>
> "Not so," said a man.
> "The voice of God whispers in the heart
> "So softly
> "That the soul pauses,
> "Making no noise,
> "And strives for these melodies,
> "Distant, sighing, like faintest breath,
> "And all the being is still to hear."
>
> (BR #39, 1312)

In The Black Riders, too, the poet contrasts a raging, jealous God with a God of mercy and understanding. When a man goes before a strange god,

> The god of many men, sadly wise.
> And the deity thundered loudly,
> Fat with rage, and puffing,
> "Kneel, mortal, and cringe

"And grovel and do homage
"To my particular sublime majesty."

The man fled.
Then the man went to another god,—
The god of his inner thoughts.
And this one looked at him
With soft eyes
Lit with infinite comprehension,
And said, "My poor child!"

(#51, 1317)

Crane's devotion to the God with soft eyes is the theme of two extended, nearly identical poems. The tender God is approachable, patient, slow to anger, and quick to forgive.

There was One I met upon the road
Who looked at me with kind eyes
He said: "Show me of your wares."
And this I did
Holding forth one.
He said: "It is sin."
Then held I forth another.
He said: "It is a sin."
Then held I forth another.
He said: "It is a sin."
And so to the end
Always He said: "It is a sin."
And, finally, I cried out:
"But I have none other."
Then did He look at me
With kinder eyes.
"Poor soul," He said.

(BR #33, 1310)

The *War Is Kind* version of this poem changes a half-dozen words; for example, "held I" becomes "I held." However, the obvious and significant differences are the capitalization of "One" and "He" in the first but not the second version. "One" and "He" remove ambiguity that the poet encountered God on the road. The *War Is Kind* version is about God, too, and "one" and "he" are appropriate for the finite God who emerges in Crane's philosophical-theological poetry.

Commentators on Crane's verses have been few, but all have wrestled with his depiction of the dark night of the soul: God's apparent unconcern in "God fashioned the ship of the world carefully" (*BR* #6, 1300); the "God is cold" refrain in "A man adrift on a slim spar"

(#126, 1348); the death of God in "Should the wide world roll away" (*BR* #10, 1302), "If I should cast off this tattered coat" (*BR* #66, 1323), and "God lay dead in Heaven" (*BR* #69, 1323); as well as the nihilism, skepticism, and cynicism in "Once there was a man" (*BR* #48, 1315), "I stood musing in a black world" (*BR* #49, 1316), and "A man toiled on a burning road" (*BR* #55, 1319).[19] Nonetheless, a great number of Crane's poems clearly affirm God: "In the night" (*WK* #86, 1333–34), "'Ah, God, the way your little finger moved" (*WK* #98, 1342), and "The patent of a lord" (#135), as well as several others.

An obvious way to reconcile this tension in Crane's poetry is through a finite God discussed by his philosophical contemporaries. Ever since David Hume's masterful short-course treatise on God and the existence of evil, an infinite God has been problematic.[20] Hume argued: Consider God the creator and the world His product. Evil exists in the created world. Either God does not know of this evil, He cannot eliminate it, or He does not care to repair the flaw. Thus God is not omniscient, omnipotent, or omnibenevolent: perhaps God lacks an infinite attribute—or even two or all three of them. Hence, God does not exist, concluded Hume, for if God is to be God, He must be infinite.

Several of Hume's philosophical successors, notably the late-nineteenth-century American pragmatists, agreed with his statement of the problem but argued that his conclusion did not necessarily follow. William James urged serious consideration of a finite God as a solution to Hume's impasse. A finite God, argued James, beyond being the God of most believers, best accords our experience of the world. "'God,' in the religious life of ordinary men, is the name not of the whole of things, heaven forbid, but only of the ideal tendency in things, believed in as a superhuman person who call us to co-operate with his purposes, and who furthers ours if they are worthy. He works in an external environment, has limits, and has enemies" (*A Pluralistic Universe* 60).

According to James, we find ourselves in an ongoing world open to growth and change. Granting the genuiness of experiences of novelty and freedom, a finite God alleviates the problems of predetermination and foreknowledge. On the other hand, James appreciated the liabilities of a finite God, especially that a God with limits cannot fully satisfy the deep-seated urge for safe and secure refuge.[21]

The God who emerges in Crane's poetry is a concrete embodiment of James's concept of a finite God. Crane's God provides a measure of religious security, giving us—in James's memorable phrases—"provisional breathing-spells" and "moral holidays."[22] However, a limited God existing in time cannot dominate the environment; He has enemies, needs human cooperation, and His designs may fail. Still, God has powers and intelligence superior to humanity's, and thus appeals to Him bring succor and relief. Crane's finite God, a quiet, caring father, helps with some problems, although His answers may require time and study on his part—and repeated requests on our side.

> The patent of a lord
> And the bangle of a bandit
> Make argument
> Which God solves
> Only after lighting more candles.
>
> (#135)

God hears but sometimes does not intervene, as in "A man adrift on a slim spar" (#126, 1348). At other times, the universe responds for Him.

> A man said to the universe:
> "Sir, I exist!"
> "However," replied the universe,
> "The fact has not created in me
> "A sense of obligation."
>
> (WK #89, 1335)

God's creation of the world was careful; it works well, although it has limitations. Although the world is not perfect, it is good, in part because progress occurs. The possibility of progress, called "meliorism" by philosophers, was a standard fixture in the nineteenth-century American mindset. Crane both endorses and challenges this belief.

> God fashioned the ship of the world carefully.
> With the infinite skill of an all-master
> Made He the hull and the sails,
> Held He the rudder
> Ready for adjustment.
> Erect stood He, scanning His work proudly.
> Then—at fateful time—a wrong called,
> And God turned, heeding.
> Lo, the ship, at this opportunity, slipped slyly,
> Making cunning noiseless travel down the ways.
> So that, forever rudderless, it went upon the seas
> Going ridiculous voyages,
> Making quaint progress,

> Turning as with serious purpose
> Before stupid winds.
> And there were many in the sky
> Who laughed at this thing.
>
> (BR #6, 1300–1301)

There are difficulties, for both God and humanity, in the world. Sometimes obstacles, like a treacherous sea, rise enough to over-match humans:

> To the maiden
> The sea was blue meadow
> Alive with little froth-people
> Singing.
> To the sailor, wrecked,
> The sea was dead grey walls
> Superlative in vacancy
> Upon which nevertheless at a fateful time,
> Was written
> The grim hatred of nature.
>
> (WK #71, 1326–27)

But nature, the sea included, can be congenial and supportive of appropriate and worthwhile goals

> "The sea bid you teach, oh, pines
> "Sing low in the moonlight.
> "Teach the gold of patience
> "Cry gospel of gentle hands
> "Cry a brotherhood of hearts
> "The sea bids you teach, oh, pines."
>
> (WK #70, 1326)

Although a finite God eliminates numerous theoretical difficulties and practical problems, a serious inconsistency remains. Crane's toughness, integrity, and trust in the validity of human experience led him to reprimand God, even a finite God, on the matter of justice.[23] He saw no compromise of a glaring contradiction: God created both humans with desires and the attractive objects of those desires. Why then, asks Crane, are naturally appealing pursuits sinful? His first writ accusing God of injustice concerns a maid trying to lay flowers on the grave of her lover. She is prevented, however, by a stern spirit who grasps her by the arm,

> "No flowers for him," he said.
> The maid wept:
> "Ah, I loved him."

> But the spirit, grim and frowning:
> "No flowers for him."

The epilogue, as skillfully as the last section of "The Blue Hotel,"
states a dilemma:

> Now, this is it——
> If the spirit was just,
> Why did the maid weep?
> (BR #25, 1307)

Crane's dilemma needs unpacking, for it applies at two levels. If the
man was wicked, why does the maid want to bring flowers for him?
On the one side, if the maid, knowing his faults and understanding
his wrongs, still loves (and forgives) the wicked man, why should
God, despite His stern spirit, not do the same? On the other side, if
the maid does not know but learns from the spirit that her lover was
wicked, why does she still desire to leave violets? In this second instance, the emotional structure of humans apparently resists correction and enlightenment. "If the spirit was just," then God has created humans either too weak in intellect or too strong in desire.

An uncollected poem, "A god came to a man," one of Crane's longest, probes God about the sin of Adam and Eve. How could it have
been just for God to create human desire, next create an appealing
apple, and then, after a predictable, understandable, and natural
course of events, hold humans liable for their "sin"?

> A god[24] came to a man
> And said to him thus:
> "I have an apple
> "It is a glorious apple
> "Aye, I swear by my ancestors
> "Of the eternities before this eternity
> "It is an apple that is from
> "The inner thought of heaven's greatest.
>
> "And this I will hang here
> "And then I will adjust thee here
> "Thus—you may reach it.
> "And you must stifle your nostrils
> "And control your hands
> "And your eyes
> "And sit for sixty years
> "But,—leave the apple."
>
> The man answered in this wise:
> "Oh, most interesting God

> "What folly is this?
> "Behold, thou has moulded my desires
> "Even as thou has moulded the apple.
>
> (#109)[25]

God, however, according to another of Crane's poems, is aware of the problematic nature of His own code of justice.

> "Have you ever made a just man?"
> "Oh, I have made three," answered God
> "But two of them are dead
> "And the third——
> "Listen! Listen!
> "And you will hear the thud of his defeat."
>
> (WK #73, 1327)

Although God's justice seems to lack fair play when viewed from earth, Crane acknowledges that things take on a different aspect from heaven.

> A man saw a ball of gold in the sky;
> He climbed for it,
> And eventually he achieved it——
> It was clay.
>
> Now this is the strange part:
> When the man went to the earth
> And looked again,
> Lo, there was the ball of gold.
> Now this is the strange part:
> It was a ball of gold.
> Aye, by the heavens, it was a ball of gold.[26]
>
> (BR #35, 1311)

Interjections like "Now this is the strange part" are signature lines in Crane's poetry. The reader is asked to reconsider, leading to the anticipation of an unusual twist, whereupon Crane often reverts to a commonplace answer. Three other poems claim that things are different in heaven and on earth: "I stood on a high place" (BR #9, 1301), "There was set before me mighty hill" (BR #26, 1307), and "There was a man who lived a life of fire" (BR #62, 1322).

The unpublished poem "Chant you loud punishments" (#115) first rejects the despotic God and then celebrates the alliance of a finite God with proud, even testy, human beings. Crane's supple-souled men and strong gods enjoy nearly equal footing.

> Chant you loud of punishments,
> Of the twisting of the heart's poor strings

Of the crash of the lightning's fierce revenge.

Then sing I of the supple-souled men
And the strong, strong gods
That shall meet in times hereafter
And the amaze of the god
At the strength of the men.
—The strong, strong gods—
    —And the supple-souled men—

(#115)

Crane's robust humanism in an indifferent, challenging, and often harsh universe is stern stuff. Although despair and doubt are at hand, Crane's tough little men do and will prevail:

Once I saw mountains angry,
And ranged in battle-front.
Against them stood a little man;
Aye, he was no bigger than my finger.
I laughed, and spoke to one near me,
"Will he prevail?"
"Surely," replied this other;
"His grandfathers beat them many times."
Then did I see much virtue in grandfathers,—
At least, for the little man
Who stood against the mountains.

(BR #22, 1306)[27]

Typical Crane prayers are not pleas for help, instead he simply requests that God remember our limited, although sufficient resources.

If there is a witness to my little life,
To my tiny throes and struggles,
He sees a fool;
And is it not fine for gods to menace fools.

(BR #13, 1303)

But all is not well with finite humanity and a finite God in Crane's indifferent universe. Because there is neither a supreme order nor an almighty ruler, there is conflict, leading to wars. War, its horror, as well as its attractiveness and its excitement, is a major theme in Crane's poetry.

War and Conflict in Crane's Poetry

Crane's bittersweet fascination with war spanned his creative career. The wonder of war, the thrill of combat, and terrible toil of battle are focuses in his short stories, tales, novels, and news dispatches. A line from a news story, "How They Leave Cuba," fittingly summarizes his sense of war, "It is human agony and human agony is not pleasant" (11:201).

Nearly two dozen of Crane's poems are about war. War's glamour and its senselessness, for instance, are important themes in both books of poetry. War's glamour is genuine. Its values are not specious—consciousness and energy are raised in war.

> A soldier, young in years, young in ambitions
> Alive as no grey-beard is alive
> Laid his heart and his hopes before duty
> And went staunchly into the tempest of war.
>
> (#113)

The martial life's strenuous mood, argues Crane, is not always due to a mindless loss of self in mob action, but can be the result of individual response to the call of duty. The mystic tie of duty is the central theme of "The Clan of No-Name," which Crane begins with a poem:

> Unwind my riddle.
> Cruel as hawks the hours fly,
> Wounded men seldom come home to die,
> The hard waves see an arm flung high,
> Scorn hit strong because of a lie,
> There exists a mystic tie,
> Unwind my riddle.
>
> (#131, see also 1033)[28]

The title poem of *War Is Kind*, too, celebrates duty, although Crane does not shy away from death in war in the heavily ironic stanzas that bracket these refrains.

> These men were born to drill and die
> The unexplained glory flies above them
> Great is the battle-god, great, and his kingdom——
> A field where a thousand corpses lie.
>
> These men were born to drill and die
> Point for them the virtue of slaughter
> Make plain to them the excellence of killing
> And a field where a thousand corpses lie.
>
> (#69, 1325)

There is no doubting that war produces praiseworthy conduct; among war's good consequences are "the braver deeds."

> "Tell brave deeds of war."
>
> Then they recounted tales,—
> "There were stern stands
> "And bitter runs for glory."
> Ah, I think there were braver deeds.
>
> (*BR* #15, 1303)

War's horror is genuine, too. If one side of war is glittering excitement, its other side is boredom, disillusionment, and pain—especially mothers' losses.

> The clang of swords is Thy wisdom
> The wounded make gestures like Thy Son's
> The feet of mad horses is one part,
> ——Aye, another is the hand of a mother
>   on the brow of a son.
>
> (#125, 1348)

In *War Is Kind*, Crane treats the sorrow of wives and children along with the grief of mothers.

Although several poems ably treat the reward and the cheat of war, perhaps a more significant and interesting contribution is a group of poems that analyzes the causes of war and provides a complex and challenging diagnosis of unnecessary war.

The causes, he argues, are to be found in the nature of reality and the limitations of human knowledge. Given that neither Reality nor Truth exists, humans are left to deal with several realities, a plurality of truths, and a variety of moral orders. Whose order, which reality, what values? Crane argues that imposed arrangements lead to war.

> Once there came a man
> Who said,
> "Range me all men of the world in rows."
> And instantly
> There was a terrific clamour among the people
> Against being ranged in rows.
> There was a loud quarrel, world-wide.
> It endured for ages;
> And blood was shed
> By those whose would not stand in rows,
> And by those who pined to stand in rows.
> Eventually, the man went to death, weeping.
> And those who staid in bloody scuffle
> Knew not the great simplicity.
>
> (*BR* #5, 1300)

Appeals to God, no longer a supreme and absolute law-giver, fall short. By the time God answers, the armies are already in the field.

> Once a man clambering to the house-tops
> Appealed to the heavens.
> With strong voice he called to the deaf spheres;
> A warrior's shout he raised to the suns.
> Lo, at last, there was a dot on the clouds,
> And—at last and at last—
> —God—the sky was filled with armies.
>
> (WK #83, 1332)

Enthusiasm for truth, order, and reality adds deadly complication. Tragically, the combative instinct is part of the human race's genetic endowment.

> At the head of the new battalions
> —Blue battalions—
> March the tools of nature's impulse
> Men born of wrong, men born of right
> Men of the new battalions
> —The blue battalions—
>
> (#125, 1347–48)

For Crane, however, any schema with a right and wrong creed is woefully simplistic. In a world with many creeds, amid problems and pain, there are many sound and fruitful agendas. So tolerance is required—"the gold of patience . . . gospel of gentle hands . . . a brotherhood hearts" (WK #70, 1326). Because, as Crane explains in "The Battle Hymn," humans find themselves "in the forest of lost standards," forbearance is requisite.

> Mark well, mark well, Father of the Never-Ending Circles
> And if the path, the new path, lead awry
> Then in the forest of the lost standards
> Suffer us to grope and bleed apace
> For the wisdom is Thine.
>
> (#130, 1350)

But nervous, insecure people, "ever waving an eager sword" (WK #76, 1328), seek quick solutions. Never doubting that their cause is righteous, they grasp "God is on our side" as a moral compass in the forest of lost standards.

> —And if the path, the new path leads straight—
> Then—O, God—then bare the great bronze arm;
> Swing high the blaze of the chained stars
> And let them look and heed

(The chanting disintegrate and the two-faced eagle)
For we go, we go in a lunge of a long blue corps
And—to Thee we commit our lifeless sons,
The convulsed and furious dead.

(#130, 1350)

Even God's supposed endorsement is secondary to the main engines
of war: tradition and patriotism.

We have already seen that Crane considers tradition an unreliable
guide to truth; it is also a specious signpost to the good:

Tradition, thou art for suckling children
Thou art the enlivening milk for babes;
But no meat for men is in thee
Then——
But, alas, we all are babes.

(BR #45, 1314–15)

Although traditions effectively unify and mobilize, they often obfus-
cate rather than enlighten.

There were many who went in huddled procession,
They knew not whither;
But, at any rate, success or calamity
Would attend all in equality.

(BR #17, 1304)

Patriotism easily outdoes tradition in causing wars:

There exists the eternal fact of conflict
And—next—a mere sense of locality.
Afterward we derive sustenance from the winds.
Afterward we grip upon this sense of locality.
Afterward, we become patriots.
The godly vice of patriotism makes us slaves,
And—let us surrender to this falsity
Let us be patriots.

(#127, 1349)

The poem's second stanza takes up the "Remember the Maine"
newspaper crusade to rush President William McKinley into the
Spanish-American War.

Then welcome us the practical men
Thrumming on a thousand drums
The practical men, God help us.
    They cry aloud to be lead to war
    Ah—
    They have been poltroons on a thousand fields

And the sacked sad city of New York is their record
Furious to face the Spaniard, these people, and crawling worms be-
    fore their task
They name serfs and send charity in the bulk to better men
They play at being free, these people of New York
Who are too well-dressed to protest against infamy.

(#127, 1349)

Note, first, in Crane's bitter pill, his observation that although "they play at being free" to face the Spaniard and to liberate the serf in Cuba and the Philippines, "the godly vice of patriotism makes us slaves." Second, the poem's lasting value is a diagnostic formula: instinctive combativeness, plus loyalty, plus the blessing of patriotism equals war fever. Neither animals, nor plants, nor angels, but only humans, it seems, suffer from the infectious and fatal war microbe.

"It was wrong to do this," said the angel.
"You should live like a flower,
"Holding malice like a puppy,
"Waging war like a lambkin."

"Not so," quoth the man
  Who had no fear of spirits;
"It is only wrong for angels
"Who can live like the flowers,
"Holding malice like the puppies,
"Waging war like the lambkins."

(BR #54, 1319)

Fortunately, not all humans rally around "the cause"; some cannot see why war is, for the majority, a necessary and even attractive alternative. Two poems examine war agnostics. In the midst of war, a questioner asking "Why is this?" is overwhelmed by countless apologists. Their answers produce what Crane calls elsewhere "the senseless babble of hens and wise men—a cluttered incoherency" (WK #82, 1332). "But, why war?"

There was crimson clash of war.
Land turned black and bare;
Women wept;
Babes ran, wondering.
There came one who understood not these things.
He said, "Why is this?"
Whereupon a million strove to answer him.
There was such intricate clamor of tongues,
That still the reason was not.

(BR #14, 1303)

Although war calls forth stamina and courage, challenging an offi-
cially sanctioned violence takes, perhaps, even greater fortitude.

> There was one who sought a new road.
> He went into direful thickets,
> And ultimately he died thus, alone;
> But they said he had courage.
>
> (*BR* #17, 1304)

Crane also addresses the skeptic of militancy in "I stood musing in a
black world," the longest of *The Black Rider* poems. (It is nearly
twice as long as other poems in the collection; only "'Intrigue': Thou
art my love" is longer.) In the poem, stated in the first person, a wan-
derer comes upon a hurrying multitude "pouring ceaselessly, filled
with eager faces, a torrent of desire." Eager for insight, explains the
poet,

> I called to them,
> "Where do you go? What do you see?"
> A thousand voices called to me.
> A thousand fingers pointed.
> "Look! Look! There!"

The poet thinks he sees something, but none of the stamina, certitude, and direction that energize the others in the "quick stream of
men" comes with his vision.

> A vision painted upon a pall;
> And sometimes it was,
> And sometimes it was not.
> I hesitated.

Pausing, he hears impatient, roaring voices from the stream and
plunges on. Looking again, he see "no radiance in the far sky, ineffa-
ble, divine; no vision painted upon a pall."

> Then I cried in despair,
> "I see nothing! Oh, where do I go?"
> The torrent turned again its faces:
> "Look! Look! There!"
>
> And at the blindness of my spirit
> They screamed,
> "Fool! Fool! Fool!"
>
> (*BR* #49, 1316–17)

Critical to philosopher Crane's "idea of life as a whole" is his contention that humans are not particularly competent at judgments of
the significant and the foolish. Still, Crane is not a defeatist; he be-

lieves that humans can profit from experience and learn from mistakes.[29] For example, a dying warrior who lived "a life of fire" reassesses his choice of vocation,

> There was a man who lived a life of fire.
> Even upon the fabric of time,
> Where purple becomes orange
> And orange purple,
> This life glowed,
> A dire red stain, indelible;
> Yet when he was dead,
> He saw that he had not yet lived.
>
> (*BR* #62, 1322)

Throughout Crane's works, animals offer direct and poignant critiques of human actions. In his poetry, animals place humans' inflated sense of self-worth in bold relief. The horse, "blowing, staggering, bloody thing, forgotten at foot of castle wall," is a poignant comment on the merit of the knight's defense of his crusade "to save my lady" (*WK* #76, 1329).[30] In one of Crane's briefest poems, a haughty warrior suffers embarrassing deflation from a bird.

> A warrior stood on a peak and defied the stars.
> A little magpie, happening there, desired the soldier's plume
> And so plucked it.
>
> (#121, 1346)

Thus, Crane's poetry contains answers to questions on the nature of truth, reality, the good, God, and the reason for war. Examination of his poetry for philosophical statement can best be concluded with this compact, freeze-dried nugget of wisdom about humankind.

> When the suicide arrived at the sky,
> The people there asked him: "Why?"
> He replied: "Because no one admired me."
>
> (#119, 1346)

Crane's Philosophy of Experience

> Your temperament makes old things new and new things amazing."
> Joseph Conrad to Stephen Crane, December 1, 1897

> Life as seen through a pair of strange oblique, temporary spectacles.
> "A Lovely Jag in a Crowded Car"

Although Crane's place in the canon of American writers is secure despite a productivity cut short by death at twenty-eight, how many more literary wonders might he have produced? What other philosophical themes might he have explored, illustrated, and anticipated? For example, it is clear that he understood the perspectives of two turn-of-the-century philosophical developments—phenomenology and process metaphysics.[31]

The central problem for late-nineteenth- and early-twentieth-century philosophers, American and European, was to replace the classical and common-sense view of the relationship between knowledge and reality. The long-held views were that epistemology's project was to identify the conditions for an objective grasp of entities, and metaphysics' task was to specify the nature of substantive entities. By the late 1890s these projects had been abandoned. The notion of knowledge as picture—as an affair of faithfully copying a determinate reality—was rejected as naive, oversimple, and a misrepresentation of both knowing and the known. Thus philosophers struggled to describe the ongoing, fluidly indeterminate character of reality and to explain how the real, in part, depends upon the active contribution of consciousness. The real they sought to capture was a product, the outcome of a transaction between experiencer and a complex, multilayered, multidimensional external world.[32] Crane understood the task. Alert and faithful to experience, he sought to disclose reality's richness and its variety as well as to safeguard the genuineness of a wide spectrum of experiencers.

Crane's startling descriptions compel assent on two counts: first, experiencers constitute realities (not reality); second, the relative value and status of experiencers and their experience are problematic.[33] The Whilomville stories, for example, examine adults' and children's experience of "the same thing." In "Lynx Hunting," Crane follows Willie Datzel and his gang as they leave town and enter "that freeland of hills and woods . . . the dark-green hemlock thickets, the wastes of sweet-fern and huckleberry, the cliffs of gaunt bluestone with the sumach burning red at their feet" (1169). Objectivity, including the neutral description of "that freeland," does not seem overly difficult; both children and adults see these spaces as "wastes." Still, "The grown folk seem to regard these wastes merely as so much distance between one place and another place or as rabbit cover, or a district to be judged according to the value of the timber; but to the boys it spoke some great inspiriting word which they knew even as those who pace the shore know the enigmatic speech of the surf" (1169).

The child-adult difference of opinion involves the relative standing of utilitarian and esthetic perspectives. The freeland's economic value as timber requires using it up; freeland left alone and appreciated for its own sake is also a measurable resource. Whether it is an expendable commodity or an undisturbed reserve is, as Crane deftly points out, an ethical question of social policy. However, as he clearly understands, that ethical question must defer to a fundamental metaphysical consideration, What is real? Is the freeland so much distance and timber for the adults, a fertile environment for rabbits and boys, or is it simply trees, thorns, and briars? It is all of these things and, of course, none of them. As William James put it, "Meanwhile the reality overflows these purposes at every pore. Our usual purpose with it, our commonest title for it, and the properties which this title suggests, have in reality nothing sacramental. They characterize *us* more than they characterize the thing" (*The Principles of Psychology* 2:961).

At a time when his philosophical contemporaries sought to simplify and structure reality's plurality, Crane pressed to uncover greater multiplicity in experience, for example, his imagination masterfully inferred the consciousness of animals. His special genius illuminated human experience, both the unnoticed contours of everyday life and the riveting intensity of nonroutine experiences of fear, grief, elation, and play.

In the replaying and retelling of human lives, Crane surpassed conventional categories. He noticed, for example, that the basic datum of our awareness is not things. Instead, because reality is not made up of discrete entities but is process, we are immersed in events. Further, because we are unaware of nearly all of the rush of reality's flow, it is no surprise that attempts to render comprehensive accounts disappoint. Instead, because we are aware of limited, isolated items in a short time-frame, episodic, quick-burst sketches best reveal human experience.

Crane's masterwork, *An Episode of the American Civil War*, follows the three-day maturing of a raw recruit. Fleming's seasoning comes by way of events, especially battles, which are chaotic and confusing for both participants and spectators. Amid reality's flux, Fleming does what all humans do—he seeks meaning and he struggles to affect outcomes. What Fleming cannot do is to render the world static, make it fully comprehensible or undo the past.

As both artist and journalist, reality as process was a given for Crane. When he imagined war in *The Red Badge of Courage* Crane used process words: waves, flows, steams, and floods. Later, witnessing war and cabling war dispatches, for example in "A Fragment of Velestino," he employed the same vocabulary and images to capture the "processes of battle" (9:40) that were made up of "little tricking streams . . . rivulets . . . whirlwinds [and] pauses" (9:40–41).[34] Ordinary, everyday life consists of flowing events, too.

In "The Men in the Storm," both the snow and the men lined up outside the mission door ebb and flow, drift and swirl. "The Joys of Sea Side Life" are both the waves of the ocean and the streams of people. The main attraction of "The Fete of Mardi Gras" is the parade of people. "At noon, Canal street was a river of human bodies moving slowly. At dusk, it was a sea in which contrary currents indolently opposed each other. . . . As soon as the procession had passed, the crowds swirled in one mass over the avenue as the waters close after the passage of a vessel" (8:460, 465).

In "Manacled," a fire in a theater sparks panic; "the body of the theater now resembled a mad surf amid rocks" (1292). In "The Detail," the frail old woman finds a "tempest" in the Sixth Avenue shopping district, "where from the streams of people and vehicles went up a roar like that heard from headlong mountain torrents" (8:111). Reality's stream nearly swamps the old woman, "she seemed then like a chip that catches, recoils, turns and wheels, a reluctant thing in the clutch of the impetuous river" (8:111). Most humans are not at such a disadvantage. Usually we can swim against the current; sometimes we can influence the flow. However, we cannot change the givens of process and sequence.

The past, securely over, ends responsibility. When Ned Trescott seeks Eldridge Margate to explain that his houseguest, "The Angel-Child," has engineered the butchering of the golden curls of the Margate twins at the barbershop, he is relieved. Old Eldridge "actually chuckled long and deeply" (1181). Trescott and Margate, at any rate, understand the irreversible flow of reality. "Whereupon Trescott perceived that the old man wore his brains above his shoulders and Trescott departed from him, rejoicing greatly that it was only women who could not know that there was finality to most disasters and that when a thing was fully done, no amount of door-slamming, rushing up stairs and down stairs, calls, lamentations, tears could bring back a single hair to the heads of the twins" (1182).

Elsewhere, in "Marines Signaling under Fire at Guantanamo," Crane recounts the most sustained display of courage he witnessed in his lifelong study of exceptional conduct. Without emotion or excitement, the signalmen stand above the trench, gesturing with their lanterns, illuminated, stationary, and easy targets for the enemy's sharpshooters. At daybreak the lantern will no longer be visible, so the signal corps and news correspondents ache for daylight. "Possibly no man who was there ever before understood the true eloquence

But, curiously enough, the one who achieved the bulk of the misery
was old Eldridge Margate, who had been picking peas at the
time. The feminine Margates stormed his positions as individuals,
in pairs, in teams and en masse. In two days they may
have aged him seven years. He must destroy the utter
Neeltje. He must midnightly massacre the angel child
and her mother. He must dip his arms in blood
to the elbows.

Trescott took the first opportunity to express to him his
concern over the affair but when the subject of the
disaster was mentioned, old Eldridge, to the doctor's
great surprise, actually chuckled long and deeply.
"Oh, well, lookahere" said he, " I never was so much in
love with them there damn curls. The curls was purty —
yes — but then I'd a darn sight rather see boys
look more like boys than like two little wax
figgers. An', ye know, the little cusses like it 'emselves.
They never took no stock in all this washin' an' combin'
an' fixin' an' goin' to church an' paradin' an'
showin' off. They stood it because they was told to. That's
all. Of course this here Neel-te-gee, er-whatever-his-name
-is, is a plum dumb yit but I don't see what's to be
done now that the kids is full-well cropped. I might go
and burn his shop over his head but that wouldn't
bring no hair back onto the kids' heads. They're
even kicking on sashes now an' that's all right
because, what fer does a boy want a sash?"

Whereupon Trescott perceived that the old man wore
his brains above his shoulders and Trescott departed from
him, rejoicing greatly that it was only women who could
not know that there was finality to most
disasters and that when a thing was fully done, no
amount of door-slamming, rushing up stairs and down
stairs, calls, lamentations, tears could bring back
a single hair to the heads of twins.

Final page of the manuscript of "The Angel-Child" (1899). From the Stephen Crane
Collection, Clifton Waller Barrett Library, University of Virginia.

of the breaking of day. We would lie staring into the east, fairly rav-
enous for the day" (1053). With the dawn, the terrible anxiety and
danger are permanently and absolutely over. "Usually it was impossible for many of the men to sleep at once. It always took me, for
instance, some hours to get my nerves combed down. But then it was
a great joy to lie in the trench with the four signalmen, and understand thoroughly that the night was fully over at last, and that, although the future might have in store other bad nights, that one
could never escape from the prison-house which we call the past"
(1054).

Reality's linear process and its relentless onward flow notwith-
standing, the rate of that flow is not a feature of external reality.
Time belongs to the inner life of the experiencer. At Guantanamo,
Crane and the signalmen are desperate for dawn as the hours crawl
by. Eventually, they see in the east "a patch of faint blue light . . . .
This patch widened and whitened in about the speed of a man's ac-
complishment if he should be in the way of painting Madison Square
Garden with a camel's hair brush" (1053).

Time's elasticity is prominent in several of Crane's war dispatches. In "The Red Badge of Courage Was His Wig-Wag Flag," Crane
contrasts ordinary, back-home, peaceful time, "little absurd indica-
tions of time, redolent of coffee, steak, porridge or what you like,
emblems of the departures of trains for Yonkers, Newark, N.J., or
anywhere," with real time on the battlefield, where "these indica-
tions of time now were sinister, sombre with the shadows of certain
tragedy, not the tragedy of a street accident, but foreseen, inexorable,
invincible tragedy" (9:136). Later in the same dispatch, Crane tries to
gauge the duration of a battle. "This terrific exchange of fire lasted a
year, or probably it was twenty minutes" (9:139). When he found
himself ahead of the march of two companies of the Sixteenth Pennsylvania Infantry that he was covering in "The Porto Rican 'Strad-
dle,'" he and his fellow journalists had to wait. "Time passed slowly,
with no change in the situation. . . . A half-hour passed as slowly as
time in the sick room" (9:180–81).

Although we are powerless to alter the past and can only partially
penetrate "the screen of the future" (9:135), human efforts are decid-
edly efficacious in other arenas. First, in obvious ways we act, react,
and alter the world we inhabit. Second, subtly but more fundamentally, our consciousness defines the world. In this second area, Crane
as well as the early philosophical phenomenologists sought to explain how consciousness constitutes the reality we experience. For
example, "A Great Mistake" follows the plottings of a babe to steal

a lemon from an Italian street vendor. "His infant intellect had defined the Italian. The latter was undoubtedly a man who would eat babes that provoked him" (531). Or, in "A Lovely Jag in a Crowded Car," the man on a spree "sang of the pearl-hued joys of life as seen through a pair of strange, oblique, temporary spectacles" (8:364). His "benign amiability" converts, for him at least, "the atmosphere of the car . . . as decorous as that of the most frigid of drawing rooms" into a "convivial party" (8:361–62). Or, in "The Duel That Was Not Fought," what Patsey says is quite different from what the Cuban prizefighter understands. "Then Patsey made a careless and rather loud comment to his two friends. He used a word which is no more than passing the time of day down in Cherry street, but, to the Cuban, it was a dagger point" (8:353–54). In addition to the individual worlds, human consciousness creates an intersubjective and public reality: culture. As we strive to comprehend both other persons and other cultures, Crane calls attention to a residual opacity in both private and public worlds.

In "The Mexican Lower Classes," Crane comments that "above all things, the stranger finds the occupations of foreign peoples to be trivial and inconsequent" (728). The impatient traveler, unwilling or unable to enter the consciousness that defines another culture, "utterly fails to comprehend the new point of view" (728) and so misjudges other persons' lives. The arrogance of judging others reveals a dangerous, deeper bias: the belief that we can sufficiently capture another's reality. "It perhaps might be said—if any one dared—that the most worthless literature of the world has been that which has been written by the men of one nation concerning the men of another" (728).

Crane prescribes a demanding regimen for understanding others. "It seems that a man must not devote himself for a time to attempts at psychological perception. He can be sure of two things, form and color. Let him then see all that he can but let him not sit in literary judgment on this or that manner of the people" (728). Next, he warns of deceptive cross-cultural similarities. "Instinctively he will feel that there are similarities but he will encounter many little gestures, tones, tranquillities, rages, for which his blood, adjusted to another temperature, can possess no interpreting power. The strangers will be indifferent where he expected passion; they will be passionate where he expected calm. These subtle variations will fill him with contempt" (728).[35] Although his initial reaction is negative bewilderment—"that such and such a man should be satisfied to carry bundles or mayhap sit and ponder in the sun all his life in this faraway country seems an abnormally stupid thing" (728)—Crane checks himself. "I refuse to commit judgment upon these lower classes of Mexico" (731).

Stephen Crane's contributions to philosophy are considerable. First, his works foster reflection and thoughtfulness. As "Mexican Lower Classes" demonstrates, with an empathetic imagination, a keen perceptiveness, and an exceptional openness, Crane discloses the distance and detachment needed to appreciate the human way of being. Second, and more generally, Crane's writings prompt wonder, which, according to Socrates, is the beginning of wisdom. His terse, astonishing style obliges readers to "begin to reflect upon elasticity and point of view." And then, on the far side of both the commonplace and the exotic, and beyond the routine and the recognizable, Crane reveals not Truth and Reality, but "the whirl, the unknown" and mystery of experience. He guides his reader, "like a creature allowed a glimpse of another world" to "encounter the dividing line between coherence and a blur."[36]

Notes

Preface

1. This phrase occurs in chapters 14 and 18 of *The Red Badge of Courage* (161 and 179) and also in an early piece for *McClure's Magazine*, "In the Depths of a Coal Mine" (605).

2. Weiss provides a thoughtful and detailed psychoanalytic treatment of Fleming's increased self-awareness and maturity. Bergon, Burhans, Satterfield, and Michael Schneider discuss the range of opinion on Fleming's moral maturation.

3. For pessimistic Darwinism in Crane, see Cox (1959), Fitelson, and Edward White; for a treatment of the positive impact of Darwin on philosophy and nineteenth-century American culture generally, see Dooley (1985).

4. In a literature fairly bristling with philosophical labels, the philosophy of Stephen Crane has been little analyzed. In addition to superficiality, most commentators have not respected the differences between foundational and derivative claims. For instance, in his near-comprehensive introduction to volume 5 of the University Press of Virginia edition of *Tales of Adventure*, Levenson fluctuates, holding that Crane espouses what he calls Crane's common-sense attitude toward an *objective* reality, that Crane believed that reality possesses unfathomable multiplicity and is ultimately chaotic. Five years later in his introduction volume 2 of the Virginia edition of *The Red Badge of Courage*, Levenson argues that "the various psychic patterns which Crane implicitly set up . . . express the multiplicity of a world which simply does not present itself to us as tradition teaches or reason hopes" (li), and then that "Crane believed that . . . the universe is only a neutral backdrop to human activity" (lvi). Levenson does not explain the supposed connection between Crane's view of a neutral universe and humanity's multiple reactions to it. Colvert (1977) makes the same omission.

Other commentators have been eager to assert that Crane's philosophical "outlook" is naturalistic (Adams, Cox [1957], and Conder); nihilistic (Autrey, Brennan [1960, 1962, 1969], Fryckstedt [1963], Griffith, Holton, Stein [1959], Swann, Wertheim [1963], and Wolford [1983, 1989]); optimistic (Bassan [1963, 1965], Greenfield, Glen Johnson [1977, 1989], Westbrook [1959, 1962 a and b, 1963]); pessimistic (Gleckner, Grenburg, Mayer [1973], Pilgrim, Robert Schneider); existential (Buitenhuis and Karlen); religious (Monteiro

[1971a, 1972a, b], Neal Osborn, Smith, Stein (1958); impressionistic (Bender [1976], Nagel, [1975b, 1978, 1980], Schnitzer, Rogers); and humanistic (Gullason [1960, 1975], Katz [1989], Solomon [1966]). I am not interested in contesting the correctness of any of these designations, but rather call attention to an error. Because attitudes toward the world or responses toward the universe have been treated as Crane's "philosophy," the power of his thought has been been underestimated drastically. This misunderstanding has reduced Crane's "philosophy" to a set of derived, second-order, reactions. For the full range of general criticism on Crane, see Dooley (1992:33–68).

My treatment of Crane's philosophy, paying close attention the relative priority of various aspects of his philosophy, focuses upon Crane's primary and fundamental philosophical position, his metaphysical stance on the nature of reality. I use "metaphysics" in John Dewey's sense of an account of the "generic traits of existence" (*Experience and Nature* 45). Dewey proposes that quality and relation, event and meaning, time and the eternal, the precarious and the stable, the genuine and the spurious, the dependable and the deceptive, the routine and the creative, need elucidation. Our reaction to the world is, of course, dependent on our perception of the character of reality and the nature of the universe. Nonetheless, reality's generic traits and human reactions thereto are separable and distinct matters.

Unlike Crane's philosophy of humanity and its philosophical "outlook," his epistemology has been examined with a degree of philosophical sophistication. For example, Nagel (1973, 1975a, 1975b, 1978, 1980) has made a sustained contribution. Although his analysis of the shifting points of view in Crane is very helpful, I depart from Nagel at two points. The first has to do with the relative priority of philosophical claims. Because our reaction to the world is mediated by and dependent upon our knowledge, Nagel has retained some philosophical leverage to justify his view. (With regard to Crane's epistemology, the positions of Bergon, Colvert [1965 and 1977], LaFrance [1973], Solomon [1961], and Trachtenberg are akin to Nagel's.) My account, on the contrary, tied to Crane's metaphysics, provides a comprehensive basis from which to discuss the positions Crane adopted on epistemological, ethical, social, and other philosophical issues. Second, there is a difference of emphasis between Nagel's position and my own on the limitations of human knowledge. Nagel decries that, in Crane, people's judgments are perpetually limited and tentative. Although I, too, acknowledge tentativeness in our knowledge, I also stress how reality's richness tolerates a good number of reliable, satisfactory, and pragmatically true human conceptions of it.

5. LaFrance (1971) is particularly confused on this score. In his enthusiastic response to Crane's emphasis on personal honesty, LaFrance misunderstands how Crane's ethical position is related to prior metaphysical and epistemological stances. As a result, he struggles to defend as *Crane's* the "moral" position "If I sincerely believe that X is right, then it *is* morally right." LaFrance's conflation of moral and personal duties has unfortunate consequences: it drains morality of content and robs moral norms of generality.

1. Mentors, Backers, and a Literary Creed

1. See Kibler for an inventory of Crane's library. Crane's curiosity about his ancestors' books led him to write to his cousin. J. K. Peck's reply of April 21, 1899 lists Crane's grandfather's and his great-uncle's books, see *Correspondence* #506. See Gullason (1968a) for details on Mrs. Crane's will, which gave Stephen one-fourth of the family library. Hoffman (1957) says of Crane's first book of poetry, *The Black Riders*, "It is almost as though Crane had taken *What Must I Be to Be Saved?* [written by his grandfather Bishop Jesse Peck] as his text, and proceeded to write commentaries on what seemed to him the monstrousness and inhumanity of the creed of his mother's family" (65).

2. See Gullason (1971, 1972, 1977, 1986) and Sorrentino (1986) for a discussion of the Crane family's literary output. Elconin describes the reports that Crane's mother wrote for the New York *Times* and the Philadelphia *Press* detailing religious news at Ocean Grove resorts.

3. On the writings of Agnes Crane, see Sorrentino (1986); for her tutelage of Crane, see Gullason (1977) and Schoberlin (1949).

4. John D. Barry wrote in 1901, "It was his mother who secured for him his first chance to write regularly for money as a New Jersey correspondent for the New York *Tribune*" (148). Crane's niece, Helen R. Crane, commented that "since the age of fifteen or sixteen he had been writing for newspapers, contributing to his mother's *Tribune* column" (24).

5. Kwiat (1980) argues that "the young writer, of course, reported the news; nevertheless, he frequently insisted upon interpreting it in an ironic mode and upon interjecting some color symbolism—two distinguishing characteristics of his short stories and novels" (131). Elconin notes of Crane's Asbury Park dispatches, "the flippant cynicism and the iconoclastic tone that are such familiar marks in his fiction are the principal notes in these pieces" (277). See also Kwiat (1953, 1976, 1979) and Weinstein.

6. Syracuse classmate and pitcher Mansfield J. French wrote the definitive article on his batterymate's baseball skills, including details of "wantonly profane" swearing and "diabolical glee" when the side was retired (13). Crane also played shortstop for Syracuse University (see Jones). In his February 2, 1896 letter to Ripley Hitchcock, at the crest of *Red Badge* fame, Crane noted: "I was very much delighted with Frederick's letter in the Times. I see also that they are beginning to charge me with having played base ball. I am rather more proud of my base ball ability than of some other things" (*Correspondence* #198). For a sample of the excitement over Crane's overnight *Red Badge* fame, see Charles K. Gaines's March 15, 1896 article, "Rise to Fame of Stephen Crane" in the Philadelphia *Press*.

7. See Crane's friend, Arthur Oliver, "'Stevie' and I were 'budding journalists'" (455) for details on the Crane brothers' dismissal, also see Willis Johnson and Eloconin.

8. See Levenson's lists: "News From Asbury Park," "Possible Attributions" (8:xvii–xviii), and Gullason (1986). Emery and Emery detail reporters

working "under a degrading time and space system" (214) during the Dana, Hearst, and Pulitzer circulation wars. On the matter of time-space rates, Smythe reports that the New York *Tribune* was among the lowest-paying and had "the meanest city department of any local paper" (3). Symthe cites (9) an article that Crane might have read, "Reporters and Oversupply" by John Livingston Wright, that appeared in the December 1898 *Arena*.

9. See Weatherford's (4) estimate based on Katz's census of located copies of the 1893 *Maggie*.

10. See Holloway (55–56) for Garland's lecture circular and for syllabuses of his addresses.

11. Garland (1914, 1930) describes playing catch with Crane.

12. Several scholars (Dickason, Cline [1940a, b], and Fairfield) have attempted to verify *Arena*'s June 1903 claim of a circulation of a hundred thousand. None has been able to find documentation of "a total higher than thirty-five thousand" (Fairfield 272). Mott (1957, 4:414) explains the discrepancy: "It is sometimes said that the *Arena* had a circulation of 100,000. This is an absurdity based on Flower's reference to a time 'when the *Arena* was being read by over one hundred thousand of the most thoughtful Americans every month' (*Arena* 29 [May 1903]:670). It was common in these times to estimate that each copy of a magazine or newspaper was read by at least five persons . . . and that is what Flower was doing here."

13. Garland boasts: "I set to work to let my editorial friends know of this youngster. I mailed two of his completed sketches to B. O. Flower of the *Arena*, asking him to be as generous as he could, 'for the author is hungry'" (1930:197). See Ayers for more about Garland's campaign on behalf of *Maggie*.

14. An analysis of the reaction to the presentation copies of *Maggie*, although interesting and important, would take us far afield, nonetheless a brief summary of the reactions of five critics is in order.

Brander Matthews, professor of English at Columbia University and an influential critic who wrote the "In the Library" column for *Cosmopolitan*, gave indirect endorsement to Crane's realism is his March 12, 1892 column, "American Fiction Again." Surveying the most widely circulated public library books, Matthews decried the popularity of romantic works (*Ben Hur, Looking Backward, The Count of Monte Cristo*) and applauded the growing interest in realistic, local-color works (*Huckleberry Finn* and Garland's *Main-Traveled Roads*): "There is nothing that we need more in fiction nowadays than careful, scientific, unsentimental portrayal of poverty, so that the reader may see the thing as it is and not illumined by any hectic flush reflected from the over-colored pictures of Dickens" (638). Oliver (1988) shows that the 1893 *Maggie* deeply disturbed Matthews and his ideal of a "truthful" romantic realism. Seven years after he received a presentation copy of the book, he responded with a short story, "Before the Break of Day," published in *Harper's*. His story was a melodramatic recast of Rum Alley in which Maggie O'Donnell, with hard work, luck, and a willing husband, buys a saloon. Matthews's "Maggie" not only blossoms in a mud puddle, but also lives happily ever after. Hers is the family living in heroic purity that Garland asked for in his review of *Maggie:* "The story fails of rounded completeness. It is only a fragment. It is typical only of the worst elements of the alley. The author should delineate the families living on the next street, who live lives of heroic purity and hopeless hardship" (*Critical Heritage* #1).

John D. Barry sent Crane a lengthy, thoughtful letter. Crane's friend and the illustrator of several of his stories, C. K. Linson, reports that Barry's letter "touched Steve for its proof of genuine interest" (1958:33). Barry was moved by *Maggie:* "I have read it with the deepest interest. It is pitilessly real and it produced its effect upon me . . . a kind of horror." Barry echoed both Matthews and Gilder: "you have painted too black a picture, with no light whatever to your shade." But there was heartening news in the letter too: "I really believe that the lesson of your story is good, but I believe, too, that you have driven that lesson too hard." Barry was an assistant editor for the reform organ *Forum,* but the drift of his advice to Crane anticipated what senior reform-periodical editors would tell him: realism is welcome when it contains exhortations prompting the belief that improvement is possible. Barry had put it that "mere brooding upon evil conditions . . . is [the] most dangerous . . . and I don't think that it often moves to action, to actual reform work" (*Correspondence* #18).

Godey's Magazine's "Chilifer" (Rupert Hughes) called *Maggie* "probably the strongest piece of slum writing we have" (*Critical Heritage* #4). Beyond "the keenness of the wit, the minuteness of the observation, and the bitterness of the cynicism," readers would find that "the foredoomed fall of a well-meaning girl reared in an environment of drunkenness and grime is told with great humanity and fearless art." Hughes closes with both an invitation and a warning: "The subjects chosen . . . compel an occasional plainness of speech which may give shock to spasmic prudishness, but there is nothing to harm a healthy mind, and they all should have the effect of creating a better understanding and a wiser, more active sympathy for the unfortunates who must fill the cellar of the tenement we call life. To do this is far better even than to be artistic" (*Critical Heritage* #4). Howells provided the final two reviews of the 1893 *Maggie.* He, too, worried about Crane's excessive fidelity to Bowery conditions and conversation.

Edward Marshall's interview of Howells in the April 15, 1894, Philadelphia *Press* actually provided *two* estimates of *Maggie:* Howells's comments and Marshall's commentary. Howells is quoted as observing "he is very young, but he promises splendid things. . . . *Maggie* is a wonderful book. There is so much realism of a certain kind in it that we might not like to have it lying on our parlor tables, but I hope that the time will come when any book can safely tell the truth as completely as *Maggie* does" (*Critical Heritage* #2). Marshall's commentary was equally supportive: "Stephen Crane . . .is still in the very early twenties and wrote *Maggie* several years ago . . . . It aims at exact truth in painting an unpleasant side of life, and approaches nearer to realizing it than any other book written by an American ever has" (*Critical Heritage* #2).

The following year in his regular column "Life and Letters" in *Harper's Weekly*, Howells explained that *Maggie* had failed to gain a wide readership because of "its grim, not to say grimy truth, and in the impossibility to cultured ears of a parlance whose texture is so largely profanity" (*Critical Heritage* #3). But Howells commended Crane's conscience and art. More positive still and more important, Howells emerged as a strong, behind-the-scenes sponsor for Crane.

15. See *Correspondence* #168 and 268 for Crane's letters of appreciation to Howells. Beyond that, Linson witnessed how much Howells's (and Garland's) support meant: "when such men as Howells and Garland, who were to him the last word in American Literature, called his book [*Maggie*] a great performance, he was seriously elate, happy beyond expression. I have often wondered if Mr. Howells knew the deep joy with which his good opinion filled Crane" (1903:20). Gullason (1957) argues that Crane's opinion of Howells cooled considerably near the end of Crane's life.

16. This was perhaps the point at which Crane's career was launched. In addition to his literary production, Crane's energy, vitality, creativity, and confidence are evident in two off-beat publications during the last half of 1894: a press agent's puff, "Miss Louise Gerard—Soprano," published in the *Musical Courier* (8:642–44) and an entire four-page newspaper parody, complete with advertisements, chronicling a camping vacation, "Pike County Puzzle" (8:608–35). Linson concurs; citing Crane's output for the year, he observes, "eighteen ninety-four was a full year" (1958:80).

17. The loan was for $15 so Crane could get the second half of the manuscript of *The Red Badge of Courage* from the typist. See Garland (1930) for more on this loan.

18. A few months later, writing again to Lily Monroe, Crane reports, "The *Arena Co* brings out a book of mine this winter" (*Correspondence* #27). Sorrentino and Wertheim explain that "apparently, Crane negotiated with the Arena company for a reissue of *Maggie* but the book was first published commercially under Crane's name by D. Appleton and Company in June 1896" (*Correspondence* #58).

19. Garland's decline from realism to Rocky Mountain romanticism has caused lively debate. Duffey (1953:59) charges that Garland "sold his Western, reformist and realistic birthright to produce a long series of inanities which comprise his later work"; George Johnson, Koerner, McCullough, and Saum defend Garland's "evolution" as an author; and then Duffey (1954) rebuts. Pizer's explanations (1954, 1960) seem to be an even-handed end to the debate. Stronks's discussion of impressionism asserts that "Garland's attempt at self-improvement may have been colored by the influence, hitherto unsuspected, of Stephen Crane" (38). Wertheim (1967) argues that the influence went in the other direction.

20. See J. L. French, Lyon, and Stinson for more on McClure's newspaper, syndicate, and magazine career; Wilson concentrates on *McClure's* and muckraking.

21. Other McClure exposes were on copper mines, dynamite factories, powder mills, the deep coal mines of Cornwall, the goldfields of the Klond-

ike, and Bonanza wheat farms in the Midwest. See Wilson (1970) for the *McClure's* worker series.

In 1895 *McClure's* ran a series on municipal reform, Tammany Hall, and Roosevelt's crusade to close New York City saloons on Sunday. The magazine assumed leadership among the muckrakers when staff writer Ida M. Tarbell was shifted from her very successful portrait series of Napoleon and Lincoln to write a history of a corporation. The result was her epic "History of the Standard Oil Co.," featured in *McClure's* from November 1902 until October 1904.

The trust-busting crusade came later. Tarbell had limited herself to the process and the power that came from consolidated wealth; while the population expanded 20 percent between 1880 and 1900, the nation's wealth doubled. *Life* magazine in 1901 printed the following revision of the catechism: "'Who made the world, Charles?' 'God made the world in 4004 B.C., but it was reorganized in 1901 by James J. Hill, J. Pierpoint Morgan and John D. Rockefeller" (quoted in Mott 1954:206). Crane's views on robber barons are contained in a *War Is Kind* poem, "The successful man has thrust himself" (#85, 1333).

The standard account of the muckrackers is by Regier, also helpful are Schultz and Harry Stein. Clark studied muckrakers in the polite magazines, finding that in the late 1890s "the *North American Review, Forum* and *Arena* published one or two reform articles in each issue, while the *Atlantic* and *Century* offered one every two months" (5). Holly's *Bookman* piece is a period discussion of muckrakers, complete with photographs of sixteen leading reform editors.

22. Controversy exists over Crane's editing of "In the Depths of a Coal Mine"; see Bowers's detailed analysis (8:923–32). Weinstein and Katz (1968, 1989) have suggested, based on the conversation between Crane and Linson (reported in Linson 1958:69–70), that McClure censored Crane. However, because Linson's *My Stephen Crane* does not discuss the full range of changes Crane made in his first draft, as well as the fact that McClure left standing preachy indictments in articles by Garland and others, it does not seem likely that McClure was the impetus for Crane's revisions.

Crane gave the first draft of "In the Depths of a Coal Mine" to Linson. Perhaps, as Levinson contends, Linson used his influence with S. S. McClure to get Crane his first magazine assignment. This manuscript, now part of the Barrett Collection at the University of Virginia, contains careful annotations (presumably by Linson) of all differences between the first draft and printed versions. The matter of Crane's editing is further complicated by differences in newspaper appearances and the fuller *McClure's* version of this article. Linson checked the first draft against the newspaper, not the magazine, version of "In the Depths of a Coal Mine."

23. It is difficult to excuse McClure's treatment of Crane during these months; McClure's grandson, however, tries hard to exonerate him (Lyon 129n). It is not clear just how long—six, eight, or nine months—McClure kept the typescript of *The Red Badge of Courage*. Crane was careless about dates, and Garland, the other source, has often to be corrected. Pizer (1960a)

has sorted out the dates and facts in "The "Garland-Crane Relationship." Apparently, however, Crane did not hold a grudge against the McClure family. The Whilomville story "The Angel-Child" has, as its central event, a visit to the barbershop of William Neeltje: "'How do you pronounce the name of that barber up there on Bridge Street hill?' And then, before anyone could prevent it, the best minds of the town were splintering their lances against William Neeltje's signboard" (1177). In 1897 McClure merged his firm with Frank N. Doubleday to form a publishing company. Among the first offerings of Doubleday & McClure were two illustrated bird books by Mrs. Frank Doubleday released under the pen name of Neltje Blachan. See Lyon (159) for more on Neltje Blachan.

The other barber in Whilomville was Reifsnyder. In his unpublished biography "Flagon of Despair: Stephen Crane," Schoberlin reveals that "on his return to the Pendennis club, Crane stopped at Reifsneider's old bookstore on East 55th Street to raid the section of Civil War volumes" (Book 2:x–8). Schoberlin's manuscript is located at the George Arents Research Library at Syracuse University. For another possible source for this odd name, see "Melange of the Class of 1892," which reveals that the Delta Upsilon chapter at Lafayette College, which Crane joined as a freshman, also had, as a sophomore pledge, one Samuel K. Reifsnyder.

24. See *Correspondence* #59 for details; Linson's beautiful oil portrait of Crane hangs in the Alderman Library of the University of Virginia. Reproductions can be found in several books, the best of which are Baum and Linson (1958).

25. Crane's difficulties in repaying Bacheller's advance were the start of a chronic pattern of securing advances by promising future works to retire past debts. For instance, while in England, despite his earlier experience with his *Red Badge* manuscript with McClure, Crane used the copy text of *The Monster* as collateral to a secure loan. McClure had no plans to publish the novella, yet blocked its publication by *Harper's* for nearly six months. At numerous times Crane (and Cora) badgered his English agent James B. Pinker for similar advances, using manuscripts, even promised manuscripts. Indeed, most of volume 2 of *Correspondence* is the sad saga of the last years of Stephen and Cora Crane at Brede Place in Sussex, England, desperately trying to catch up so they might fend off bankruptcy.

26. See "Irving Bacheller" (1904) for the club members' account in *The Lanthorn Book;* see Bacheller (1928) for the story of Mark Twain stopping in for an hour or so but staying all afternoon. McBride, an artist friend, recalled seeing Crane after "the Lantern Club had honored him with a banquet-luncheon" (46).

27. This is the title of Mott's article in the *Proceedings of the American Antiquarian Society.*

28. See Heddendorf on James, lay audiences, and significant philosophizing. Fredson Bowers, the general editor for the University Press of Virginia's Crane edition, was also the textual editor for Harvard University Press's critical edition of William James. Bowers notes, "James was a conscious and

dedicated stylist, less perhaps for aesthetic reasons than for purposes of clarity, precision and readability, on which he set high store" (1980:10).

29. For example, in 1894–95 James was president of both the American Psychological Association and the English Society for Psychical Research.

30. For more on *Century's* growth because of the Civil War series, see Mott (1954:3); for a discussion of *Century's* book publishing enterprises as Appleton-Century-Crofts (including, of course, publishing *The Red Badge of Courage*), see Chew.

31. See Hungerford for the case—including evidence from the standard reference book, *Century's Battles and Leaders of the Civil War*—that "the battle in Crane's novel is closely and continuously parallel to the historical Chancellorsville" (522).

32. C. K. Linson was commissioned by *Scribner's* to cover the first modern Olympic games.

33. Allen has the exchange of letters between Gilder and Reynolds concerning removing "B'Gawd" from "A Man and Some Others," along with details on Reynolds as Crane's literary agent. Whether or not Gilder was a prude has been widely debated. See Berkelman, Charvat, and Wagenknecht.

34. This is the title of Colvert's excellent analysis (1986) of Schoberlin's "Flagon of Despair." Colvert makes a convincing case for a new biography of Crane.

35. On Crane's inscribed gift volumes of *The Black Riders* and *Active Service*, see *Correspondence* #85 and #619. On Brown as editor and literary agent, see *Correspondence* #334.

36. For details on Crane's dismissal, see Colvert (1986) and Seitz, who also explains that "between the *World* and the *Journal* we barked President McKinley into a war that was none of our business" (137). Seitz was the *World's* business manager at the time. Later, in his biography of Pulitzer, he criticized Crane for sending only one dispatch of worth from Cuba. In fact, some twenty of Crane's dispatches, many featured on page one, were used by the *World*. See Weinstein for details of Crane, Seitz, and Pulitzer. See also Brown, Churchill, and Emery and Emery for the headline war Hearst and Pulitzer fought for circulation during the Spanish-American War. See Marshall for more on Crane's rescue of his journalist friend.

37. The address by the former mayor of Newark, Thomas Raymond, at the dedication of a memorial to Crane at the Newark Public Library captures, as well as any scholar's, Crane's vibrance. "Crane was a lovable fellow, inspiring affection in all who knew him, every one calling him 'Stevie,' 'dear Stevie,' 'poor Stevie'; he was careless of his material affairs; he liked the active life—horseback riding, baseball playing; he was fond of the sea, of horses, of guns; he loved adventure, free living, and outdoor life" (Raymond 19).

2. Metaphysics and Epistemology

1. For an extended discussion of "interested selection" in James, see Dooley (1974).

2. See Bergon (1975) for a helpful analysis of the stylistic techniques Crane uses to surprise and disorient his reader. In this connection, Fried calls attention to Crane's "formidable powers of defamiliarization" (93); La France (1971) and Milne give useful explications of Crane's style and technique; Albrecht discusses doubleness and ambiguity in Crane; and Kamholtz notes Crane's knack of presenting unlabeled and uncaptioned pictures of "disordered detail" (395). Frohock suggests that what makes Crane's style so potent is its modern syntax and "the general absense of causal connections that allows him to juxtapose visual responses instead of asserting the relationship between them" (228). Tanner argues that "the particular combination of conveyed intensity and apparent disengagement" (142) is unique to Crane.

3. As Nagel aptly put it, Crane arranges "the irony of the inversion of knowledge relative to rank" (1980:102). Stallman's simplistic metaphysical scheme, with ontological categories limited to appearance/reality, leads him to misread the story as "the withdrawal of the wounded lieutenant from the real world into an imaginary world" (1958:376).

Covici has resurrected Stallman's faulty *either* appearance *or* reality premise by his assertion that, for Crane, humans can not know the thing-in-itself. Although Corvici calls this an "agnostic perspective," he has actually made Crane into a philosophical solipsist, "whatever that truth might in infinite actuality be, each individual could know and belive only what that specifically particular individual was able to know and believe" (13). See also Delbanco, who flatly asserts that Crane's "real subject [was] . . . the solipsistic condition of the human mind, which he regarded as not a pathology restricted to certain social classes, but as a universal human failing" (34).

4. In a letter to the editor of the *Youth's Companion* after they had ageed to publish this story, Crane wrote, "I have some thought of writing a Part II to it but that is a matter the next two weeks will decide. As it stands it is of course complete." Crane then adds, "This lieutenant is an actual person" (*Correspondence* #225). See May for more on this story.

5. For contrary readings, see Gerstenberger, Kent (1981, 1982, 1986), La France (1971), and Nettles, who find epistemological pessimism, including the conclusion that the world is unknowable, in Crane. In Bergon's Crane (1975), human judgments are extremely tentative: human meanings have an elusive and spectral quality, imposed on a reality which is, in the last analysis, demonic in character. Marovitz also sees much that is demonic in Crane.

6. Ethical philosophers use the term *slippery slope* (see Thompson) to refer to the argument that, without moral absolutes, radical subjectivism cannot be prevented. Similar slippery-slope thinking is obvious in Crane's commentators. Some critics (Perosa and, to a lesser extent, Mayer and Overland), uncomfortable with anything less than the Truth, have attempted to argue that Crane's characters move from appearances and distorted beliefs to full possession of the Truth. At the bottom of the slippery slope, other writers (Gerstenberger, Glen Johnson, Kent, Wolford) assert that any subjectivity in humans is sufficient to preclude reliable knowledge.

Happily, the majority of commentators (Bassan, Colvert, Davidson,

Metzger, and Nagel) have rejected dichotomous appearance-reality, subjectivity-objectivity, and belief-truth distinctions and opted for midway positions on the slippery slope. I also reject the slippery-slope position, defending instead a middle position. That is, I spell out how concepts, without claiming to possess the Truth, can nevertheless be useful, reliable, and "pragmatically" true. Shulman's sensible and perceptive essay deserves careful study in this regard.

Crane, it seems, anticipated the slippery-slope image. The newspaper story "Tent Life at Ocean City" contains the striking phrase, "a sort of moral toboggan slide" (78). This story, attributed to Crane by Schoberlin, is reprinted by Gullason (1986), who, however, thinks its authorship is "conjectural" (60).

7. H. G. Wells's review essay "An English Standpoint" deftly captured Crane's project, "the persistent selection of the essential elements of an impression, in the ruthless exclusion of mere information, in the direct vigor with which selected points are made" (*Critical Heritage* #115). To the same effect, Schoberlin cites an undated letter by Crane to an unidentified recepient, "a novel ... to my mind, should be a succession of ... clear, strong, sharply-outlined pictures which pass before the reader like a panorama, leaving each its definite impression" (1949:20).

8. The standard philosophical treatments of "skilled seeing" are by Polanyi (1962, 1967). See Levinson's (1975) discussion of Fleming's second engagement, wherein he "seems to see everything in minute detail.... Practice disciplines the soldier's vision" (2:lxxi–lxxii) and Nagel's (1980) analysis of Crane's ability to involve the reader in problems of seeing. Crane was also interested in "skilled hearing." In "The Red Badge of Courage Was His Wig-Wag Flag," he explains how to discriminate between the sounds of Lee and Mauser rifle fire: "the firing broke out. It needs little practice to tell the difference in sound between the Lee and the Mauser. The Lee says 'Prut!' It is a fine note, not very metallic. The Mauser says 'Pop!'—plainly and frankly pop, like a soda-water bottle being opened close to the ear. We could hear both sound now in great plenty. Prut—prut—pr-r-r-rut—pr-rut! Pop—pop—poppetty—pop!" (9:137).

9. Harris's detailed drawing "A Typical Spanish Blockhouse in Cuba" (132) is helpful in following Crane here.

10. The first reviews of *The Third Violet* found Stanley to be the book's chief merit. *Athenaeum* noted, "*The Third Violet* incidentally contains the best dog that we have come across in modern fiction" (*Critical Heritage* #75); the New York *Times* added, "there is a good dog, too, in Stephen Crane's new story, a large orange and white setter, whose geniality and constancy almost reconcile one to Mr. Crane's manner of telling a story" (*Critical Heritage* #76); and the *Spectator* commented, "'Stanley,' Hawker's dog ... is quite one of the most delightful animals we have encountered in recent fiction" (*Critical Heritage* #77).

Conrad (among others) noted Crane's habit of sharing his study with his dog. Crane would have warmly endorsed William James's recreation of his dog's disgust with another afternoon "wasted" while his master reads in the library. "Take our dogs and ourselves, connected as we are by a tie more intimate than most ties in this world; and yet, outside of that tie of friendly fondness, how insensible, each of us, to all that makes life significant for the other!—we to the rapture of bones under hedges, or smells of trees and lampposts, they to the delights of literature and art. As you sit reading the most moving romance you ever fell upon, what sort of a judge is your fox-terrier of your behavior? With all his good will towards you, the nature of your conduct is absolutely excluded from his comprehension. To sit there like a senseless statue, when you might be taking him to walk and throwing sticks for him to catch! What a queer disease is this that comes over you every day, of holding things and staring at them like that for hours together, paralyzed of motion and vacant of all conscious life?" ("On a Certain Blindness in Human Beings" 132–33).

11. For a parallel account in Wallace Stevens of the need to transcend cultural, habitual, and personal ways of looking at things, see Scott. Shaw, exploring the "genuine consistency of outlook between [Robert] Frost and [William] James" (180), concludes, "Frost believes it is the function of poets and eccentrics, of prophets and madmen to keep open the possibility of other frameworks" (188).

12. The concept of games as a key to Crane's vision, originally suggested by Cady (1961) and George Johnson, has been extended by Deamer, Edwards, Overton James, and McFarland.

13. For a discussion of fellow journalists' opinions of Crane, see Carmichael, Davis, Kaufmann, and Scott C. Osborn. In "The Filibustering Industry" (9:94–99), Crane forthrightly confesses a newspaper correspondent's difficult conflicting obligations to public, employer, sources, and personal causes. In "Some Curious Lessons from the Transvaal" (9:240–43), he discusses the role of national security in reporting defeats on the battlefield.

14. See Dooley (1974, chs. 2 and 4) for more on James's treatment of "knowledge about" and "knowledge by acquaintance." For the role of experiential knowledge in Crane, see Bender (1979).

15. "Ol' Bennet" was Crane's great-great grandfather, and the lost button incident can be found in a history of the Wyoming Massacre written by Crane's great grandfather, the Reverend Dr. George Peck. See Arnold for details.

16. Colvert (1984) gives an excellent rendering of the surrealistic distortions and anxiety-directed misperceptions in *The Red Badge of Courage.* More generally, Brooks notes Crane's skill in disclosing how "an acute sensibility [makes] . . . trifling situations assume for the moment a prodigious importance" (*Critical Heritage* #142). The distorting impact of anxiety is clearly present in Crane's first story (written at the age of fourteen), "Uncle Jake and the Bell-Handle" (Hoffman 1960).

17. See Budd and Kwiat (1952) for a discussion of honesty, discipline, and objectivity from the literary standpoint of journalists.

18. On this point, see especially Cazemajou, as well as Cady (1962, 1980) and William Stein (1958).

19. The essay by Westbrook (1963) on the God of perspective and the God of arrogance covers this ground admirably. See also Hoffman (1957) and Miller.

20. McIntosh's *The Little I Saw of Cuba* describes the Rough Rider ambush and the balloon: "The taking of that balloon down there [to Cuba] was one of the most criminally negligent acts of the entire war. Not only were many men killed by the explosion of shells aimed at it, but it also gave those in San Juan a clue to the fact that the road was filled with our men" (125). McIntosh's book is valuable for more than two hundred pictures, including two of Crane (72 and 156) and one of "that balloon" (162). See Freidel (48–49) for additional photographs.

3. Brotherhood in an Indifferent Universe

1. Conder has given extended discussion to environmental behaviorism in the writings of Crane. Unfortunately, Condor restricts himself to impoverished paradigms of the freedom-determinism problem. Only two philosophers—Hobbes and Bergson—are considered, and he commits a category confusion by mixing the causes of physical movements with the reasons for actions. See MacIntyre on this last point.

With regard to *Maggie*, Conder refers to Crane's often-cited expression of philosophical determinism, the inscription on the cover of the copy of *Maggie* he presented to the Reverend Thomas Dixon, but he ignores three qualifications Crane made. "It is inevitable that this book will greatly shock you, but continue, pray, with great courage to the end, for it tries to show that environment is a *tremendous* thing in this world, and *often* shapes lives regardlessly. If one could prove that theory, one would make room in Heaven for all sorts of souls (notably an *occasional* street girl) who are not confidently expected to be there by many excellent people" (*Correspondence* #73, emphasis added).

Conder's assertion, "He [Crane] suggests that people are so much a part of their environment that only the environment, not the individual, can be judged morally" (45), is at odds with the declaration in Crane's letter of January 26, 1896 to Nellie Crouse. He noted his newfound fame for *The Red Badge of Courage*, "the majestic forces which are arrayed against man's true success—not the world—the world is silly, changeable, any of it's decisions can be reversed—but man's own colossal impulses [are] more strong than chains, and I perceived that the fight was not going to be with the world but with myself" (*Correspondence* #186). See Meyer for an analysis of "a confusion of determinism with fatalism" (567), and Morgan and Pizer (1965) for the compatibility of literary naturalism, morality, and freedom. For a detailed description, with photographs and drawings, of the slum environment and the Bowery during Crane's time, see Maurice.

2. See McDermott's discussion (1986) of the harmful effects of this polarization, and, in his view, Americans' unconscious, benefit-of-the-doubt endorsement of "nature."

3. See Hunt, who argues that in Canadian literature nature is predominantly portrayed as a harsh, threatening, "amoral counterforce" (49). The premise of Hunt's discussion is the view that the Canadian frontier was "hard," whereas America's was "soft." See Burns, Colvert (1982), and Wolford (1983) for readings of Crane that stress humanity's war against an essentially hostile nature.

4. Murphy notes parallels between the battlegrounds of George and Mrs. Kelcey. Brennan (1960) finds disparities in the battles of son and mother. Giamo and Halliburton give extended discussion to *George's Mother*, the latter shows a "remarkable symmetry" (185) in *Maggie* and *George's Mother*.

5. In "Two Books by Stephen Crane," June 1896, an anonomous reviewer for *The Critic* found striking comparisons between the rites and shrines that bolster George and Mrs. Kelsey (*Critical Heritage* #58).

6. Deamer (1972, 1980) makes a detailed and persuasive case for Berryman's earlier claim that the West changed Crane. On the West and Crane, see also Bassan (1967), Fryckstedt (1963), Kimball, Paredes, Robertson, and Weinstein. Bergon (1975) is undecided if the West changed Crane's orientation; however, he later (1979) traces changes in Crane's style to his western trip. Deamer (1977) charges Bergon with confusion in trying to have it both ways.

7. Crane's November 8, 1895 letter to Willis Brooks Hawkins argues that easterners are hemmed in by culture and social regulations: "I have always believed the western people to be much truer than the eastern people. We in the east are overcome a good deal by detestable superficial culture which I think is the real barbarism. . . . Damn the east! I fell in love with the straight out-and-out, sometimes-hideous, often-braggart westerners because I thought them to be the truer men. . . . They are serious, those fellows. When they are born they take one big gulp of wind and then they live. . . . Garland will wring every westerner by the hand and hail him as a frank honest man. I wont. No, sir. But what I contend for is the atmosphere of the west which really is frank and honest and is bound to make eleven honest men for one pessimistic thief. More glory be with them" (*Correspondence* #128).

It seems likely that simple factors like open space, social informality, the importance of basic necessities, and the need to fend for one's self impressed Crane out west. For example, the poverty of the Nebraska farmers easily equaled that of the Johnson's and the Kelcey's in the Bowery. Perhaps because westerners face natural foes (hail, heat, wind, cold, drought, and floods) they believe their own initiative and efforts will be adequate, whereas easterners must combat human constructs and social conventions. See Edwards and George Johnson for helpful discussions of conformity and convention in Crane, and Daskam for a turn-of-the-century analysis of American literature's celebration of frontier-survival qualities.

In any case, Crane holds that poverty by itself is an insufficient obstacle to human freedom. Recall the qualifications in his inscription of *Maggie* to Hamlin Garland and consider his comment, "I have said that a man has a right to rebel if he is not given a fair opportunity to be virtuous. Inversely then, if he possesses this fair opportunity, he cannot rebel, he has no complaint. I am of the opinion that poverty of itself is no cause. For example, there is Collis P. Huntington and William D. Rockefeller. . . .their opportunities are not greater. They can give more, deny themselves more in quality, but not relatively. We can each give all that we possess and there I am at once their equal. . . . There is in fact no advantage of importance which I can perceive them possessing over me" ("The Mexican Lower Classes" 730).

Some fifty years earlier, in *The Maine Woods*, Thoreau anticipated Crane's views on rural penury and urban poverty: "How much more respectable also is the life of the solitary pioneer or settler in these, or any woods,— having real difficulties, not of his own creation, drawing his subsistence directly from nature,—than that of the helpless multitudes in the towns who depend on gratifying the extremely artificial wants of society and are thrown out of employment by hard times" ("The Allegash and East Branch" 244).

8. For details on the severe drought and the harsh winter in Nebraska, see Katz (1970). For Crane's travels in Nebraska, see Cather and Slote (1969b).

9. See Crane's letter of September 18, 1895 to Willis Brooks Hawkins and the note "Crane had been pursued in Mexico by a bandit named Ramon Colorado" (*Correspondence* #108). See Levenson (1970) and Colvert (1982, 1984) for more on this episode.

Even away from civilization, individual efforts have their limits. Later, in full daylight, when the banditos catch up to Richardson and José in the desert, "a detachment of rurales, that crack cavalry corps of the Mexican army which polices the plains" ("One Dash—Horses" 742) saved them by running off the Mexican pursuers.

Crane's rugged individualism sometimes has been overstated, see Edwards and LaFrance, for example. Crane welcomed group efforts, and he valued the support of fire and police departments (with an obvious exception taken to the New York City Police, see note 19), trains, street cars, ships, and other social institutions. Recall, for instance, his keen interest in fire engines. His long-standing fascination appears early, in *Maggie* ("a fire-engine was enshrined in his [Jimmie's] heart as an appalling thing that he loved with a distant dog-like devotion" [23]); late in a European report, "London's Firemen Fall From Grace" ("nothing in London strikes Americans as being more quaint than the London fire engine. Compared with the great engines of New York they seem like toys" [8:763]); and in several intervening works.

10. In this story, the Americans, a stranger and Bill, are ambushed by a band of Mexicans; during the second attack, Bill is killed. Theodore Roosevelt wrote to Crane that the Americans, not the Mexicans should have prevailed. "Some day I want you to write another story of the frontiersman and the Mexican Greaser in which the frontiersman shall come out on top; it is more normal that way!" (*Correspondence* #270).

11. White offers the standard treatment the West as a health tonic, with special attention to the experiences of Theodore Roosevelt, Frederic Remington, and Owen Wister. On Crane and the strenuous life, see Cady (1961).

12. See Frus for a comparison of Crane's initial newspaper dispatch with his later story. Day, Hagemann, and Stallman (1968) offer exhaustive analyses of the precise nautical situation: details including drawings of the dingey and the *Commodore* before, during, and after it sunk, information about the tides, winds, water, and air temperature, and annotated maps of the route taken by the four in the open boat. For firsthand accounts, see the selection of newspaper reports collected in Stallman and Watters. Begley describes scholar-skindiver Elizabeth Friedman's discovery of the wreck of the *Commodore*.

13. Because the term *existentialism* has been stretched to an almost limitless range of doctrines—see MacIntyre, "that two writers both claim to be existentialist does not seem to entail their agreement on any one cardinal point . . . any formula sufficiently broad to embrace all the major existentialist tendencies would necessarily be so general and vague as to be vacuous" (147)—it is perhaps futile to deny that Crane is an existentialist. He is sensitive to the indifference of the universe and the precariousness of human existence. Writing in 1925 before existentialism was in vogue, Beer astutely described Crane's sense of the universe as a neutral backdrop for human activity: "In this landscape, the animal called man moves without the slightest importance, supplying himself with that quality as best he can, between his misfortunes, for this human body, 'this citadel of wisdom, virtue, power,' is nothing but X in a problem of irregular mathematics infested with unknown quantities. . . . The animal called man, in short, is still the animal called man and never flattered by the psychological reporter at his elbow" (426). Craven, reviewing Beer's biography, makes the point equally well: "we discover [in Crane's writings] the inherent futility of the grand programme, and are made to understand how proud and impotent a thing is the talking mammal" (476).

The case for nihilism in Crane, specifically that he espouses the arbitrariness of choice, the futility of action, and the absurdity of the human situation, is unconvincing. If Crane is an existentialist, his existentialism is peculiarly American, both pragmatic and hopeful. The encounter with indifference leads to ringing affirmations of self-initiative and brotherhood, hope and energy. For the contrary view, see Buitenhuis, Fryckstedt (1961), Gleckner, Grenberg, Griffith, Holton, Karlen, Kent (1981, 1986), Najui, Pilgrim, and William Stein.

14. For more on earning qualification by way of experience in Crane's writings, see Bender (1979, 1988), Colvert (1959), and Shulman. Levenson makes the interesting claim that Crane was handicapped by too great a reliance on personal experience: "he was slow to learn that culture is man's substitute for experience and that without it a young man is prey to deceptions" (1962:383). Follett holds the opposite, "Crane was greatest when imagination and intuition enabled him to present experiences which he had never had" (1926:xii). Colvert has argued that by the time Crane turned his attentions to *The Red Badge of Courage*, "he was in command of formidable literary resources" (1982:110).

15. Dietz points out that several respected commentators have attributed running "like a rabbit" to Fleming. The attentive reader will note that a man near Fleming first runs like a rabbit, then as "others began to skamper away," Fleming yells, panics, and "like a proverbial chicken" (119) runs.

16. I take up Crane's treatment of courage as an animal reflex in *The Red Badge of Courage* in the second section of chapter 4.

17. These terms are from William James's "The Will to Believe." See Dooley (1972) for a discussion of the precursive faith that prompts effort and often success.

18. During September 1896, Crane angered the New York City police and their commissioner Theodore Roosevelt with his newspaper story "Adventures of a Novelist," an eyewitness account of the framed arrest of Dora Clark, a prostitute. In his article, Crane called her "a chorus girl" (865). In the lively controversy that followed, Crane's credibility was attacked through rumors that he was an opium fiend. Fryckstedt (1962b), Trachtenberg, and Wertheim (1975) discuss Crane in New York City's "Tenderloin." See Gallagher for an even-handed discussion of the whole incident.

19. Westbrook (1959, 1962a, b) effectively argues that the attitude toward life in Crane's writings is melioristic and cautiously affirmative; for a discussion of meliorism, especially in the writings of William James, see Dooley (1975, 1985). Meliorism was a staple aspect of late-nineteenth-century American thinking. Browne's "The Philosophy of Meliorism" in the 1897 *Forum* is typical. Recall Crane's dealings with *Forum*'s assistant editor, John Barry (chapter 1).

20. The death of William (Billie or Billy) Higgins has been widely discussed. Going discusses basic biographical matters. Regarding his death and its significance in "The Open Boat," early commentators (Adams, Shroeder) seemed to expect that either all or none would drown and so accused Crane of an inconsistent naturalism. Autry, Horsford, Kent (1986), Solomon (1966), Stallman (1958), and William Stein (1959) see an image of the futility of human efforts. Cady (1962), Greenfield, Griffith, Shulman, and Stallman (1968) stress the role of chance, either the good fortune of the three or the bad luck of Billie. Burns and Gerstenberger see a Darwinian allegory about survival, while Ross rejects Darwinism. Halliburton finds his death "particularily unjust" (253). Emphasizing that three of the four men make it safely to shore, I find in Crane a mature acknowledgment of the limitations of human knowledge and efforts. This reading is shared by the majority of commentators: Alternbernd and Lewis, Berryman (1976), Colvert (1958, 1959), Davidson, Denny, Gibson (1968), Marcus (1962), and Oliviero.

21. For analogous, micro versions of Crane's evolution, see Marcus's (1962) discussion of kinds of indifferent nature in "The Open Boat," and Greenfield's treatment of three senses of nature in *The Red Badge of Courage*.

22. Royce extended C. S. Peirce's stress upon the place of community in classical American philosophy. Royce warned that loyalty to one's group is so strong a human instinct that reflex narrowness and blind provincialism

are constant threats. As a safeguard he proposed loyalty to a universal human community. His vision of genuine community was essentially religious: "Loyalty . . . has the value of a love which does not so much renounce the individual self as devote the self, with all its consciousness and its powers, to an all-embracing unity of individuals in one realm of spiritual harmony" (*The Problem of Christianity* 188). See Conser, Oppenheim, and McDermott (1985) for helpful general essays on Royce; see also Clendenning's biography of him.

4. Tolerance, Compassion, and Duty

1. The observation comes from Conrad's "Introduction" (20) to Beer's biography of Crane. For more on Conrad and Crane, see Fox, Bruce Johnson, and Nettles (1978).

2. Woollcott points out that early publishers worried that Crane's readers would notice his irony, "the 'Whilomville Stories' were first printed at a time when any editor or publisher, on discovering traces of irony in a manuscript, hastily engaged Peter Newell to illustrate it lest any reader overlook the humorous intent. And I remember that in *Harper's* each story had as a headpiece a line-drawing by Edward B. Edwards" (14). Proof of Woollcott's contention is that Crane's first magazine story, "A Tent in Agony" (*Cosmopolitan*, December 1892) a scant three pages long, was nearly overwhelmed by illustrations—twenty-three cartoon drawings by F. P. Bellow and F. S. Church.

3. Crane's moral character remains elusive. Phelps has captured some of his complexity, however: "Stephen Crane was a curious compound of patience and impatience. As a man he was wildly impatient with hypocracy, cant, pretence, falsehood, brutality, sentimentalism, injustice, and cruelty; as an artist, he was unendingly patient in dealing with these very things" (xii–xiii).

4. Crane's substantive stances are interesting: what conduct does he condemn and which actions does he applaud. Global assertions about Crane's moral vision are commonplace: that morality is a crucial concern in his works (Cady [1962, 1969, 1980], Cazemajou, Ellison, Stallman [1952, 1955]); that Crane attacked the confusion of morality with middle-class respectability and sentimentality (Bergon [1975], Brennan [1969], Lenehan, Pizer [1965], Walcutt); or that Crane held that individuals in choosing their own values must accept responsibility for their actions (LaFrance [1971], Nagel [1980], Oliviero, Warner). However, little or no attention has been paid to Crane's ethics, properly speaking. My concern is to lay out the specific moral norms contained in his works to see whether a coherent, workable moral theory emerges.

5. In "Stephen Crane: A Note without Dates," Conrad remarks, "He never appeared so happy or so much to advantage as on the back of a horse" (530). And also living near Brede, Ford recalled, "Crane used to ride over, perched on the top of one of his two enormous carriage horses, which gave him the air of a frail eagle astride a gaunt elephant" (41).

Crane's proficiency with horses so amazed Michelson, a fellow-reporter of the Cuban war, that almost thirty years later he recalled "the telepathic sympathy of the rider and the horse" (xxi) that Crane managed with even a rank horse. "During the Porto Rico campaign he rode a hammer-headed, spur-scarred, hairy-hoofed white horse hardly bigger than a goat, with all the bad habits that could be grafted on original sin by ignorance and bad treatment. 'El Dog' was his name while Crane had him. He was always picketed apart from the other horses, for he was both a biter and a kicker, but he and Crane got along together like sweethearts" (xxii). An interview, "The Author of *The Red Badge of Courage*," published by *The Critic* in 1896, contains one of Crane's earliest comments on his love of horses, "I think a good saddle-horse is one of the blessings of life" (163). His enthusiasm is also clear in two early letters: "what can be finer than a fine frosty morning, a runaway horse, and only the still hills to watch. Lord, I do love a crazy horse with just a little pig-skin between him and me." And also, "my idea of happiness is the saddle of a good-riding horse," *Correspondence* #115, 169). For more on the Crane family's love of riding, the outdoors, hunting, camping, and fishing, see Gullason (1968).

6. A more serious blind spot, jingoism, became obvious in Crane's later writings. For example, in "Stephen Crane's Vivid Story of the Battle of San Juan," he slurs both Cuban insurgents—"the average Cuban here will not speak to an American unless to beg. . . . there is no more useless body of men anywhere!" (1010)—and also loyalists, "the rummiest-looking set of men one could possibly imagine . . . slim, dirty, bad-eyed boys. They were all of a lower class than one could find in any United States jail" (1011–12). In "War Memories," he likens fighting the Cubans to flushing out a covey of quail, "then began the great bird shooting. . .the Spaniards were the birds" (6:232–33), and in "The Red Badge of Courage Was His Wig-Wag Flag," "now began one of the most extraordinary games ever played in war. . . . It was trap-shooting. The thicket was the trap. . .coveys of guerillas got up in bunches of five or six and flew frantically up the opposite hillside" (9:140). Although it is sometimes overstated, Paredes has made an impressive analysis of Crane's derogatory stereotypes of Mexicans. See Robinson for more on Crane's depiction of Mexicans. On a related matter, see Beards for comments on solitary Swedish madmen in Crane.

7. On the matters of good manners and morality, Van Doren credits Crane with "teach[ing] later novelists to lift their stories, out of the low place of domestic sentimentalism, with its emphasis on petty virtues and vices, to the plane of the classics, with their emphasis on the major vices of meanness and cruelty and the major virtues of justice and magnanimity" (12). Kwiat (953, 1976, 1980) suggests that Crane's early newspaper experience provided close contact with vital moral issues. For brief comments on responsiveness to animals as a clue to moral character, see Noxon; on the confusion of morals with manners, see Beer (1926).

8. In his comparison of detachment in the styles of Crane and Hemingway, Nagel observes: "There is no background, no expression of sympathy by the narrator, no moral opinion offered, no conclusions drawn. The

events . . . are made the more forceful and compelling by having them thrust directly onto the reader with no intervening consciousness to soften the blow or suggest the reaction" (1980:173). Although he does not cite the ending of "A Dark-Brown Dog," Nagel's analysis fits perfectly. As early as 1900, H. G. Wells noted directness and lack of mediation in Crane's style. Also on this point, Brooks explains that early readers of *Maggie* and *George's Mother* thought Crane callous and cold because "he left the reader to invest with sentiment the facts that he related barely and boldly" (6).

9. Crane's father, the Reverend Jonathan Townley Crane, had a similar appreciation for animals, including views about treating them with justice. See Gullason (1971) for three animal stories by Crane's father.

10. Influential discussions of the rights of the subhuman world have been offered by Hartshorne (1979), Passmore, and Singer (1979). Useful, too, are Dombowski and the special 1987 animal rights issue of *Monist*.

11. *Academy*, reviewing *The Open Boat and Other Tales of Adventure*, captured Crane's aptitude in two happy phrases. He was "the analytic chemist of the subconscious and the occasional betrayer of the night side of heroism" (*Critical Heritage* #87).

12. For accounts of animal imagery in *The Red Badge of Courage* see Marcus (1959, 1960) and Taylor. On a closely related issue, Taylor comments that Fleming's mental resolve is worthless because in Crane's account both courage and cowardice are matters of "biochemical processes" (132); and Frohock describes Fleming as "a packet of vulnerable flesh, capable of craven panic and unreasoning courage" (231). Of Fleming's courage and cowardice, Lively observes that "one had been as senseless as the other" (155); Kazin finds "in this book courage is as mechanical as desertion" (xiii); Beaver criticizes "the passionate heroism of Crane's pseudo-heroes" (193); and Kaplan notes that "at the boundaries of biological fate [Crane discovers] . . . the essence of naturalist heroism" (122).

As both screen writer and director, John Huston described his intention to portray in the movie version of *The Red Badge of Courage* "the ironically thin line between cowardice and heroism" and how "courage is as unreasoning as cowardice" (Ross 1964:228, 396). Huston's interpretation echoed, with some sixty years intervening, Higginson's comment that Fleming "first stumbles into cowardice, to his own amazement, and then is equally amazed at stumbling into courage" (*Critical Heritage* #46). Stevenson has contended that even though Stanley Kubrick's "grand sense of the ironic" dominates *Full Metal Jacket* (1987), the film is, nonetheless, "a twentieth-century parody of a famous nineteenth-century novel, *The Red Badge of Courage*" (43).

It is clear that the sort of courage involved in group actions *is* problematic for Crane. In *The Red Badge of Courage*, Fleming chafes when "the regiment . . . inclosed him. And there were iron laws of tradition and law on four sides. He was in a moving box" (101). In "The Price of the Harness," Nolan has similar suspicions, "although he himself was in the assault with the rest of them . . . his part, to his mind, was merely that of a man who was going along with the crowd" (1029–30).

In his study of naturalists London, Norris, Crane, and Dreiser, Mitchell argues that impoverished selves rather than oppressive environments rob naturalistic protagonists of autonomy and moral responsibility. Thus Fleming's lack of self-possession not "the madness of war" (110) makes his panic and his heroism equivalent.

13. Several reliable commentators, Bergon (1975), Gibson (1968), Holton, Solomon (1961), and Stallman (1952, 1958) among others, miss this moral point. The moral difference between the egoism of Collins's getting the water and his selfless compassion toward the wounded officer has been noted by La France (1971), but only Nagel (1975a) has offered a sustained analysis. Among the others, Gargano's note calls attention to two sorts of courage, and Krauth suggests that Crane was attempting a moral redefinition of courage. Both accounts, however, lack a discussion of what counts as moral, what as heroic, and what are the characteristics of hybrid, moral heroism.

This story strikingly anticipates Crane's own behavior under fire. Noxon reports that in Cuba "the moment the fighting began Crane started carrying buckets of water to the wounded" (6). Cora Crane pasted in her diary, "Oxtenbridges," this account by George Lynch, war correspondent in Cuba for the London *Chronicle:*

"A company under fire was badly in need of water, and water was seven miles away, down hill at that. Stephen collected all the tin canteens he could find and trotted off for the refreshment. Coming warily back, there was a sharp ping against one of the cans, and it began to leak. Stephen turned up the can and tried to stop the leak. An officer in the woods near by shouted to him:

"'Come here, quick! You're in the line of fire!'

"'If you've got a knife, cut a plug and bring it to me,' replied the young man, and, as he spoke, bang went a bullet against another can.

"'Come under cover, or you'll loose every can you've got!'

"This warning had its effect. The loss of the precious fluid terrified him in a way that the danger to himself had failed to do. He finally brought the water up to the thirsty company, and then fainted through exhaustion." (Identified in Cora's hand as an article from the *Saturday Evening Post,* April 8, 1899, part of the Barrett Collection, Alderman Library, University of Virginia, accession #5505e, box titled "Oxtenbridges Slipcase.")

14. Another philosophically interesting issue is whether Collins's reckless, selfish dare is not only pointless, false heroism but also an immoral act. Taking a serious risk without the possibility of comparable gain would be immoral in light of one's duties toward other soldiers, oneself, and God to preserve one's own life. Crane broached the possibility of a morally questionable suicide in Fleming's rescue of the colt, but not in Collins's dash for the water.

15. It is important to note that genuine human needs, as opposed to wants or desires, form the basis of Crane's moral position. For a discussion of needs versus wants, see Dooley and Ring.

16. To address the controversy surrounding the "flawed ending" of *The

Red Badge of Courage, I hold that Henry has significantly matured. Crane has allowed us to witness only two days in the development of a young man. They have been full days, replete with crucial experiences, but he is still a young man, and the war is not over. On the basis of his sobering moral realizations, Fleming has crossed the threshold into manhood. Wasserstrom calls Fleming, at the end of the novel, "an apprentice adult" (228).

Fleming's transformation is traceable to his realization that he alone has to carry the burden of self-forgiveness. Crane's language is clear. Fleming does not deny or block out his moral failure, "he mustered force to put the sin at a distance" (212). Within six months of his own death, in "War Memories," Crane reiterates "you can't fling [it] . . . carelessly over your shoulder and lose it. It follows you like the haunting memory of a sin" (6:247). With different emphases, the readings of Conder, Greenfield, Kapoor, Solomon (1966), and Stallman (1951) are compatible with this view of Fleming's growth. My interpretation that self-forgiveness, including self-acceptance, was the crucial event in Fleming's development was triggered by a sermon on the need to forgive oneself as well as others given in 1986 by Rev. Donald Staib of Immaculate Conception Church, Durham, N.C.

For sharply contrary readings, see Dunn, Schmitz, and Vidan. Dunn argues that *The Red Badge of Courage* is "a mock epic in prose" (280) and concludes that "Henry's acceptance of a self-assessment based on repression and denial of responsibility manifests his continuing self-deception" (276). Schmitz holds that "Fleming stumbles out of his ordeal a supple neurotic, busily revising his delusions" (450). Vidan, with no leniency for Fleming's immaturity, sees the novel as "essentially a study in bad faith . . . where Crane . . . presented Henry as a person without a moral centre and with no integrity" (108). Horsford concludes that even though Fleming has "undergone a kind of development . . . whether the figure Crane has presented would, in his future life, make anything constructive from those experiences is doubtful in the extreme" (126). Crews tries to have it both ways: Fleming, at the end, has "acquired new poise . . . he is no longer a boy but a competent soldier" (xx), but Crews also finds that Fleming settles into "manly self-deception" (xxiii).

Several commentators (see Mailloux and Schneider for listings of the spectrum of opinion) see varying degrees of irony in the ending of *The Red Badge of Courage.* Of most interest is Binder (1978), who, although emphasizing that Fleming's "betrayal of the tattered man haunts him as a sin more serious than his violation of conventional codes of heroism" (29), still contends that Crane's last chapter is fully ironic; "Henry does not change" (41). The first British review of *The Red Badge of Courage* by Marriott-Watson, writing for the Pall Mall *Gazette* in November 1895, also focused on Fleming's ill-treatment of the tattered man. Marriott-Watson concluded, however, that "out of this panic comes the redemption . . . [a] mental evolution"(*Critical Heritage* #30).

Much of Binder's case is tied to textual changes that he alleges were "forced upon" Crane by Appleton's editor Ripley Hitchcock. However, when

Stallman first published Crane's letters to Hitchcock, he offered the contrary opinion. "In the business of selling his stuff Crane was as shrewd a dealer as Hitchcock. . . . He had a hardheaded bargaining drive uncommon among artists" (1956:320).

On Crane's manuscript revisons, see Binder (1982) and Parker (1984, 1986). Pizer's 1979 article is an even-handed examination of the Binder-Parker stance. For the participants' view of the textual controversies surrounding the manuscript, before and after Crane presented it to Hamlin Garland and Ripley Hitchcock, and the debate over Fredson Bowers's version of *The Red Badge of Courage* for the University Press of Virginia's edition, see Mailloux, Parker (1984), and Pizer (1985). With regard to the expanded Norton edition, I agree with Pizer's conclusion that the 1895 Appleton first edition is clearly preferable for "the [expanded 1979] Norton *Red Badge* is just another new civil war novel, not as good as the novel it resembles and without its historical resonance" (1985a:156). Gibson concurs, arguing that the expunged passages so crucial to the Binder-Parker interpretation clearly do not "have the same standing as evidence drawn from the text as he [Crane] presented it to his publisher" (1988:48). See also Dooley (1992:69–70).

17. This view of Scully is shared by Gardner and Dunlap and Satterwhite. Satterwhite, in addition, sees all the characters involved in social complexity due to a failure to understand the Swede. While misinformation is surely a factor in his murder, the ethically significant fact is that no one is moved by the simple, moral datum that a human being needs help. The Swede's abrasive manner is also ethically irrelevant to the moral duty to aid him. See Dillingham, Holton, LaFrance (1971), Rooke, Westbrook (1959, 1962), and Wolter.

For contrary readings, see Geismar for Scully as a warm and generous host; Conder for a Scully with "good intentions" (35); and Gibson (1964) for a patient Scully who "does all within the range of his possibilities to protect the Swede" (391) so that "the Swede is primarily responsible for his own death" (395). McFarland sees Scully as the victim. Kent (1981) argues that all the characters, including the Swede, suffer from a lack of knowledge so that "at least three possible and contradictory interpretations for the meaning of the murder are presented" (266).

Crane's short story has been made into both a play and a film. The former, by Alberts, emphasizes Scully's fairness as a referee of the Johnny-Swede fistfight; the latter, by Kadar, features Scully's well-meaning hospitality and substantially changes the ending. Leaving the hotel, the Swede is knifed by a stranger. On Kadar's adaption, see Petrakis, Skaggs, and also Keenan, who argues that Kadar and screenwriter Harry Mark Petrakis have diminished "the story to a pointless reductive ending in which nothing more significant happens than an offensive boor is given his fatal comeuppance" (265).

18. For more on the Swede's hysteria, see Berryman (1950), who finds that "the Swede is wild to die" (213), and Monterio (1985), who sees the tale as "the chronicle of a loner moving toward self-destruction" (296). Stone stresses determinism to the point of reducing the story to a study of morbid ma-

nia, of the Swede's "not-to-be-denied death wish" (62). Unable to counte-
nance any interference in the Swede's behavior, Stone repudiates the entire
theme of collaboration as "Crane's failure to control the materials of his story" (65). Similarly, Law accounts for "the grim determinism of the story" (11)
by appealing to a demonic Scully. On fear in "The Blue Hotel," Sutton, as
well as Davidson and Knapp, sees the Swede as both instigator and victim.
Bergon (1979) casts the Swede as a traditional Western hero.

19. Follet first raised questions about the last section of Crane's story in
1929, but Stallman's strenuous and vociferous objections to it, "the off-key
tone of the appended section . . . the trumped-up theme announced in the
irrelevant and non-ironic conclusion" (1952:258) framed the issue for subsequent commentators. For example, Tanner has called the last section of
"The Blue Hotel" "a fairly clumsy addition to a brilliant psychological
study" (146).

20. For readings of Crane that ignore the contextual nature of ethical
judgments, see Lenehan and LaFrance (1967, 1971, 1972). The former argues
that ethical values, if not based on an absolute standard, become totally relative; the latter believes that values are a personal idiosyncrasy and simply a
matter of personal choice. LaFrance's "boot strap" morality reduces ethical
considerations to a single factor—personal sincerity. See Shulman for a balanced discussion of the role of context in both ethical and epistemological
judgments.

21. Another philosophical controversy is contained in a moral position
that requires positive aid (love) instead of refraining from harm (justice). The
history of ethics has seen extended discussion of the good samaritan. Was he
a minimally good and moral man, or was he an exemplary, ethically splendid person who should have been called the *heroically moral* samaritan? For
treatments of good samaritanism, the duty to rescue and heroic actions, see
Gewirth, Glebe-Moller, and Ratcliffe.

The distinction between ethical and heroic actions also turns upon the
extent of sacrifice involved and the potential good to be gained (Singer 1972),
and upon whether a biocentric, a homocentric, or theocentric worldview is
assumed (Dooley 1986.)

22. With regard to practical competence, French offers the interesting
suggestion that Fleming's achievement by the end of *The Red Badge of Courage* is a matter of practical maturation, "Henry Fleming has learned to make
the world work for him" (160). French concludes that Crane's contribution
to literary modernism was his depiction of the achievement of personal autonomy *within* society: "that the same individual might be both shrewd and
unexploitive enough to rise above the victimizing power of institutions
while remaining a functioning and even respected member of his home-town
society" (166). In effect, my analysis extends French's point, stressing
Crane's celebration of the steady, valuable contribution of society's everyday
heroes. For more on depictions of everyday competence in late-nineteenth-
century American literature, see McElderry's account of a Hamlin Garland-
Walt Whitman conversation about "the heroism of the common man" (373).

Crane's admiration for the heroic competence of ordinary soldiers is prominent in his Cuban war pieces "Regular Soldiers Get No Glory" and "War Memories." On the conduct of American soldiers in the Spanish-American War, see Bullard and Axeen, who perceptively analyzes late-nineteenth-century America's struggles with military valor when "the implements of modern war were manned by groups, not heroic individuals" (499). Another reporter in Cuba, Charles Michaelson, recalled Crane's intense curiosity about the businesslike bravery of the men in the ranks. Michaelson notes that while other news correspondents "were wondering if the next volley would splatter their way he was commenting on the rigidity of the men in columns of four, and the imperturbability of birds scolding each other while bullets cut the bushes on which they perched. He endowed his heroes with the same mental attitude, whose business of sheep-herding or boat-steering was not to be interfered with" (xv).

Crane's celebration of everyday competence has caused consternation in some of his interpreters. For example, Swann, insistent that Crane's worldview is radically nihilistic—"the world that Crane sees is one without sense" (100)—finds it necessary to renounce, as ironic and patronizing, Crane's endorsement of ordinary moral values, "it is hard to resist the impression that Crane is desperate to try to find positive, unironic values in the simplest places possible—and vilely over-playing his hand as he tries" (120).

23. Gullason (1975) casts Crane as a crusader, Elconin finds him cynical about reform efforts, and Edwards stresses the tension between intense individualism and strong humanitarian impulses in Crane.

24. Cooley, Ellison, Mayer (1973), Stallman (1968), and Starke have briefly discussed blacks in Crane; Halliburton's lengthy treatment of *The Monster* (particularly his section "The Question of Race") deserves careful reading. See also Mitchell (1990) and Wertheim (1989) on whether Henry Johnson's blackness is a central or an accidental element in Crane's story.

25. Written immediately after *George's Mother* was published, Boyce's review said of Mrs. Kelsey, "there is a touch of heroism in her soul, but it is the feminine heroism which endures rather than dares" (*Critical Heritage* 63). Trescott easily surpasses the ethical stamina of George's Mother. Gale's description of Trescott's behavior as "suicidal gratitude" (89) is a provocative and accurate assessment. Also helpful is Levinson's contention that *The Monster* retraces a pattern in Crane's own life: "the imprudent commitment and its consequences" (7:xvii).

26. Typical readings—Gibson (1968), Gullason (1960), Hilfer, Kahn, Mayer (1973), and Westbrook (1972)—of the moral issues involved in *The Monster* assume that Trescott stands for virtue and the rest of Whilomville represents vice. Wolford (1989) is especially insistent on this point. Crane, however, perceptively explores a wide range of behaviors (amoral, immoral, premoral, moral, and heroic) in the face of the challenges of life. Westbrook (1972), Spofford, Gullason (1960, 1972), Cooley (1983), and Pizer (1983) have difficulty handling the suggestions of the Twelve-Hagenthorpe delegation. On this point Ahnebrink is especially insistent, "they acted as they did be-

cause of their inability to oppose public opinion" (380). In my reading, the delegation's suggestions are not hypocritical and self-serving, but prudent and moral.

In addition, Gibson (1968), Gullason (1960), Kahn, and Mayer (1973) accuse Martha Goodwin of hypocrisy. As Quinn also notes, although no paragon of virtue, Martha Goodwin shows common sense and makes a sincere effort to head off fresh gossip about Dr. Trescott. It is notable that Gibson, Gullason (1960, 1972), and Kahn tie their condemnations of Martha to a remark in chapter 19 about Trescott, "'Serves him right if he was lose all his patients'" (434). However, this remark is not made by Martha but by her sister Kate.

For accounts that do not equate Trescott as good and Wilomville as bad, see Glen Johnson (1989), Monteiro (1972a), Nettles (1983), and Solomon (1966). In his informative analysis of the various games played by Whilomvillites, Morace, more than any other commentator, sees complexity and ambiguity in *The Monster*. However, his condemnation of the townspeople, criticism of the Twelve-Hagenthorpe delegation, and unstinting praise of Trescott's virtue fail to respect differences between moral and heroic behavior.

27. Among contemporary moral theorists, Toulmin's *An Examination of the Place of Reason in Ethics* has been an influential account of the contextual nature of ethical judgments. Toulmin argues that because morality's function is to harmonize desires within a community or culture, judgments of good and bad, right and wrong involve a calculation of the hurtful or beneficial consequences of changing an ongoing practice.

Because the normal frame of reference for ethical questions is an existing social practice, intercommunity and cross-cultural comparisons are unusual. Toulmin explains, for example, that wondering whether monogamy or polygamy is really good or really bad is logically equivalent to wondering whether the shortest distance between two points is a straight or curved line. In both disputes, a context (Christian versus Islamic society, or Euclidian versus non-Euclidian geometry) must be specified. Toulmin, like Crane, believes that ethical questions that transcend communities or cultures involve special difficulties. It is also is clear that Toulmin's approach endorses Crane's view that appreciating another culture and judging the value of its life-style requires tolerance, patience, and wisdom.

5. Philosoher-Poet

1. Colvert (1982) comments that Crane's Syracuse friends found him "giftedly profane" (102). Forty years later, his teammate French vividly remembered Crane's swearing skills on the baseball field.

2. Recall Crane's description of the crew in "The Open Boat," frustrated that no one on the shore notices their plight. "Four scowling men sat in the dingey and surpassed records in the invention of epithets" (893).

For more on swearing and boats, see Crane's letter to Willis Brooks Hawkins, November 19, 1895, "I lost my temper to-day—fully—absolutely—for the first time in a good many years. I sailed the cat-boat up to the lake in the stiffest breeze we've had in moons. When I got near to the head of the lake, the boat was scudding before the wind in a manner to make your heart leap. Then we got striking snags—hidden stumps, floating logs, sunken brush, more stumps, . . . Up to the 5th stump I had not lost my philosophy but at the 22nd I was swearing like cracked ice. At the appearance of the 164th, I perched on the rail, a wild and gibbering maniac" (*Correspondence* #138). Crane's letter was posted at Hartwood, where he no doubt had profited from an outstanding swearing role model, a guide at the Hartwood Club, Lewis C. Boyd. Cambell's history of Hartwood, *Traditions of Hartwood*, says of Boyd: "'Lew,' as he was familiarly known, served the Club in various important capacities during the first six years of the organization's existence [1893–99], particularly as guide on hunting expeditions. As a young man he was gaunt, rugged and powerful and admirably adapted to the necessities of the wilderness. He possessed an unconscious and continuous efficiency in picturesque profanity—seldom equalled and perhaps never surpassed. He knew the country and the game trails and was an agreeable companion in spite of his vehement and at times embarrassing speech" (56).

3. The typed letters are in the Barrett Crane Collection, accession #5505, box 5, University of Virginia Library.

4. Crane felt handicapped not knowing the native language when he covered the Greco-Turkish War.

5. Ironically, William, Stephen's older brother and executor of his estate, selected as the inscription on his gravemarker, "Stephen Crane, Poet-Author/1871–1900." On the matter of an inscription, Cora consulted William Dean Howells, who wrote her, "I would so willingly help you about words for your husband's monument if I were good for anything in that way" (*Stephen Crane: Letters* 306).

For details on the estate, which William had to administer, see Katz (1982). On William's well-deserved reputation as a skinflint, see Sorrentino (1981). Schoberlin's unpublished biography, "Flagon of Despair," contains details of William's earlier questionable handling of the estate of his and Stephen's mother. "His twenty-fifth birthday, however, was important in other ways—and to his brothers and sister as well. By the terms of his mother's will, inasmuch as he had refused to continue in college, her estate was now liable to division among her seven surviving children. More than likely Stevie had abandoned reporting in anticipation of receiving a sizeable inheritance—one-seventh share of twenty thousand dollars, $2,857, or about that figure. Nevertheless, William Crane, who was now administering the estate alone, had discouraging news to report to the family: their mother's estate was worth only an insignificant fraction of the value he had sworn in court; furthermore, he said, the coal royalties did not even pay his fee as trustee; to all ostensible purposes the leases were practically worthless. His mathematics is disturbing, to say the least. Actually, as trustee of the estate, he was receiving for each one-seventh share an annual royalty payment of $186.83, of which, if we ignore the rest of Mrs. Crane's estate, her Asbury Park properties and whatever remained of Jonathan's fortune, and after deducting William's fees—each of the heirs should have received [a yearly royalty share of] $182.96. They received nothing, but William volunteered or agreed to purchase the other six shares at ridiculously low figures. By this means he eventually came to control five-sevenths of his mother's estate. The exact amount he paid to Stevie for his share is irretrievably obscured by legend; certainly it did not exceed one thousand dollars, and it was probably considerably less" (Book 2:8, 43–44). Also see Gullason (1968b) for more on Mrs. Crane's estate and will.

6. Wertheim and Sorrentino argue that Crane's attempts to distance himself from poetry were a ploy to present himself to Nellie Crouse as a respectable, established author. "Crane wished to convey an image of himself as a conventional, ambitious young man who shunned the bohemian and effete application of 'poet'" (172). At least with respect to *The Black Riders*, Blair takes the matter of ploys the other direction, depicting Crane as a youthful, bohemian poseur

Crane's allergic reaction to "poet" was evident in numerous ways. He had several reasons for absenting himself from John Barry's reading of his "lines" before the Uncut Leaves Society. First, the guest of honor that evening was Mrs. Frances Burnett, whose *Little Lord Fauntleroy* Crane despised. Many of Crane's Whilomville stories have as their target the Little Lord Fauntleroy image of childhood. (Linson's version of the Uncut Leaves affair insists that "it was Fauntleroy's fault" [1958:55] that Crane refused to read his own lines.) Second, also in attendance were Mrs. Edmund Clarence Stedman and Mrs. Richard Henry Stoddard, whose poetry, along with that of Richard Watson Gilder, Crane also disliked. Third, and more generally, Crane abhorred the nineteenth-century schoolroom practice of memorizing poetry. His "Making an Orator" (7:158–63) is a satirical retelling of his own painful experience with a recitation of Tennyson's "The Charge of the Light Brigade."

Crane must have enjoyed a review in the New York *World* during February 1896 in which Jeannette Gilder (Richard Watson Gilder's sister) complained that "Do not weep, maiden, for war is kind" was "not poetry as Tennyson understood it" (quoted by Stallman, 1958:567).

7. Levenson has not reprinted eighteen of the poems from the University Press of Virginia's critical edition. In this chapter, then, I will cite the number of the poem from the Virginia edition, followed by, if appropriate, the page number from Levenson's *Crane: Prose and Poetry. BR* indicates a poem from *The Black Riders; WK*, a selection from *War Is Kind.*

In most cases, I have quoted Crane's poems in their entirety for three reasons. His poems are short; most readers are unfamiliar with all but a handful; and, most important, in an examination of Crane's poetry for philosophical statement, a poem, as a whole, states an argument. On this last point, Stallman (1958) sees a "syllogistic" (574) structure in many of Crane's poems, Untermeyer notes their "clenched" (448) argumentation, and Waggoner finds that argument is "primary" in Crane's verses.

8. Colvert (1984) estimates that the whole period of composition was about three months. See Fryckstedt (1962a) for an exhaustive attempt to date Crane's composition of *The Black Riders*, including the story that he "wrote the poems during three days in a fit of inspiration" (291–92).

9. Katz (1966b) explains that Barry and Copeland were Harvard college mates, prompting Barry to put Crane in touch with Copeland and Day, publishers of *The Black Riders*. Also see Wertheim and Sorrentino on this point. Cady and Wells have reprinted the April 26, 1894 New York *Daily Tribune* article, "They Read from Unpublished Stories," on the Uncut Leaves affair. "John D. Barry read several unnamed poems from the pen of Stephen Crane, who, according to Mr. Barry, was too modest to read them himself, in fact, the poet made the assertion that he 'would rather die than do it'" (48).

Garland (1900) and Linson (1903, 1958) have more on Barry's reading of Crane's poetry for the Uncut Leaves Society. Linson describes how flattered Crane was with Barry's invitation: "So when John D. Barry wanted some of his 'Lines' read at a gathering of notables [the Uncut Leaves Society], Steve was naturally elated, but it was not because of the notables. It was because Mr. Barry, whom he respected as critic and valued as a friend, thought enough of his work to want to read it. It was the seal of a high approval" (1958:54). Although Crane refused to read his poetry in public, he was eager for news about its reception, asking Garland in a letter of April 18, 1894, "I hope you have heard about the Uncut Leaves affair" (*Correspondence* #33).

10. Hubbard's support of Crane was extensive—twenty-one of his items, mostly poems, were published in the *Philistine;* see Dickason (1943). Bruce White's account is even better. Harry Thurston Peck's *Bookman* also gave important endorsement, printing twelve of Crane's poems, see Katz (1966b).

11. See Miller for a helpful discussion of Crane's "conception of poetry as the rendering of dramatic conflict" (342).

12. Crane's "Legends" poems (#118–23, 1346–47) were the poems printed as prose in the May 1896 *Bookman;* see Hoffman (1957:224, 281–82). Also see Schoberlin (1949) for several excerpts of Crane's prose arranged as poetry and Hoffman's comments about "the enigma of Crane's apparently 'prosiac' verse and 'poetic' fiction" (220). The conclusion of Hoffman's study puts the point dramatically. After a brief consideration of themes and symbols in "The Open Boat," Hoffman turns to Crane's final line, "and they felt that they could then be interpreters" (909). He argues, "The truth of the correspondent's interpretation lies not in his last impressions but in the manner in which he recreates the entire experience in the reader's imagination. And the techniques Crane uses for this purpose, I suggest, are essentially the techniques of poetry. 'The Open Boat' is his greatest poem. We may take license for so considering it from Crane's own repudiation of the formal distinctions between prose and verse, as well as from his incorporation into the tale of formal elements apparently of poetic derivation" (278).

13. Opinions vary on the relationship between Crane's early and later poetry. Berryman (1950), Colvert (1975), and Gillis see sharp differences. Blair, Hoffman (1957), and Monroe see the later as a sophistication of the

early. Katz (1966b) sees in the later "commercial qualities" (xlix), and Lowell judges the later to be a retrograde of the early. I agree with LaFrance (1971) that "*all* of Crane's poetry . . . forms a distinct unit" (131), and Westbrook (1963), who finds in his poetry "a single and coherent standard of values" (25). Halliburton's lengthly chapter "The Farther Shore: Poems" discusses virtually all of Crane's published and unpublished poems.

14. Miller observes that "among the sixty-eight poems in *The Black Riders* there are twenty-three poems in which a character says this man is a fool or laughs outright at him" (335). She agrees that epistemology is a primary concern in Crane's poetry: "in *The Black Riders* fourteen [poems] ponder the nature of truth. The next largest number, thirteen, inquire into the nature of God. But since Crane wonders if God can be known, what are His attributes, what is the truth about God, his quest for truth and his search for the meaning of God are so interrelated we may look upon all twenty-seven poems as having a similar concern. The remaining forty-one poems, indeed all the rest of the poems in the canon, have for their subject matter various applications of this pervasive search for truth" (334).

15. Elsewhere, Socrates' contention that inflicting harm on his own soul by committing an injustice was more fatal than his enemies' ability to injure his body is mirrored in another of Crane's poems: "A man feared that he might find an assassin;/Another that he might find a victim./One was more wise than the other" (*BR* #56, 1319). Bergon (1975) applies this poem to the Swede and the gambler in "The Blue Hotel."

16. Nelson (1963) praises Crane's skill at "dramatic irony" although he, inexplicably, takes the line "Old, old man, it is the wisdom of the age" literally, stating that the poet-speaker believes that a newspaper provides "the analysis and judgment of events which provides a basis of wisdom" (572). Itabashi argues that the sage's reliance on a newspaper creates a "comic situation" (9). See Marcus (1966) for more on irony in Crane's poetry.

17. This poem is a gloss on Revelation 10:9–10: "So I went to the angel and he told me to give me the little scroll; and he said to me, 'Take it and eat; it will be bitter to your stomach, but sweet as honey in your mouth.' And I took the little scroll from the hand of the angel and ate it; it was sweet as honey in my mouth, but when I had eaten it my stomach was made bitter." Likewise, "I stood upon a highway" (*BR* #36, 1310) is a gloss on Revelation 6:5–6.

18. On this point, as well as for most other matters in Crane's poetry, especially family influences and literary sources, Hoffman (1957) is the standard reference. On the former, his chapter "War in Heaven" analyzes the theology of Crane's father, his mother, and his mother's father, Bishop Jesse Peck. His treatment (53–62) of "The Depraved Heart" from Peck's treatise *What Must I Do to Be Saved?* is illuminating. On the latter, his chapter "Styles, Sources, Symbols," convincingly establishes the influence of the fables of Ambrose Bierce and the verses of the South African Olive Schreiner. For more on Crane and Schreiner, see Kindelien. James M. Cox suggests that Bunyan's *The Pilgrim's Progress* was the source for *The Black Riders*.

La France (1971) and Wertheim (1963) also discuss differences between the theologies of Crane's parents.

19. See Westbrook (1963) for a treatment of the soul's despair in Crane's poetry.

20. Hume's argument is contained in *Dialogues Concerning Natural Religion,* especially Parts 10 and 11. The most accessible discussion of Hume's argument is found in Pike.

21. For more on James's finite God see Dooley (1976).

22. These phrases occur in *The Meaning of Truth.*

23. In late August 1894 Crane wrote to Copeland and Day, "I would like to hear from you concerning my poetry" (*Correspondence* #42). Their response included the news that several of the poems he had submitted were unacceptable. He responded on September 9: "Dear sirs:—We disagree on a multitude of points. In the first place I should absolutely refuse to have my poems printed without many of those which you just as absolutely mark 'No.' It seems to me that you cut all the ethical sense out of the book. All the anarchy, perhaps. It is the anarchy which I particularly insist upon. From the poems which you keep you could produce what might be termed a 'nice little volume of verse by Stephen Crane' but for me there would be no satisfaction. The ones which refer to God, I believe you condemn altogether. I am obliged to have them in when my book is printed. There are some which I believe unworthy of print. These I herewith enclose. As for the others, I cannot give them up—in the book" (*Correspondence* #44). A compromise was struck, with Crane withdrawing seven poems. Three of these were lost. Of those remaining, "There was a man with a tongue of wood" (*WK* #84, 1332), "A god came to a man" (109), and "One came from the sky" (#110) reflect Crane's ethical sense, while "To the maiden" (*WK* #71, 1326–27) is anarchical. Anarchical, too, "The ocean said to me once" (*BR* #38, 1312) depicts the sea as the grim reaper.

24. In this poem, the word *god* is not capitalized except when the man responds to *God.* Crane did not seem to follow a particular pattern on the matter of God or god, Gods or gods. He was, however, clearly attentive to *One* and *He* in the *Black Riders* version and *one* and *he* in the *War is Kind* versions of "There was One I met upon the road." Although the *Black Riders* version initially appeared in capital letters throughout, Crane's holograph manuscript (at Columbia University) contains *One* and *He.* See Bowers (1975) for details on textual variants. Both Baron and Crosland have compiled concordances of Crane's poetry; Crosland's is keyed to the University Press of Virginia's edition.

25. Hoffman (1957:50) has reprinted from *Holiness the Birthright of All God's Children* (1874) Crane's father's treatment of Eve's temptation. Also see the second stanza of Crane's "There was a man and a woman" (*BR* #61, 1321) for another treatment of the sin of Adam and Eve. Itabashi explicates the second and third stanzas with reference to Dr. Trescott and *The Monster,* as well as Crane's defense of Dora Clark, "Adventures of a Novelist" (865–70). The poem's first stanza applies to Pete of *Maggie.*

26. See Westbrook (1963) for more on this poem. Westbrook (and I concur) paraphrases the last line as "the value represented by the ball of gold exists, but must be seen in perspective—obliquely, from a distance—or else be distorted" (29). For a contrary view, see Hoffman (1957:201–2), whose interpretation requires an ironic reading.

27. See Colvert (1967, 1975) and Halliburton for the little man in Crane's poetry and in the Sullivan County tales.

28. See Nagel (1975) and Neal J. Osborn for discussions of this poem in "The Clan of No-Name."

29. Westbrook's (1963) phrase "the theme of experience as a discipline" (33) succently captures the pragmatic impulse in Crane's writings. Katz (1966a) argues that Crane's experiences in the Greco-Turkish War are evident in "The Blue Battalions."

30. I heartily endorse Hoffman's remark, "one does not forget this poem. The simplicity of the concluding image is the source of its power" (1958:143).

31. See Earle, Gadamer, and Wild for accessible general discussions of phenomenology; the standard full-length treatment, as foreboding as it is valuable, is Speigelburg. On process metaphysics, Hartshorne (1932) and Rescher are of value. See Whitehead for a lengthy treatment, including the place of change and process in the thought of Peirce, James, Royce, and Dewey.

32. See Rosenblatt (1978, 1985) for accounts of her use of "transactions" for readers-text interaction as well as for the use of the same term in *Knowing and the Known* by Dewey and Bently.

33. Benfey is quite correct: "even the slightest of his newspaper sketches is worth reading, for his angular vision and luminous, unexpected sense of detail" (34). Earlier, Weimer commented, "it is as though what others accept as normal Crane sees as tortured; or as though he detects what is fantastic in the accustomed" (57).

34. "Death and the Child" is replete with process images; Levinson's (1970) comparison (5:lxxvii–lxxxii) of the draft and final version of this tale stresses this point. See also Colvert's (1971) comments on "the imagery of violent motion of which Crane was a particular master" (9:xxviii).

35. Crane's most powerful account of the tragedies of illusion, conceit, and cultural naiveté occur when he follows the "shaky and quick-eyed" (799) Swede from Scully's Blue Hotel to the saloon.

36. The quotations in this last paragraph are taken from "New Invasion of Britain" (8:680), "'God Rest Ye, Merry Gentlemen'" (1069), "The Bride Comes to Yellow Sky" (798), and "The Devil's Acre" (8:667). Many commentators have attempted to capture Crane's spare and episodic style. Two of the best attempts occur in early reviews. Norris, reviewing *Maggie* in 1896, described Crane's craft as a "habit and aptitude for making phrases—short, terse epigrams struck off in the heat of composition, sparks merely, that cast a momentary gleam of light upon whole phases of life" (13). In the November 2, 1895 review in *Bookman*, Banks said of *The Red Badge of Courage*:

"The short, sharp sentences hurled without sequence give one the feeling of being pelted from different angles by hail—hail that is hot" (*Critical Heritage* #32). Also helpful is Beer's description: "He wrote a staccato, nervous prose with selected adjectives placed in a manner that astonished Henry James" (1922:63). Bates explains Crane's technique in utilizing episodes as a "method by which the story is told not by the carefully engineered plot but by the implication of certain isolated incidents, by the capture and significant arrangement of casual, episodic moments" (70).

Works Cited

Adams, Richard P. "Naturalistic Fiction: 'The Open Boat.'" *Tulane Studies in English* 4 (1954):137–46.

Ahnebrink, Lars. "Ibsen and Crane." In *The Beginnings of Naturalism in American Fiction, 1891–1903*, 378–81. 1950. Reprint. New York: Russell and Russell, 1961.

Alberts, Frank. "*The Blue Hotel:* A Play in Three Acts Based on the Story by Stephen Crane." *Theater* 2 (1960):27–42.

Albrecht, Robert, C. "Content and Style in *The Red Badge of Courage.*" *College English* 27 (1966):487–92.

Allen, Frederic Lewis. *Paul Revere Reynolds.* New York: Printed privately, 1944.

Alternbernd, Lynn, and Leslie L. Lewis. "The Elements of Fiction: Stephen Crane's 'The Open Boat.'" In *A Handbook for the Study of Fiction*, 29–80. London: Macmillan, 1966.

"Animal Rights." Special issue of *Monist* 70 (January 1987).

Arnold, Hans. "Stephen Crane's 'Woming Valley Tales': Their Source and Their Place in the Author's War Fiction." *Jahrbuch fur Amerikastudien* 4 (1959):161–69.

"The Author of *The Red Badge of Courage.*" *The Critic*, March 7, 1896, 163.

Autrey, Max L. "The Word out of the Sea: A View of Crane's 'The Open Boat.'" *Arizona Quarterly* 30 (1974):101–10.

Axeen, David. "'Heroes of the Engine Room': American 'Civilization' and the War with Spain." *American Quarterly* 36 (1984):481–502.

Ayers, Robert W. "W. D. Howells and Stephen Crane: Some Unpublished Letters." *American Literature* 28 (1957):469–77.

Bacheller, Irving. "The Rungs in My Little Ladder." *American Magazine* 85 (April 1918):19, 79–80, 83–84, 86, 88.

———. "The High-Brow Decade." In *Coming Up the Road*, 267–316. Indianapolis: Bobbs-Merrill, 1928.

———. "Genius." In *From Stores of Memory*, 110–18. New York: Farrar & Rinhart, 1938.

Baron, Herman. *A Concordance of the Poetry of Stephen Crane.* Boston: G. K. Hall, 1974.

Barry, John D. "A Note on Stephen Crane." *The Bookman* 13 (April 1901):148.

Bassan, Maurice. "Misery and Society: Some New Perspectives on Stephen Crane's Fiction." *Studia Neophilologia* 35 (1963):104–20.

———. "The Design of Stephen Crane's Bowery 'Experiment.'" *Studies in Short Fiction* 1 (1964):129–32.

———. "Stephen Crane and 'The Eternal Mystery of Social Condition.'" *Nineteenth-Century Fiction* 19 (1965):387–94.

———. Introduction. In *Stephen Crane: A Collection of Critical Essays*, 1–11. Englewood Cliffs: Prentice-Hall, 1967.

Bates, H. E. "Americans after Poe: Crane." In *The Modern Short Story*, 65–71. Boston: The Writer Inc., 1941.

Baum, Joan H., ed. *Stephen Crane: An Exhibition*. New York: Columbia University Library, 1956.

Beards, Richard D. "Stereotyping in Modern American Fiction: Some Solitary Swedish Madmen." *Moderna Sprak* 63 (1969):329–37.

Beaver, Harold. "Stephen Crane: The Hero as Victim." *Yearbook of English Studies* 12 (1982):186–93.

Beer, Thomas. "Stephen, Henry and the Hat." *Vanity Fair* 18 (1922):63, 88.

———. *Stephen Crane: A Study in American Literature*. New York: Knopf, 1923.

———. "Fire Feathers." *Saturday Review of Literature* 2 (1925):425–27.

———. *The Mauve Decade: American Life at the End of the Nineteenth Century*. New York: Knopf, 1926.

Begley, Sharon. "Found: Crane's 'Open Boat.'" *Newsweek*, January 5, 1987, 52.

Bender, Bert. "Hanging Stephen Crane in the Impressionist Museum." *Journal of Aesthetics and Art Criticism* 35 (1976):47–55.

———. "The Nature and Significance of 'Experience' in 'The Open Boat.'" *Journal of Narrative Technique* 9 (1979):70–80.

———. "The Experience of Brotherhood in 'The Open Boat.'" In *Sea Brothers: The Tradition of American Sea Fiction from "Moby Dick" to the Present*, 68–82. Philadelphia: University of Pennsylvania Press, 1988.

Benfy, Christopher. "The Courage of Stephen Crane." *New York Review of Books*, March 16, 1989, 31–34.

Bergon, Frank. *Stephen Crane's Artistry*. New York: Columbia University Press, 1975.

———. Introduction. In *The Western Writings of Stephen Crane*, 1–27. New York: New American Library, 1979.

Berkelman, Robert. "Mrs. Grundy and Richard Watson Gilder." *American Literature* 4 (1952):66–72.

Berryman, John. *Stephen Crane*. New York: William Sloan, 1950.

———. "The Open Boat." In *The Freedom of the Poet*, 176–84. New York: Farrar, Straus & Geroux, 1976.

Binder, Henry. "*The Red Badge of Courage* Nobody Knows." *Studies in the Novel* 10 (1978):9–47.

————. "*The Red Badge of Courage* Nobody Knows: Expanded Version." In Stephen Crane, *The Red Badge of Courage,* 111–58. New York: Norton, 1982.

Blair, John. "The Posture of a Bohemian in the Poetry of Stephen Crane." *American Literature* 61 (1989):215–29.

Bowers, Fredson. "The Text, History and Analysis." In *The Works of Stephen Crane.* Vol. 10: *Poetry and Literary Remains,* 189–281. Charlottesville: University Press of Virginia, 1975.

————. "Editing a Philosopher: The Works of William James." *Analytical and Enumerative Bibliography* 4 (1980):3–36.

Brennan, Joseph. "The Imagery and Art of *George's Mother.*" *College Language Association Journal* 4 (1960):106–15.

————. "Ironic and Symbolic Structure in Crane's *Maggie.*" *Nineteenth-Century Fiction* 16 (1962):303–35.

————. "Stephen Crane and the Limits of Irony." *Criticism* 11 (1969):180–220.

Brooks, Van Wyke. Introduction. In Stephen Crane, *Maggie and George's Mother,* 5–8. Greenwich: Fawcett, 1960.

Brown, Charles. *The Correspondents' War: Journalists in the Spanish-American War.* New York: Charles Scribner's Sons, 1967.

Brown, Curtis. "Some Old *Press* Men." In *Contacts,* 254–80. New York: Harper and Brothers, 1935.

Browne, Junius Henri, "The Philosophy of Meliorism." *Forum* 22 (1897):624–32.

Budd, Louis, J. "Objectivity and Low Seriousness in American Naturalism." *Prospects* 1 (1975):41–61.

Buitenhuis, Peter. "The Essentials of Life: 'The Open Boat' as Existentialist Fiction." *Modern Fiction Studies* 5 (1959):243–50.

Bullard, Frederick. L. "Reporting the Spanish American War." In *Famous War Correspondents,* 409–24. New York: Beckman, 1974.

Burhans, Clinton S. "Judging Henry Judging: Point of View in *The Red Badge of Courage.*" *Ball State University Forum* 15 (1974):38–48.

Burns, Landon C. "On 'The Open Boat.'" *Studies in Short Fiction* 3 (1966):455–57.

Cady, Edwin H. "Stephen Crane and the Strenuous Life." *English Literary History* 28 (1961):376–82.

————. *Stephen Crane.* Boston: Twayne, 1962. Rev. ed. 1980.

————. "Stephen Crane: *Maggie, A Girl of the Streets.*" In *Landmarks of American Writing,* 172–81. Ed. Henning Cohen. New York: Basic Books, 1969.

————, and Lester G. Wells, eds. *Stephen Crane's Love Letters to Nellie Crouse.* Syracuse: Syracuse University Press, 1954.

Cambell, Charles A. *Traditions of Hartwood.* Winter Park: Orange Press, 1930.

Carmichael, Otto. "Stephen Crane in Havana." *Prairie Schooner* 42 (1969):200–204.

Cassady, Edward E. "Muckraking in the Gilded Age." *American Literature* 13 (1941):134–41.

Cather, Willa. "When I Knew Stephen Crane." *Prairie Schooner* 23 (1949):231–36.

Cazemajou, Jean. *Stephen Crane.* Minneapolis: University of Minnesota Press, 1969.

Charvat, William. "Literature as Business." In *Literary History of the United States,* 953–68. Ed. Robert Spiller et al. New York: Macmillan, 1948.

Chew, Samuel C. "The House of Appleton." In *Fruit Among the Leaves: An Aniversary Anthology,* 3–66. New York: Appleton-Century- Crofts, 1950.

Churchill, Allen. "The Pulitzer World" and "The Favored Ones: Stephen Crane and Richard Harding Davis." In *Park Row,* 27–44, 194–213. New York: Rinehart & Company, 1958.

Clark, John G. "Reform Currents in Polite Monthly Magazines, 1880–1900." *Mid-America* 47 (1965):3–23.

Clendenning, John. *The Life and Thought of Josiah Royce.* Madison: University of Wisconsin Press, 1985.

Cline, H. F. "Benjamin Orange Flower and the Arena, 1889–1909." *Journalism Quarterly* 17 (1940a):139–50, 171.

———. "Flower and the Arena: Purpose and Content." *Journalism Quarterly* 17 (1940b):247–57.

Cockerill, John A. "Some Phases of Contemporary Journalism." *Cosmopolitan* 13 (October 1892):695–703.

Colvert, James. "Style and Meaning in Stephen Crane: 'The Open Boat.'" *Texas Studies in English* 38 (1958):34–45.

———. "Structure and Theme in Stephen Crane's Fiction." *Modern Fiction Studies* 5 (1959):199–208.

———. Introduction. In *Great Short Works of Stephen Crane,* vii–xv. New York: Harper and Row, 1965.

———. "Stephen Crane's Magic Mountain." In *Stephen Crane: A Collection of Critical Essays,* 95–105. Ed. Maurice Bassan. New York: Prentice-Hall, 1967.

———. Introduction. In *The Works of Stephen Crane.* Vol 9: *Reports of War,* xix–xxix. Ed. Fredson Bowers. Charlottesville: University of Virginia Press, 1971.

———. "Stephen Crane: Style as Invention." In *Stephen Crane in Transition,* 127–52. Ed. Joseph Katz. DeKalb: Northern Illinois University Press, 1972.

———. Introduction. In *The Works of Stephen Crane.* Vol. 10: *Poems and Literary Remains,* xvii–xxix. Ed. Fredson Bowers. Charlottesville: University of Virginia Press, 1975.

———. "Stephen Crane's Literary Origins and Tolystoy's *Sebastopol.*" *Comparative Literature Studies* 15 (1977):66–82.

———. "Stephen Crane." In *American Realists and Naturalists,* 100–124. Ed. Donald Pizer and Earl N. Harbert. Detroit: Gale Research, 1982.

———. *Stephen Crane*. New York: Harcourt Brace Jovanovich, 1984.

———. "Searching for Stephen Crane: The Schoberlin Collection." *Courier* 21 (1986):5–34.

Conder, John J. *Naturalism in American Fiction: The Classical Phase*. Lexington: University Press of Kentucky. 1984.

Conrad, Joseph. "Stephen Crane: A Note without Dates." *The Bookman* 50 (1920):529–31.

———. Introduction. In Thomas Beer, *Stephen Crane: A Study of American Letters*, 1–33. New York: Knopf, 1923.

Conser, Walter, Jr. "The Reassessment of Josiah Royce." *American Studies* 27, no. 2 (1986):54–60.

Cooley, John R. "*The Monster*—Stephen Crane's 'Invisible Man.'" *Markham Review* 5 (1975):10–14.

———. "Stephen Crane's 'The Monster.'" In *Savages and Naturals: Black Portraits by White Authors in Modern American Literature*, 38–49. Newark: University of Delaware Press, 1982.

Covici, Pascal, Jr. Introduction. In Stephen Crane, *The Red Badge of Courage*, 7–34. New York: Penguin Books, 1983.

Cox, James M. "*The Pilgrim's Progress* as Source for Stephen Crane's *The Black Riders*." *American Literature* 28 (1957):478–87.

Cox, James Trammell. "Stephen Crane as Symbolic Naturalist: An Analysis of 'The Blue Hotel.'" *Modern Fiction Studies* (1957):147–58.

———. "The Imagery of *The Red Badge of Courage*." *Modern Fiction Studies* 5 (1959):209–19.

Crane, Helen R. "My Uncle, Stephen Crane." *American Mercury* 31 (1934):24–29.

Crane, Stephen. "A Tent in Agony." *Cosmopolitan* 14 (December 1892):241–44.

———. *Stephen Crane: Letters*. Ed. Robert Stallman and Lillian Gilkes. New York: New York University Press, 1960.

———. *Works of Stephen Crane*. Ed. Fredson Bowers. Charlottesville: University Press of Virginia, Vol. 2, 1975; Vol. 6, 1970; Vol. 8, 1973; Vol. 9, 1971; Vol. 10, 1975.

———. *Stephen Crane: Prose and Poetry*. Ed. J. C. Levenson. New York: Library of America, 1984.

———. *The Correspondence of Stephen Crane*. Ed. Stanley Wertheim and Paul Sorrentino. New York: Columbia University Press, 1988.

Craven, Thomas. "Stephen Crane." *The Freeman* 8 (1924):475–77.

Crews, Frederic. Introduction. In Stephen Crane, *The Red Badge of Courage*, vii–xxii. Indianapolis: Bobbs-Merril, 1964.

Crosland, Andrew T. *A Concordance to the Complete Poetry of Stephen Crane*. Detroit: Gale Research, 1975.

Daskam, Josephine Dodge. "The Distinction of Our Poetry." *Atlantic* 87 (May 1901):696–705.

Davidson, Richard Allen. "Crane's 'Blue Hotel' Revisited: The Illusion of Fate." *Modern Fiction Studies* 15 (1970):537–39.

Davis, Richard Harding. "Our War Correspondents in Cuba and Puerto Rico." *Harper's New Monthly Magazine* (May 1899):938–48.

Day, Cyrus. "Stephen Crane and the Ten-foot Dinghy." *Boston University Studies in English* 3 (1957):193–213.

Deamer, Robert Glen. "Stephen Crane and the Western Myth." *Western American Literature* 7 (1972):111–23.

———. Review of Frank Bergon, *Stephen Crane's Artistry. Western American Literature* 12 (1977):335–37.

———. "Remarks on the Western Stance of Stephen Crane." *Western American Literature* 15 (1980):123–41.

Delbanco, Andrew. "The Disenchanted Eye." *New Republic,* July 11, 1988, 33–36.

Denny, Neville. "Imagination and Experience in Stephen Crane." *English Studies in Africa* 9 (1966):28–42.

Dewey, John. *Experience and Nature.* 2d ed. LaSalle: Open Court, 1925.

———, and A. F. Bently. *Knowing and the Known.* Boston: Beacon Press, 1949.

Dickason, David H. "Benjamin Orange Flower, Patron of the Realists." *American Literature* 14 (1942):148–56.

———. "Stephen Crane and the *Philistine.*" *American Literature* 15 (1943):279–87.

Dietz, Rudolph F. "Crane's *The Red Badge of Courage.*" *The Explicator* 42 (1984):37–38.

Dillingham, William. B. "'The Blue Hotel' and the Gentle Reader." *Studies in Short Fiction* 1 (1964):224–26.

Dombrowksi, Daniel A. *Hartshorne and the Metaphysics of Animal Rights.* Albany: State University of New York Press, 1988.

Dooley, Patrick K. "The Nature of Belief: The Proper Context for William James's 'The Will to Believe.'" *Transactions of the C. S. Peirce Society* 8 (1972):141–51.

———. *Pragmatism as Humanism: The Philosophy of William James.* Chicago: Nelson-Hall, 1974.

———. "William James's Concept of Rationality and a Finite God." In *Bicentennial Symposium of Philosophy,* 356–61. New York: CUNY Press, 1976.

———. "Darwinian Survival in James's Psychology and Religious Philosophy." *Research Journal of Philosophy and Social Sciences* 5 (1985):17–25.

———. "The Ambiguity of Environmental Ethics: Duty or Heroism." *Philosophy Today* 30 (1986):48–57.

———, and Raymond J. Ring. "Ethical and Economic Responsibilities of Affluence." *Philosophy Today* 27 (1983):77–84.

———. *Stephen Crane: An Annotated Bibliography of Secondary Scholarship.* New York: G.K. Hall, 1992.

Duffey, Bernard I. "Hamlin Garland's 'Decline' from Realism." *American Literature* 25 (1953):69–74.

———. "Mr. Koener's Reply Considered." *American Literature* 26 (1954):432–35.

Dunn, N. E. "The Common Man's *Iliad*." *Comparative Literature Studies* 21 (1984):270–81.

Earle, William. "Husserl's Phenomenology and Existentalism." *Journal of Philosophy* 57 (1960):75–95.

Edwards, Forest C. "Decorum: Its Genesis and Function in Stephen Crane." *Texas Quarterly* 18 (1975):131–43.

Elconin, Victor A. "Stephen Crane at Asbury Park." *American Literature* 20 (1948):275–89.

Ellison, Ralph. Introduction. In *The Red Badge of Courage and Four Great Stories by Stephen Crane*, 7–24. New York: Dell, 1960.

Emery, Micheal, and Edwin Emery. *The Press in America: An Interpretative History of the Mass Media.* 6th ed. Englewood Cliffs: Prentice–Hall, 1988.

Fairfield, Roy P. "Benjamin Orange Flower: Father of the Muckrakers." *American Literature* 22 (1956):272–82.

Fitelson, David. "Stephen Crane's *Maggie* and Darwininism." *American Quarterly* 16 (1964):182–94.

Flower, B. O. *Progressive Men, Women and Movements of the Past Twenty-five Years.* Boston: The New Arena, 1914.

Follett, Wilson. Introduction. In *The Monster and The Third Violet: The Works of Stephen Crane*, Vol. 3, ix–xxii. New York: Knopf, 1926.

———. "The Second Twenty-Eight Years: A Note on Stephen Crane, 1871–1900." *The Bookman* 68 (1929):532–37.

Ford, Madox Ford. "Stephen Crane." *American Mercury* 37 (1936):36–45.

Fox, Austin. "Stephen Crane and Joseph Conrad." *Serif* 6 (1969): 16–20.

Freidel, Frank. *The Splendid Little War.* New York: Bramhall House, 1958

French, J. L. "The Story of McClures." *Profitable Advertizing,* October 15, 1897, 139–45.

French, Mansfield J. "Stephen Crane, Ball Player." *Syracuse University Alumni News* 15, no. 4 (1934):3–4.

French, Warren. "Stephen Crane: Moment of Myth." *Prairie Schooner* 55 (1981):155–67.

Fried, Michael. *Realism, Writing, Disfiguration: On Thomas Eakin and Stephen Crane.* Chicago: University of Chicago Press, 1987.

Frohock, W. M. "American Realism and the Elegaic Sensibility: Stephen Crane and Frank Norris." In *Geschichte und Fiction: Amerikanische Prosa im 19. Jahrhundert*, 216–37. Ed. Alfred Weber and H. Grandel. Gottingen: Vandenhoeck and Ruprecht, 1972.

Frus, Phillis. "Two Tales 'Intended to be after the Fact,' 'Stephen Crane's Own Story' and 'The Open Boat.'" In *Literary Nonfiction: Theory, Criticism, Pedagogy*, 125–51. Ed. Chris Anderson. Carbondale: Southern Illinois University Press, 1989.

Fryckstedt, Olaf W. "Henry Fleming's Tupenny Fury: Cosmic Pessimism in Stephen Crane's *The Red Badge of Courage.*" *Studia Neophilologica* 33 (1961):256–81.

———. "Crane's *Black Riders:* A Discussion of Dates." *Studia Neophilologica* 34 (1962a):282–93.

———. "Stephen Crane in the Tenderloin." *Studia Neophilologia* 34 (1962b):135–63.

———. Introduction. In *Stephen Crane: Uncollected Writings*, xvii–lxvii. Upsala: Studia Anglistica Upsaliensia, 1963.

Gadamer, Georg. "The Phenomenological Movement" (1963). In *Philosophical Hermeneutics*, 130–81. Ed. and trans. David E. Inge. Berkeley: University of California Press, 1976.

Gaines, Charles K. "Rise to Fame of Stephen Crane." Philadelphia *Press*, March 15, 1896, 34.

Gale, Robert. L. *Barron's Simplified Approach to The Red Badge of Courage.* Woodbury: Barron's Educational Series, 1966.

Gallagher, Robert S. "Stephen Crane's Tenderloin Adventure." In *New York: New York*, 128–33. Ed. David G. Lowe. New York: Amererican Heritage, 1968.

Gardner, John, and Lennis Dunlap. "Stephen Crane: 'The Blue Hotel.'" In *The Forms of Fiction*, 329–57. New York: Random House, 1962.

Gargano, James, W. "Crane's 'A Mystery of Heroism': A Possible Source." *Modern Language Notes* 74 (1959):22–23.

Garland, Hamlin. "Stephen Crane as I Knew Him." *Yale Review* 3 (1919):494–506.

———. "Stephen Crane." In *Roadside Meetings*, 189–206. New York: Macmillan, 1930. Reprinted with slight revisions in *The Bookman* 70 (1930):523–28.

Geismar, Maxwell. "Stephen Crane: Halfway House." In *Rebels and Ancestors: The American Novel, 1890–1915*, 69–136. Boston: Houghton Mifflin, 1953.

Gerstenberger, Donna. "'The Open Boat': Additional Perspective." *Modern Fiction Studies* 17 (1971):557–61.

Gewirth, Allan. *Reason and Morality.* Chicago: University of Chicago Press, 1978.

Giamo, Benedict. *On the Bowery.* Ames: University of Iowa Press, 1989.

Gibson, Donald, B. "'The Blue Hotel'and the Ideal of Human Courage." *Texas Studies in Language and Literature* 6 (1964):388–97.

———. *The Fiction of Stephen Crane.* Carbondale: Southern Illinois University Press, 1968.

———. *The Red Badge of Courage: Redefining the Hero.* Boston: Twayne, 1988.

Gillis, Everett A. "A Glance at Stephen Crane's Poetry." *Prairie Schooner* 28 (1954):73–79.

Glebe-Moller, Jens. "The Good Samaritan in Recent American Moral Philosophy." *Philosophical Investigations* 4 (1981):35–52.

Gleckner, Robert F. "Stephen Crane and the Wonder of Man's Conceit." *Modern Fiction Studies* 5 (1959):271–81.

Going, William T. "William Higgins and Crane's 'The Open Boat.'" *Papers on English Language and Literature* 1 (1965):79–82.

Greenfield, Stanley B. "The Unmistakable Stephen Crane." *PMLA* 73 (1958):562–72.

Grenberg, Bruce L. "Metaphysic of Despair: Stephen Crane's 'The Blue Hotel.'" *Modern Fiction Studies* 14 (1968):203–13.

Griffith, Clark. "Stephen Crane and the Ironic Last Word." *Philological
Quarterly* 47 (1968):83–91.

Gullason, Thomas A. "New Light on the Crane-Howells Relation ship."
New England Quarterly 30 (1957):389–92.

———. "The Symbolic Unity of *The Monster*." *Modern Language Notes* 75
(1960):663–68.

———. "A Stephen Crane Find: Nine Newspaper Sketches." *Southern Humanities Review* 2 (1968a):1–37.

———. "The Last Will and Testament of Mrs. Mary Helen Peck Crane."
American Literature 40 (1968b):232–34.

———. "The Fiction of Reverend Jonathan Townley Crane, D. D." *American Literature* 43 (1971):263–73.

———. "A Family Portfolio" and "Stephen Crane's Short Stories: The True
Road." In *Stephen Crane's Career: Perspectives and Evaluations*, 7–50,
470–85. New York: New York University Press, 1972.

———. "Stephen Crane: In Nature's Bosom." In *American Literary Naturalism: A Reassesment*, 37–56. Ed. Yoshinobu Hakutani and Lewis Fried.
Heidelberg: Carl Winter, 1975.

———. "Stephen Crane's Sister: New Biographical Facts." *American Literature* 49 (1977):234–38.

———. "The 'Lost' Newspaper Writings of Stephen Crane." *Courier* 21
(1986):57–87.

Hagemann, E. R. "'Sadder than the End': Another Look at 'The Open Boat.'"
In *Stephen Crane in Transition: Centenary Essays*, 66–85. Ed. Joseph
Katz. DeKalb: Northern Illinois University Press, 1972.

Halliburton, David. *The Color of the Sky: A Study of Stephen Crane*. Cambridge: Cambridge University Press, 1988.

Hartshorne, Charles. "Contingency and the New Era in Metaphysics." *Journal of Philosophy* 29 (1932):421–31, 457–69.

———. "The Rights of the Subhuman World." *Environmental Ethics* 1
(1979):49–60.

Harris, Kenneth F. "Rough Rider O'Neill." In *The Chicago* Record's *War Stories by Staff Correspondents in the Field*, 131–33. Chicago: Chicago
Record, 1898.

Heddendorf, David. "Filling Out the What: William James, Josiah Royce
and Metaphor." *American Transcendental Quarterly* 2, no. 2 (1988)
125–38.

Hilfer, Anthony Channel. *Revolt From the Village, 1915–1930*. Chapel Hill:
University of North Carolina Press, 1969.

Hoffman, Daniel, G. *The Poetry of Stephen Crane*. New York: Columbia
University Press, 1957.

———. "Stephen Crane's First Story." *Bulletin of the New York Public Library* 64 (1960):273–78.

Holloway, Jean. *Hamlin Garland: A Biography*. Austin: University of Texas
Press, 1960.

Holly, Flora Mai. "Notes on Some American Magazine Editors." *The Bookman* 12 (December 1900):357–68.

Holton, Milne. *Cylinder of Vision: The Fiction and Journalistic Writings of Stephen Crane.* Baton Rouge: Louisiana State University Press, 1972.

Horsford, Howard C. "He Was a Man." In *New Essays on* The Red Badge of Courage, 109–27. Ed. Lee Mitchell. Cambridge: Cambridge University Press, 1986.

Hume, David. *Dialogues Concerning Natural Religion* (1874). Ed. Norman Kemp Smith. Indianapolis: Bobbs-Merrill, 1947.

Hungerford, Harold, R. "'That Was Chancellorsville': The Framework of *The Red Badge of Courage.*" *American Literature* 34 (1963):520–31.

Hunt, Patricia. "North American Pastoral: Contrasting Images of the Garden in Canadian and American Literature." *American Studies* 23 (1982):39–68.

"Irving Bacheller." *Current Literature* 37 (1904):323–25.

Irving, Washington. *A Tour of the Prairies* (1835). Oklahoma City: Harlow Publishing, 1955.

Itabashi, Yoshie. "The Modern Pilgrimage of *The Black Riders:* An Interpretation." *Tsuda Review* 12 (1967):1–41.

Jackson, John, A. "The Map of Society: America in the 1890s." *Journal of American Studies* 3 (1969):103–10.

James, Overton Phillip. "The 'Game' in 'The Bride Comes to Yellow Sky.'" *Xavier University Studies* 4 (1969):3–11.

James, William. *The Meaning of Truth.* Ed. Fredson Bowers and Ignas Skrupskelis. Cambridge: Harvard University Press, 1975.

———. *Pragmatism.* Ed. Fredson Bowers and Ignas Skrupskelis. Cambridge: Harvard University Press, 1975.

———. *A Pluralistic Universe.* Ed. Fredson Bowers and Ignas Scrupskelis. Cambridge: Harvard University Press, 1977.

———. "Great Men and Their Environment," "Reflex Action and Theism," and "The Sentiment of Rationality." In *The Will to Believe,* 57–89, 163–89. Ed. Fredson Bowers and Ignas Skrupskelis. Cambridge: Harvard University Press, 1979.

———. *The Principles of Psychology.* 2 vols. Ed. Fredson Bowers and Ignas Skrupskelis. Cambridge: Harvard University Press, 1981.

———. "On Certain Blindness in Human Beings." In *Talks to Teachers,* 132–49. Ed. Fredson Bowers and Ignas Skrupskelis. Cambridge: Harvard University Press, 1983.

Johnson, Bruce. "Joseph Conrad and Crane's *Red Badge of Courage.*" *Papers of the Michigan Academy of Science, Arts and Letters* 48 (1963):649–55.

Johnson, George W. "Stephen Crane's Metaphor of Decorum." *PMLA* 78 (1963):250–56.

Johnson, Glen M. "Stephen Crane's 'One Dash—Horses': A Model of 'Realistic' Irony." *Modern Fiction Studies* 23 (1977):571–78.

———. "Stephen Crane." In *American Short-Story Writers, 1880–1910,* Vol. 78, 117–35. Ed. Bobby Ellen Kimbel. Detroit: Gale Research, 1989.

Johnson, Jane. Introduction. In Hamlin Garland, *Crumbling Idols*, ix–xxviii. Cambridge: Harvard University Press, 1960.

Johnson, Willis Fletcher. "The Launching of Stephen Crane." *Literary Digest International Book Review* 4 (1926):288–90.

Jones, Claude. "Stephen Crane at Syracuse." *American Literature* 7 (1935):82–84.

Kahn, Sy. "Stephen Crane and the Giant Voice in the Night: An Explication of *The Monster*." In *Essays in Modern American Literature*, 35–45. Ed. Richard Langford. De Land: Stetson University Press, 1963.

Kamholtz, Jonathan. "Literature and Philosophy: The Captioned Vision vs. The Firm, Mechanical Impression." *Centennial Review* 24 (1980):384–402.

Kaplan, Harold. "Vitalism and Redemptive Violence." In *Power and Order: Henry Adams and the Naturalistic Tradition in American Fiction*, 115–30. Chicago: University of Chicago Press, 1981.

Kapoor, Kapil. "Desertion in the Fields: A Note on the Interpretation of *The Red Badge of Courage*." *Journal of the School of Languages* 7 (1980–81):65–69.

Karlen, Arno. "The Craft of Stephen Crane." *Georgia Review* 28 (1974):470–84.

Katz, Joseph. "'The Blue Battalions' and the Uses of Experience." *Studia Neophilologica* 38 (1966a):107–16.

———. Introduction. *The Poems of Stephen Crane*, xvii–li. New York: Cooper Square Publishers, 1966b.

———. "Stephen Crane: Muckraker." *Columbia Library Columns* 17 (1968):2–7.

———. Introduction. In *Stephen Crane in the West and Mexico*, ix–xxv. Kent: Kent State University Press, 1970.

———. "The Estate of Stephen Crane." *Studies in American Fiction* 10 (1982):135–50.

———. "Stephen Crane: The Humanist in the Making." In *William Carlos Williams, Stephen Crane, Philip Freneau*, 75–85. Ed. W. John Bauer. Trenton: New Jersey Historical Commission, 1989.

Kaufmann, Reginald Wright. "The True Story of Stephen Crane." *Modern Culture* 12 (October 1900):143–45.

Kazin, Alfred. Introduction. In Stephen Crane, *The Red Badge of Courage*, vii–xviii. New York: Bantan Books, 1983.

Keenan, Richard. "The Sense of an Ending: Jan Kadar's Distortion of Stephen Crane's *The Blue Hotel*." *Literature Film Quarterly* 16 (1988):265–68.

Keet, Alfred Ernest. *Stephen Crane: In Memoriam*. Folcroft: Folcroft Press, n.d.. Reprint 1969.

Kent, Thomas L. "The Problem of Knowledge in 'The Open Boat' and 'The Blue Hotel.'" *American Literary Realism* 14 (1981):262–68.

———. "Epistemological Uncertainty in *The Red Badge of Courage*." *Modern Fiction Studies* 27 (1982):621–28.

———. "The Epistemological Text: *The Red Badge of Courage*, 'The Open

Boat,' 'The Blue Hotel.'" In *Interpretation and Genre*, 124–42. Lewisburg: Bucknell University Press, 1986.

Kibler, James E. "The Library of Stephen and Cora." *Proof* 1 (1977):199–246.

Kimball, Sue. "Circles and Squares: The Designs of Stephen Crane's 'The Blue Hotel.'" *Studies in Short Fiction* 17 (1980):425–30.

Kindelien, Carlen T. "Stephen Crane and the 'Savage Philosophy' of Olive Schreiner." *Boston University Studies in English* 3 (1957):97–107.

Klotz, Marvin. "Romance or Realism? Plot, Theme, and Character in *The Red Badge of Courage*." *College Language Association Journal* 9 (1962):98–106.

Knapp, Bettina L. *Stephen Crane*. New York: Ungar, 1987.

Koerner, James D. "Comments on 'Hamlin Garland's "Decline" from Realism.'" *American Literature* 26 (1954):427–32.

Krauth, Leland. "Heroes and Heroics: Stephen Crane's Moral Imperative." *South Dakota Review* 10 (1973):86–93.

Kwiat, Joseph, J. "Stephen Crane and Painting." *American Quarterly* 4 (1952):331–38.

———. "The Newspaper Experience: Crane, Norris, and Dreiser." *Nineteenth-Century Fiction* 8 (1953):99–117.

———. "Stephen Crane and Frank Norris: The Magazine and the 'Revolt' in American Literature in the 1890's." *Western Humanities Review* 30 (1976):311–22.

———. "Stephen Crane's Literary Theory: 'The Effort Born of Pain.'" *Amerikastudien* 24 (1979):152–56.

———. "Stephen Crane, Literary-Reporter: Commonplace Experience and Artistic Transcendence." *Journal of Modern Literature* 8 (1980):129–38.

LaFrance, Marston. "Stephen Crane's 'Private Fleming: His Various Battles.'" In *Patterns of Committment in American Literature*, 113–33. Toronto: University of Toronto Press, 1967.

———. *A Reading of Stephen Crane*. Oxford: Clarendon Press, 1971.

———. "*George's Mother* and the Other Half of *Maggie*." In *Stephen Crane in Transition: Centenary Essays*, 35–53. Ed. Joseph Katz. DeKalb: Northern Illinois University Press, 1972.

———. "Stephen Crane in Our Time." In *The Chief Glory of Every People: Essays on Classic American Writers*, 27–51. Ed. Matthew Bruccoli. Carbondale: Southern Illinois University Press, 1973.

Law, Richard A. "The Morality Motif and Imagery of Diabolism in 'The Blue Hotel.'" *Wisconsin English Journal* 13 (Fall 1970):11–15.

Lenehan, William T. "The Failure of Naturalistic Techniques in Stephen Crane's *Maggie*." In *Maggie: Text and Context*, 166–73. Ed. Maurice Bassan. Belmont: Wadsworth, 1966.

Levenson, J. C. "Stephen Crane." In *Major American Writers*, 383–97. Ed. Perry Miller. 2 vols. New York: Harcourt, 1962.

———. Introduction. In *The Works of Stephen Crane*. Vol. 7: *Tales of Whilomville*, xi–lx. Ed. Fredson Bowers. Charlottesville: University Press of Virginia, 1969.

———. Introduction. In *The Works of Stephen Crane*. Vol. 5: *Tales of Adventure*, xv–cxxxii. Ed. Fredson Bowers. Charlottesville: University Press of Virginia, 1970.

———. Introduction. In *The Works of Stephen Crane*. Vol. 2: *The Red Badge of Courage*, xiii–xcii. Ed. Fredson Bowers. Charlottesville: University Press of Virginia, 1975.

Lindberg-Seyersted, Brita. *Ford Madox Ford and His Relationship to Stephen Crane and Henry James*. Atlantic Highlands: Humanities Press International, 1987.

Linson, Corwin K. "Little Stories of 'Steve' Crane." *Saturday Evening Post*, April 11, 1903, 20–21.

———. *My Stephen Crane*. Ed. Edwin Cady. Syracuse: Syracuse University Press, 1958.

Lively, Robert A. *Fiction Fights the Civil War*. Chapel Hill: University of North Carolina Press, 1957.

Lowell, Amy. Introduction. In *The Works of Stephen Crane*. Vol. 4: *The Black Riders and Other Lines*, ix–xxix. Ed. Wilson Follett. New York: Knopf, 1922.

Lyon, Peter. *Sucess Story: The Life and Times of S. S. McClure*. New York: Charles Scribner's Sons, 1963.

MacIntyre, Alasdair. "Existentialism." In *The Encyclopedia of Philosophy*, Vol. 3, 147–54. Ed. Paul Edwards. 8 vols. New York: Macmillan, 1976.

Mailloux, Stephen. "Literary History and Reception Studies." In *Interpretative Convention: The Reader in the Study of American Fiction*, 159–91. Ithaca: Cornell University Press, 1982

Marcus, Erin, and Mordecai Marcus. "Animal Inagery in *The Red Badge of Courage*." *Modern Language Notes* 74 (1959):108–11.

Marcus, Mordecai. "The Unity of *The Red Badge of Courage*." In *Stephen Crane's The Red Badge of Courage: Text and Context*, 189–95. Ed. Richard Lettis. New York: Harcourt, Brace, 1960.

———. "The Three-fold View of Nature in 'The Open Boat.'" *Philological Quarterly* 41 (1962):511–15.

———. "Structure and Irony in Stephen Crane's 'War Is Kind.'" *College Language Association Journal* 9 (1966):274–78.

Marovitz, Sanford E. "Scratchy the Demon in 'The Bride Comes to Yellow Sky.'" *Tennessee Studies in English* 16 (1971):137–40.

Marshall, Edward. "The Santiago Campaign, Some Episodes: A Wounded Correspondent's Recollections of Guasimas." *Scribner's Magazine* 24 (September 1898):273–76.

Matthews, Brander. "Recent Essays in Criticism." *Cosmopolitan* 12 (November 1891):124–28.

———. "American Fiction Again." *Cosmopolitan* 12 (March 1892):636–40.

Maurice, Arthur Bartlett. *The New York of the Novelists*. New York: Dodd, Mead, 1917.

May, Charles E. "The Unique Effect of the Short Story: A Reconstruction and an Example." *Studies in Short Fiction* 13 (1976):289–97.

194 Works Cited

Mayer, Charles W. "Social Forms vs. Human Brotherhood in Crane's *The Monster.*" *Ball State University Forum* 14 (1973):29–37.

———. "Stephen Crane and The Realistic Tradition: 'Three Miraculous Soldiers.'" *Arizona Quarterly* 30 (1974):128–33.

McBride, Henry. "Stephen Crane's Artist Friends." *Art News* (1949):46.

McCullough, Joseph B. *Hamlin Garland.* Boston: Twayne, 1978.

McDermott, John J. *The Culture of Experience: Philosophical Essays in the American Grain.* New York: New York University Press, 1976.

———. "Josiah Royce's Philosophy of Community." In *American Philosophy*, 153–76. Ed. Marcus Singer. Cambridge: Cambridge University Press, 1985.

———. *Streams of Experience: Reflections on the History and Philosophy of American Culture.* Amherst: University of Massachusetts Press, 1986.

McElderry, Jr., B. R. "Hamlin Garland's View of Whitman." *The Personalist* 36 (1955):369–78.

McFarland, Ronald E. "The Hospitality Code and Crane's 'The Blue Hotel.'" *Studies in Short Fiction* 18 (1981):447–51.

McIntoch, Burr. *The Little I Saw of Cuba.* New York: F. Tennyson Neeley, 1899.

Melange of the Class of '92. Easton: Lafayette College, 1892.

Metzger, Charles R. "Realistic Devices in Stephen Crane's 'The Open Boat.'" *Midwest Quarterly* 4 (1962):47–54.

Meyer, George W. "The Original Purpose of the Naturalistic Novel." *Sewanee Review* 50 (1942):563–70.

Michaelson, Charles. Introduction. In *The Open Boat and Other Tales: The Works of Stephen Crane*, xi–xxiv. Ed. Wilson Follett. New York: Knopf, 1927.

Miller, Ruth. "Regions of Snow: The Poetic Style of Stephen Crane." *Bulletin of the New York Public Library* 72 (1968):328–49.

Milne, W. Gordon. "Stephen Crane: Pioneer in Technique." *Die Neueren Sprachen* 8 (1959):297–303.

Mitchell, Lee Clark. "The Spectacle of Character in Crane's *The Red Badge of Courage.*" In *Determined Fictions: American Literary Naturalism*, 96–116. New York: Columbia University Press, 1989.

———. "Face, Race and Disfiguration in Stephen Crane's *The Monster.*" *Critical Inquiry* 17 (1990):174–92.

Monroe, Harriet. "Comment: Stephen Crane." *Poetry* 14 (1919):148–52.

Monteiro, George. "Society and Nature in Stephen Crane's 'The Men in the Storm.'" *Prairie Schooner* 45 (1971):13–17.

———. "Stephen Crane and the Antinomies of Christian Charity." *Centennial Review* 16 (1972a):91–104.

———. "The Logic Beneath 'The Open Boat.'" *Georgia Review* 26 (1972b):326–35.

———. "Crane's Coxcomb." *Modern Fiction Studies* 31 (1985):295–305.

Morace, Robert A. "Games, Play, and Entertainments in Stephen Crane's 'The Monster.'" *Studies in American Fiction* 9 (1981):65–81.

Morgan, Wayne H. "Stephen Crane: The Ironic Hero." In *Writers in Transition*, 1–22. New York: Hill and Wang, 1963.

Mott, Frank Luther. "The Magazine Revolution and Popular Ideas in the Nineties." *Proceedings of the American Antiquarian Society* 64 (April 1954):195–214.

———. *A History of American Magazines.* 5 vols. Cambridge: Harvard University Press, 1957. Vols. 3 and 4.

"Mr. Irving Bacheller." *The Bookman* (1900):218–21.

Murphy, Brenda. "A Woman without Weapons: The Victor in Stephen Crane's *George's Mother.*" *Modern Language Studies* 11 (1985):88–93.

Nagel, James. "Stephen Crane's 'The Clan of No-Name.'" *Studies in Short Fiction* 1 (1975):230–40.

———. "The Narrative Method of 'The Open Boat.'" *Revue Des Langues Vivantes* 39 (1973):409–17.

———. "Stephen Crane's Stories of War: A Study of Art and Theme." *North Dakota Quarterly* 43 (1975a):5–19.

———. "Impressionism in 'The Open Boat' and 'A Man and Some Others.'" *Research Studies* 43 (1975b):27–37.

———. "Stephen Crane and the Narrative Methods of Impressionism." *Studies in the Novel* 10 (1978):76–85.

———. *Stephen Crane and Literary Impressionism.* State College: Pennsylvania State University Press, 1980.

Najui, James. "Indifference in Crane and Camus." *CEA Critic* 28 (1966):11–12.

Nelson, Harland S. "Stephen Crane's Achievement as a Poet." *Texas Studies in Language and Literature* 4 (1963):564–82.

Nettles, Elsa. "Crane and Conrad." *Conradiana* 10 (1978):276–83.

———. "'Amy Foster' and Stephen Crane's 'The Monster.'" *Conradiana* 15 (1983):181–90.

Norris, Frank. Review of *Maggie. Wave,* July 4, 1986, 13.

Noxon, Frank, W. "The Real Stephen Crane." *Stepladder* 14 (1928):4–9.

Oliver, Arthur. "Jersey Memories—Stephen Crane." *Proceedings New Jersey Historical Society* 16 (1931):454–62.

Oliver, Lawrence J. "Brander Matthews' Re-visioning of Crane's *Maggie.*" *American Literature* 60 (1988):645–68.

Oliviero, Toni H. "'People as They Seem to Me': Determinism and Morality as Literary Devices in Three Novels of Stephen Crane." *Seminaires* 2 (1976):167–81.

Oppenheim, Frank M. "A Roycean Road to Community." *International Philosophical Quarterly* 10 (1970):341–77.

Osborn, Neal J. "The Riddle of 'The Clan': A Key to Crane's Fiction." *Bulletin of the New York Public Library* 69 (1965):247–58.

Osborn, Scott, C. "The 'Rivalry-Chivalry' of Richard Harding Davis and Stephen Crane." *American Literature* 28 (1956):50–61.

Overland, Orm. "The Impressionism of Stephen Crane: A Study in Style and Technique." *America Norvegica* 1 (1966):239–85.

Paredes, Raymund, A. "Stephen Crane and the Mexican." *Western American Literature* 6 (1971):31–38.

Parker, Hershel. *"The Red Badge of Courage:* The Private History of a Campaign That—Succeeded?" In *Flawed Text and Verbal Icons: Literary Authority and American Fiction,* 147–79. Evanston: Northwestern University Press, 1984.

———. "Getting Used to 'The Original Form' of *The Red Badge of Courage."* In *New Essays on* The Red Badge of Courage, 25–47. Ed. Lee Mitchell. Cambridge: Cambridge University Press, 1986.

Passmore, John. *Man's Responsibility for Nature.* New York: Scribners, 1974.

Peirce, C. S. Preface. In *Collected Papers of Charles Sanders Peirce,* Vol. 1, vii–xi. 6 vols. Ed. Charles Hartshorne and Paul Wiess. Cambridge: Harvard University Press, 1931–35.

Perosa, Sergio. "Naturalism and Impressionism in Stephen Crane's Fiction." In *Stephen Crane: A Collection of Critical Essays,* 80–94. Ed. Maurice Bassan. New York: Prentice-Hall, 1967.

Petrakis, Harry Mark. "Scene from 'The Blue Hotel.'" In *The American Short Story,* 65–69. Ed. Calvin Skaggs. New York: Dell, 1977.

Peterson, Theodore. "The Birth of the Modern Magazine." In *Magazines in the Twentieth Century,* 1–17. Urbana: University of Illinois Press, 1964.

Phelps, William Lyon. Introduction. In *Whilomville Stories: The Work of Stephen Crane,* Vol. 5, xi–xii. 12 vols. Ed. Wilson Follett. New York: Knopf, 1925–27.

Pike, Nelson. *God and Evil: Readings on the Theological Problem of Evil.* Englewood Cliffs: Prentice-Hall, 1964.

Pilgrim, Tim A. "Repetition as a Nihilistic Device in Stephen Crane's 'The Blue Hotel.'" *Studies in Short Fiction* 11(1974):125–29.

Pizer, Donald. "Hamlin Garland and the *Standard."* *American Literature* 26 (1954):401–15.

———. "The Garland-Crane Relationship." *Huntington Library Quarterly* 24 (1960a):75–82.

———. *Hamlin Garland's Early Work and Career.* Berkeley: University of California Press, 1960b.

———. "The Concept of Nature in Frank Norris' *The Octopus."* *American Quarterly* 14 (1962):73–80.

———. "Stephen Crane's *Maggie* and American Naturalism." *Criticism* 7 (1965):168–75.

———. "'*The Red Badge of Courage* Nobody Knows': A Brief Rejoinder." *Studies in the Novel* 11 (1979):77–81.

———. "Stephen Crane's 'The Monster' and Tolstoy's 'What to Do': A Neglected Allusion." *Studies in Short Fiction* 20 (1983):127–29.

———. "Self-censorship and Textual Editing." In *Textual Criticism and Literary Interpretation,* 144–61. Ed. Jerome J. McGann. Chicago: University of Chicago Press, 1985a.

———. "*The Red Badge of Courage:* Text, Theme and Form." *South Atlantic Quarterly* 84 (1985b):302–13.

Polanyi, Michael. *Personal Knowledge.* Chicago: University of Chicago Press, 1962.

———. *The Tacit Dimension.* New York: Doubleday, 1967.

Pugh, Edwin. "Stephen Crane." *The Bookman* 74 (1924):162–64.

Quinn, Arthur Hobson. "The Journalists." In *American Fiction,* 532–38. New York: Appleton-Century-Crofts, 1936.

Ratcliffe, James. "The Duty to Rescue: A Comparative Analysis." In *The Good Samaritan and the Law,* 91–134. Garden City: Doubleday, 1966.

Raymond, Thomas L. *Stephen Crane.* Newark: Carteret Book Club, 1923.

Regier, C. C. *The Era of the Muckrakers.* Glouster: Peter Smith, 1957.

Rescher, Nicholas. "The Revolt against Process." *Journal of Philosophy* 59 (1962):410–17.

Robertson, James. "Stephen Crane, Eastern Outsider in the West and Mexico." *Western American Literature* 13 (1978):243–57.

Robinson, Cecil. "Mexican Traits—A Later Look." In *Mexico and the Hispanic Southwest in American Literature,* 164–209. Tucson: University of Arizona Press, 1977.

Rogers, Rodney O. "Stephen Crane and Impressionism." *Nineteenth-Century Fiction* 24 (1969):292–304.

Rooke, Constance. "Another Visitor to the 'The Blue Hotel.'" *South Dakota Review* 14 (1977):50–56.

Rosenblatt, Louise M. *The Reader, the Text, the Poem: The Transactional Theory of the Literary Work.* Carbondale: Southern Illinois University Press, 1978.

———. "Viewpoints: Transaction versus Interaction—A Terminological Rescue Operation." *Research in the Teaching of English* 19 (February 1985):96–107.

Ross, Danforth. *The American Short Story.* Minneapolis: University of Minnesota Press, 1961.

Ross, Lillian. "Picture: John Huston and the Film Version of *The Red Badge of Courage.*" In *Reporting,* 223–442. New York: Simon and Shuster, 1964. Originally published in the *New Yorker,* May 24–June 21, 1952.

Royce, Josiah. "The Problem of Christianity." In *The Religious Philosophy of Josiah Royce,* 134–239. Ed. Stewart Gerry Brown. Syracuse: Syracuse University Press, 1952.

Satterfield, Ben. "From Romance to Reality: The Accomplishment of Private Fleming." *College Language Arts Journal* 24 (1981):451–64.

Satterwhite, Joseph, N. "Stephen Crane's 'The Blue Hotel': The Failure of Understanding." *Modern Fiction Studies* 2 (1956):238–41.

Saum, Lewis O. "Hamlin Garland and Reform." *South Dakota Review* 10 (1972):36–62.

Schmitz, Neil. "Stephen Crane and the Colloquial Self." *Midwest Quarterly* 13 (1972):437–51.

Schneider, Michael. "Monomyth Structure in *The Red Badge of Courage.*" *American Literary Realism* 20, no. 1 (1987):45–55.

Schneider, Robert W. "Stephen Crane: The Promethean Protest." In *Five Novelists of the Progressive Era,* 60–111. New York: Columbia University Press, 1965.

Schnitzer, Deborah. "'Ocular Realism': The Impressionist Effects of an 'Innocent Eye.'" In *The Pictorial in Modern Fiction from Stephen Crane to Ernest Hemmingway,* 7–62. Ann Arbor: University of Michigan Press, 1988.

Schoberlin, Melvin. Introduction. In *The Sullivan County Sketches of Stephen Crane,* 1–20. Syracuse: Syracuse University Press, 1949.

———. "Flagon of Despair: Stephen Crane." Stephen Crane Collection of the George Arents Research Library of Syracuse University.

Schultz, Stanley K. "The Morality of Politics: The Muckraker's Vision of Democracy." *Journal of American History* 52 (1965):527–47.

Scott, Stanley J. "Wallace Stephens and William James: The Poetics of Pure Experience." *Philosophy and Literature* 1 (1976):183–91.

Seitz, Don C. "Stephen Crane: War Correspondent." *The Bookman* 72 (1933):137–40.

Shaw, W. David. "The Poetics of Pragmatism: Robert Frost and William James." *New England Quarterly* 59 (1986):159–88.

Shroeder, John. "Stephen Crane Embattled." *University of Kansas City Review* 17 (1950):119–29.

Shulman, Robert. "Community, Perception and the Development of Stephen Crane: From *Red Badge* to 'The Open Boat.'" *American Literature* 50 (1987):451–60.

Singer, Peter. "Famine, Affluence and Morality." *Philosophy and Public Affairs* 1 (1972):229–43.

———. "Not For Humans Only: The Place of Nonhumans in Environ mental Issues." In *Ethics and Problems of the 21st Century,* 191–206. Ed. K. E. Goodpaster and K. M. Sayre. Notre Dame: Notre Dame University Press, 1979.

Skaggs, Calvin. "Interview with Jan Kadar." In *The American Short Story,* 70–76. Ed. Calvin Skaggs. New York: Dell, 1977.

Slote, Bernice. "Stephen Crane and Willa Cather." *Serif* 6 (1969a):3–15.

———. "Stephen Crane in Nebraska." *Prairie Schooner* 43 (1969b):192–99.

Smith, Herbert. *Richard Watson Gilder.* New York: Twayne, 1970.

Smith, Leverett. "Stephen Crane's Calvanism." *Canadian Review of American Studies* 2 (1971):13–25.

Smythe, Ted Curtis. "The Reporters, 1880–1900: Working Conditions and Their Influence on the News." *Journalism History* 7 (1980):1–10.

Solomon, Eric. "Stephen Crane's War Stories." *Texas Studies in Language and Literature* 3 (1961):67–80.

———. *Stephen Crane: From Parody to Realism.* Cambridge: Harvard University Press, 1966.

Sorrentino, Paul. "Stephen and William Howe Crane: A Loan and Its Aftermath." *Resources for American Literary Study* 11 (1981):101–8.

———. "New Evidence on Stephen Crane at Syracuse." *Resources for American Literature Study* 15 (1984):179–85.

———. "Newly Discovered Writings of Mary Helen Peck Crane and Agnes Elizabeth Crane." *Courier* 21 (1986):103–35.

Spiegelburg, Herbert. *The Phenomenological Movement.* 2 vols. The Hague: Martinus Nijhoff, 1960.

Spofford, William K. "Crane's *The Monster.*" *Explicator* 36 (1977):5–7.

Stallman, Robert Wooster. Introduction. In Stephen Crane, *The Red Badge of Courage,* v–xxxvii. New York: Modern Library, 1951.

———. "Stephen Crane: A Revaluation." In *Critiques and Essays on Modern Fiction: 1920–1951,* 244–69. Ed. John Aldridge. New York: Ronald Press, 1952.

———. "Stephen Crane's Primrose Path." *New Republic,* September 19, 1955, 17–18.

———. "Stephen Crane's Letters to Ripley Hitchcock." *Bulletin of the New York Public Library* 60 (1956):319–32.

———. Introductions. "War Tales," "A Tale of the Sea," and "Poems." In *Stephen Crane: An Omnibus,* 373–78, 415–20, 565–75. New York: Knopf, 1958.

———. "Crane's Short Stories." In *The Houses that James Built and Other Literary Studies,* 103–10. East Lansing: Michigan State University Press, 1964.

———. "Journalist Crane in that Dinghy." *Bulletin of the New York Public Library* 72 (1968):261–77.

———. *Stephen Crane: A Biography.* New York: George Braziller, 1968.

———, and R. E. Watters. "Newspaper Reports of the Wreck of the *Commodore.*" In *The Creative Reader: An Anthology of Fiction, Drama, and Poetry,* 232–41. 2d ed. New York: Ronald Press, 1962.

Starke, Catherine Juanita. "Alter-Ego Symbols." In *Black Portraiture in American Fiction,* 155–62. New York: Basic Books, 1971.

Stein, Harry. "American Muckrakers and Muckraking: The 50 Year Scholarship." *Journalism Quarterley* 56 (1979):9–17.

Stein, William Bysshe. "New Testament Inversions in *Maggie.*" *Modern Language Notes* 73 (1958):268–72.

———. "Stephen Crane's *Homo Absurdus.*" *Bucknell Review* 8 (1959):168–88.

Stevenson, James. "Kubrick and Crane in *Full Metal Jacket.*" *Humanist* 48 (March–April 1988):43–44.

Stinson, Robert. "McClure's Road to *McClure's:* How Revolutionary Were the 1890's Magazines?" *Journalism Quarterly* 47 (1970):256–22.

Stone, Edward. "Stephen Crane." In *A Certain Morbidness: A View of American Literature,* 53–69. Carbondale: Southern Illinois University Press, 1969.

Stronks, James. B. "A Realist Experiments with Impressionism: Hamlin Garland's Chicago Sketches." *American Literature* 36 (1964):38–52.

Sutton, Walter. "Pity and Fear in 'The Blue Hotel.'" *American Quarterly* 4 (1952):73–78.

Swann, Charles. "Stephen Crane and a Problem of Interpretation." *Literature and History* 7 (1981):91–123.

Tanner, Tony. "Stephen Crane." In *Scenes of Nature, Signs of Men,* 133–47. Cambridge: Cambridge University Press, 1987.

Taylor, Gordon O. "The Laws of Life: Stephen Crane." In *Passages of Thought: Psychological Representation in the American Novel, 1870–1900,* 110–35. New York: Oxford University Press, 1969.

Thompson, Judith Jarvis. "A Defense of Abortion." *Philosophy and Public Affairs* 1 (1971):47–66.

Thoreau, Henry David. "A Chapter on Bravery—Script." In *Journal.* Vol. 1, 1837–1844. 91–98. Ed. John Broderick. Princeton: Princeton University Press, 1981.

———. "The Allegash and East Branch." In *The Maine Woods,* 157–297. Ed. Joseph J. Moldenhaur. Princeton: Princeton University Press, 1972.

Toulmin, Stephen. *An Examination of the Place of Reason in Ethics.* Cambridge: Cambridge University Press, 1958.

Trachtenberg, Alan. "Experiments in Another Country: Stephen Crane's City Sketches." *Southern Review* 10 (1974):265–85.

Untermeyer, Louis. "Stephen Crane." In *Makers of the Modern World,* 444–49. New York: Simon and Schuster, 1945.

Van Doren, Carl. "Stephen Crane." *American Mercury* 1 (1924):11–14.

Vidan, Ivo. "*The Red Badge of Courage:* A Study in Bad Faith." *Studica Romanica et Anglica Zagrabiensia* 33–36 (1972–73):93–112.

———. "Forms of Fortuity in the Short Fiction of Stephen Crane." *Studica Romanica et Anglica Zagrabiensia* 38 (1974):17–48.

Vosberg, R. G. "The Darkest Hour in the Life of Stephen Crane." *The Criterion* 1 (1901):26–27.

Wagenknecht, Edward. "Richard Watson Gilder: Poet and Editor of the Transition." *Boston University Studies in English* 1 (1955):84–95.

Waggoner, Hyatt H. "Stephen Crane." In *American Poets from the Puritans to the Present,* 240–44. Boston: Houghton Mifflin, 1968.

Walcutt, Charles Child. *American Literary Realism: A Divided Stream.* Minneapolis: University of Minnesota Press, 1956.

Warner, Michael D. "Value, Agency, and Stephen Crane's 'The Monster.'" *Nineteenth-Century Fiction* 40 (1985):76–93.

Wasserstrom, William. "Hydraulics and Heroics: William James and Stephen Crane." *Prospects* 4 (1979):215–35.

Weatherford, Richard M. *Stephen Crane: The Critical Heritage.* Boston: Routledge & Kegan Paul, 1973.

Weimer, David R. "Landscapes of Hysteria: Stephen Crane." In *The City as Metaphor,* 52–64. New York: Random House, 1966.

Weinstein, Bernard. "Stephen Crane: Journalist." In *Stephen Crane in Transition: Centenary Essays,* 3–34. Ed. Joseph Katz. Northern Illinois University Press, 1972.

Weiss, Daniel. "The Red Badge of Courage." *Psychonalytic Review* 52 (1965):176–96, 460–84.

Wertheim, Stanley. "Stephen Crane and the Wrath of Jehova." *Literary Review* 7 (1963):499–508.

———. "Crane and the Garland: The Education of an Impressionist." *North Dakota Quarterly* 35 (1967):23–28.

———. "Stephen Crane's 'A Detail.'" *Markham Review* 5 (1975): 14–15.

———. "Stephen Crane's *The Monster* as Fiction and Film." In *William Carlos Williams, Stephen Crane, Philip Freneau,* 97–105. Ed. W. John Bauer. Trenton: New Jersey Historical Commission, 1989.

———, and Paul Sorrentino, eds. *The Correspondence of Stephen Crane.* New York: Columbia University Press, 1988.

Westbrook, Max. "Stephen Crane: The Pattern of Affirmation." *Nineteenth-Century Fiction* 14 (1959):219–29.

———. "Stephen Crane and the Personal Universe." *Modern Fiction Studies* 8 (1962a):351–60.

———. "Stephen Crane's Social Ethic." *American Quarterly* 14 (1962b):587–96.

———. "Stephen Crane's Poetry: Perspective and Arrogance." *Bucknell Review* 11 (1963):24–34.

———. "Whilomville: The Coherence of Radical Language." In *Stephen Crane in Transition: Centenary Essays,* 86–105. Ed. Joseph Katz. DeKalb: Northern Illinois University Press, 1972.

Wheeler, Post. "Rebel in Embryo" and "Sign O' the Lanthern." In *Dome of Many-Coloured Glass,* 19–22, 98–104. New York: Doubleday, 1955.

Whitehead, Alfred North. *Process and Reality.* Cambridge: Cambridge University Press, 1929.

Wild, John. *Existence and the World of Freedom.* Englewood Cliffs: Prentice–Hall, 1963.

Wilson, Harold S. *McClures's Magazine and the Muckrakers.* Princeton: Princeton University Press, 1970.

White, Bruce A. "Stephen Crane and the 'Philistine.'" In *Elbert Hubbard's The Philistine: A Periodical of Protest: A Major Little Magazine,* 52–87. Lanham: University Press of America, 1988.

White, Edward G. *The Eastern Establishment and the Western Experience.* New Haven: Yale University Press, 1968.

White, W. M. "The Crane-Hemingway Code: A Reevaluation." *Ball State University Forum* 10 (Spring 1969):15–20.

Wolford, Chester L. *The Anger of Stephen Crane: Fiction and the Epic Tradition.* Lincoln: University of Nebraska Press, 1983.

———. *Stephen Crane: A Study of the Short Fiction.* Boston: Twayne, 1989.

Wolter, Jergen. "Drinking, Gambling, Fighting and Paying: Structure and Determinism in 'The Blue Hotel.'" *American Literary Realism* 12 (1979):295–98.

Woollcott, Alexander. "Stephen Crane's 'Whilomville Stories.'" *Saturday Review,* October 23, 1937, 14.

Indexes

Names and Topics

Crane's Works: Prose Titles

Crane's Works: Poetry Titles

PATRICK K. DOOLEY is professor of philosophy at St. Bonaventure University, St. Bonaventure, New York. He received his Ph.D. from the University of Notre Dame and is the author of *Pragmatism as Humanism: The Philosophy of William James* and *Stephen Crane: An Annotated Bibliography of Secondary Scholarship*, as well as numerous articles on American philosophy, ethics, social and political philosophy, American studies, and American literature. He is editor of the newsletter of the Society for the Advancement of American Philosophy and a member of that society's executive committee.